Saboteurs

Saboteurs

WIEBO LUDWIG'S WAR
AGAINST BIG OIL

Andrew Nikiforuk

Macfarlane Walter & Ross
Toronto

Macfarlane Walter & Ross
An Affiliate of McClelland & Stewart Ltd.
37A Hazelton Avenue
Toronto, Canada M5R 2E3
www.mwandr.com

National Library of Canada Cataloguing in Publication

Nikiforuk, Andrew, 1955-
Saboteurs : Wiebo Ludwig's war against big oil / Andrew Nikiforuk.

Includes index.
ISBN 1-55199-053-9 (bound).—ISBN 1-55199-101-2 (pbk.)

1. Ludwig, Wiebo 2. Vandalism – Alberta – Hythe.
3. Murder – Alberta – Hythe. 4. Trickle Creek Farm (Hythe, Alta.)
5. Right of property – Alberta – Hythe. I. Title.

HV6669.C32T74 2001   364.1′64′0971231   C2001-901888-6

Quote on page 46 from *A Month and a Day: A Detention Diary*, by Ken Saro-Wiwa (Penguin Books, 1995), page 79. Copyright ®The Estate of Ken Saro-Wiwa, 1995. Reprinted by permission.

Macfarlane Walter & Ross gratefully acknowledges support for its publishing program from the Canada Council for the Arts, the Ontario Arts Council, and the Government of Canada through the Book Publishing Industry Development Program.

Printed and bound in Canada

To all downwinders

Contents

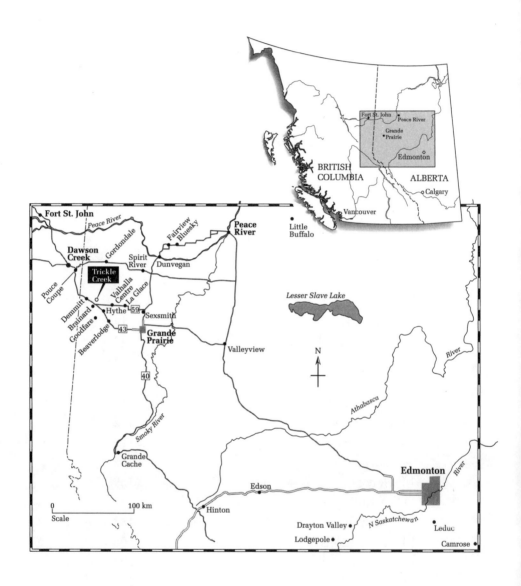

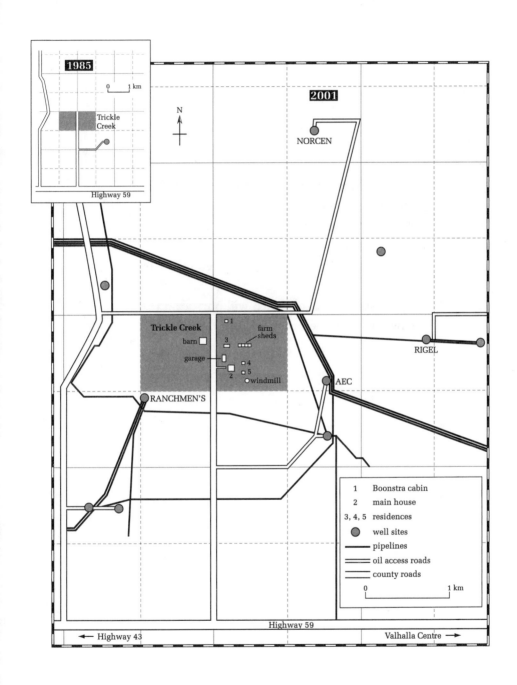

1985

0   1 km

Trickle
Creek

Highway 59

2001

N

NORCEN

RANCHMEN'S

RIGEL

Trickle Creek

barn

garage

1

farm
sheds

3

4
5

2   windmill

AEC

1   Boonstra cabin
2   main house
3, 4, 5   residences
●   well sites
──   pipelines
═══ oil access roads
─── county roads

0   1 km

Highway 59

← Highway 43   Valhalla Centre →

There is in my heart as it were a burning fire,
Shut up in my bones,
And I am weary with holding it in,
And I cannot.

– Jeremiah 20:9

Wherever a man goes, men will pursue and
paw him with their dirty institutions.

– Henry David Thoreau

Chapter 1
Genesis

The forest of the Mighty Peace is a poor man's Amazon that covers 16 million acres of northwestern Alberta and northeastern British Columbia. While Brazil's tropical forests boast millions of creatures and plants, the thin boreal gets by with the odd moose and cinnamon-coloured bear and just 12 species of trees, including spruce and aspen. The muddy river that gives the region its name and cuts the forest into the north Peace and the south Peace is one of Canada's oldest and deepest waterways. The river rises in the Rockies near Fort St. John, B.C., and snakes 1,900 kilometres through open prairie, dry forest, and wet muskeg before emptying into Lake Athabasca and, eventually, the loneliness of the Arctic Ocean. Besides being home to some 50,000 people, this broad frontier supplies Americans with an occasional hunting trip, oriented strand board, and lots of natural gas.

For nearly 100 years Canadians have trekked to the Mighty Peace to cut trees, grow wheat, or remake a life. When a farm goes broke, a marriage goes sour, or the law comes knocking, the Peace can be

1

counted on to embrace you like an all-forgiving mother. That's what Wiebo Ludwig was looking for in the summer of 1985: a respite from the storms of life.

As the leader of a Christian Reformed Church in Goderich, Ontario, on the shores of Lake Huron, the 39-year-old, Dutch-born cleric had set off ecclesiastical storms in 1980. He had started out speaking gently and smoothly but then had taken up his God-given burden of preaching directly, as Jeremiah and Ezekiel had done, verbally painting excrement on the faces of unbelievers and transgressors. Prophetic missions are never diplomatic. Micah told his people to roll in dust; Ezekiel lay on his side for 390 days to make a point; Hosea wed a harlot; Jeremiah said it was better to remove the foreskins of one's heart than to submit to circumcision. The prophets often behaved like rude performance artists and were not terribly well liked. And a true Protestant like Ludwig understood that there was much to protest against in the world.

With the endorsement of a council of elders, Ludwig asked members of his Goderich congregation to live their Christianity. He chastised parents who sent their children to Sunday school but not to Christian schools during the week. He asked working women why they weren't home caring for their children, and women with one or two offspring why they hadn't begotten "a full quiver." He questioned the wisdom of marriages that didn't take account of deep spiritual differences, since these unions often created dissension and unhappiness. He challenged a rich man who wanted to build a church gym instead of focusing on godly needs. He demanded that women submit to men as men must submit to Christ and Christ to God. He preached that when a man asks a woman to scrub the floor with a toothbrush, she should get down on her hands and knees and do so with gusto. That's a better way to shamefully expose the man's foolishness, he said, than creating "a huge argument out of everything."

Goderich's Dutch community, a quarrelsome lot, had not expected such uncompromising views. Thirty families rebelled. Many parishioners openly called Ludwig a chauvinist, "a little Hitler." The elders held heated debates about Ludwig's ministry but came to no resolution. Tired of the endless political battles, Ludwig left the community twice in the 1980s but was called back by nine families who wanted something different.

These dissenters called their new church Our Shepherd King. According to Ezekiel, a good shepherd fed his flock with judgment, tended to the weak, and ruled with love. Ludwig did his best. In these trying times he flirted and "fussed" with one of his female parishioners, Stefanie Schilthuis, and got involved in a bitter child custody battle between her and her husband, Bill. After more internal debates Ludwig resigned from the Christian Reformed Church. Shortly afterwards its officials deposed him for "challenging ecclesiastical authority" and "schismatic activity," things that the Dutch, perhaps the most religiously fractious people in the world, have been doing for years. As Ludwig later put it, "I got into a lot of trouble and they tried to hang me high and dry." After a 10-month odyssey across the United States with Bill Schilthuis and another family, Ludwig drove north into Alberta in 1985 to find solace.

His 15-member entourage camped in Rotary Park by Bear Creek in Grande Prairie, a booming oil and pulp and paper town 450 kilometres northwest of Edmonton. His breakaway church included Richard Boonstra, a genial social worker; his wife, Lois Boonstra, a legal secretary from New Jersey; and their three daughters, Kara, 16, Dania, 13, and Renée, 11. Boonstra, a Dutch immigrant who'd been raised in Michigan, was banished for misbehaving during the trek across the States but showed up in Alberta a year later.

Boonstra saw in Ludwig the kind of no-nonsense leadership his life desperately needed. Middle-aged, he felt he didn't know his children well enough. He and Lois had talked about finding sexual fulfillment outside their marriage – as Boonstra puts it, "the whole shiteree." Boonstra had met Ludwig in Goderich, where he realized that God had laid His hand on the man. Both Richard and Lois say the good reverend helped point the couple to the balm of Gilead. "The office of a prophet is an office where the spirit of God speaks through a person, and I've seen Wiebo do that to a religious community," says Boonstra. "I know what makes him tick, and it's his love of Scriptures. People don't believe that's possible."

The remainder of the church consisted of Ludwig's own family.

His wife, Mamie Lou, had large lively eyes, a generous spirit, and a heartwarming smile. An Iowa-born schoolteacher, she was the daughter of B.J. Hann, a leading member of the Christian Reformed Church in the United States. Ludwig wanted a wife who was spiritually focused and well brought up, and Mamie fit the bill. After meeting at a Bible camp, they married in 1968, and there have been no dull moments since. By the time the couple arrived in the Peace, Mamie had borne Ludwig nine robust children: Harmony, Ben, Fritz, Bo (Wiebo Jr.), Josh, Mamie Jr., Salome, Charity, and Caleb. The eldest, Harmony, was 16, and little Caleb was just a baby.

At first the church struggled. The children collected pop bottles in Grande Prairie to help make ends meet. The two families lived on soup made from bones that local butchers set aside for dogs. After looking at 50 properties, Ludwig finally found a well-treed quarter-section (160 acres) 45 minutes northwest of Grande Prairie near the British Columbia border. It had towering spruce trees, a trickling creek, lots of berries, even a log cabin. It lay at the end of a county road, a dead-end gravel strip running north from Highway 59 on which grass grew between the tire tracks. The seller gave the family a loan of $50,000 (the full purchase price) and a Winchester 30-30 and warned them to watch out for bears. To Ludwig's city-raised children, the place seemed wild as wild could be.

Over the gate they hung a painted sign that named the property Trickle Creek. On its back it declared, "The Lord: He is God." Everyone remembers those pioneer days without running water and electricity as a great adventure. Their old vehicles got stuck in the mud more times than they could count. Mamie often thawed frozen laundry by the wood stove. The Boonstra girls recall lying in the grass on long summer days, watching over the goats and playing with the younger kids. Having lived in 40 different places, Harmony loved the certainty of a place everyone could call home.

Ludwig made it known to the locals and to his own relatives in Alberta and Iowa that he wanted to be left alone. A Christian community based on the Scriptures couldn't be built with interruptions or naysayers at the door. When the nearby town of Hythe proposed to hold a social to welcome the family to the Peace, Ludwig told them not to bother. The soil in Hythe, he reasoned, was just as rocky as the soil around Lake Huron, and he didn't want to do more futile plowing. "We wanted to show them that things can be different, and that we have other values." People, he believed, are like water bugs; they skate across the surface, ignorant of the monsters beneath.

Ludwig had no illusions about the hardships of a pioneer life or the temptations of a secular one. He knew it was within his grasp to live the North American dream and buy a big house with four bathrooms, to have an entertainment system and vacations in Florida. He understood that he could raise his kids without knowing them. He knew he could get divorced and sleep around and rush through life like one possessed by empty dreams. But he wanted something more real and intense, a decent family life grounded in a belief in God – no compromises.

In particular he didn't want to relive the mistakes of his own immigrant family. In 1952 his parents, Harm and Anna Ludwig, had come to Rocky Mountain House, in central Alberta, from Zwaagwesteinde in Friesland, an independent-minded region of northern Holland that has its own language. Like many newcomers, the Ludwigs worked like beavers to make it in the New World. As a boy, Wiebo sold tomatoes and cucumbers door to door to help out. Over time the boy came to feel that his parents concentrated too much on material things and getting ahead. As the seventh of eight children, Wiebo felt neglected and lost.

School was a mixed bag for him. Kids called the intense blue-eyed boy "Bill" and made fun of his broken English. "I just didn't plug in." He ran away from home for a while, listened to the bums riding the rails, and learned about the brokenness of life. He worked as a logger and then returned to high school. The 1963 yearbook of Ludwig's high school in Red Deer simply records that he spent "much time at swimming and diving and track and field. Woodwork is Bill's hobby."

Alienated by the money-grabbing focus of immigrant life, Ludwig decided to heal some of the damage by becoming a minister. To support that goal he took all kinds of odd jobs, including stints as a cleaning product salesman, a drywaller, and an orderly in a mental institution. He even drove a hearse for a time while taking psychology at Dordt College in Iowa and then divinity studies at Calvin College in Michigan.

Ludwig respected and loved his father but hardly knew him. His mother was angry and moody but always friendly to strangers. Harm had been a leader in the Dutch resistance, and like most veterans he had seen more betrayal and death than he cared to talk about. A tailor, he chewed a lot of tobacco and slept in a separate bed from Anna, which disturbed young Wiebo. When Harm lay dying of cancer, Wiebo borrowed a van and drove up to Red Deer from Dordt College to say farewell. "It was the first time Father was personal and emotional with me," Ludwig recalls. "It was like a fresh pool of water in a long desert trek. I didn't shy away from it." Ludwig vowed that his own family would not regard him as an emotional desert, would not hunger as he had for the meaning of life. "The system has its own momentum. It catches you and we had to break with it, get off the treadmill."

For four years, from 1985 to 1989, the families worked diligently to pay off their debts. While Mamie and Lois looked after the children and raised chickens, Ludwig did drywall jobs in Grande Prairie or on the nearby Horse Lakes Indian reserve, where he saw the effects of alcohol on a family. His children helped out at job sites. He sometimes hid them in a closet when an employer came along because they looked younger than they were.

At least four RCMP officers in Grande Prairie hired Ludwig to drywall their garages and basements, because he was the cheapest and best around. When one constable tried, as Ludwig recalls it, to "jew him down" – lower the price on a difficult job by $100 – Ludwig picked up his tools and walked away.

"You don't have to pay me."

"Sir, you can't do that," stammered the constable.

"You can have it all. Give your kids some nice Christmas presents."

In those early years Ludwig often didn't come home till midnight, sweat-stained and exhausted. Boonstra also worked, taking up his father's old calling and painting homes. Together with his girls he painted, among many other places, the holding cells of the RCMP detachment in Beaverlodge, a prosperous oil and gas town 25 kilometres away.

But the real work was building a community based on the Scriptures, and it proved no easier than quelling the restless and hostile spirits of the Christian Reformed Church. Over campfires the two families held long conversations, debating how to live like true Christians. They read and reflected on the Scriptures after breakfast – sometimes for hours. They reassessed the meaning of being born again, of giving themselves to Christ. "Words tend to fail, if you don't live them," Ludwig reminded them.

Like early Christians, they shared all their goods. They also forbade the ungodly influence of television and its endless consumerist messages. They elected to educate their children at home because Ludwig believed that a public school was an ungodly place that didn't respect the needs of families or children. Tying a child to a desk at five years of age was a sure way to create osteoporosis of the spirit. "We shouldn't have to bury childhood in a straitjacketed school system," he reasoned. Over time the families agreed that formal literacy and math training should start at age 10, as in Scandinavia. Instead of teaching about abstract things, such as trigonometry or China, they taught how to do real things, such as how to dry grain or build a windmill.

They also debated the role of men and women in a family. Ludwig believed in equality before God but felt there were historical differences between the genders that society had ignored at its peril. A woman was a woman, a man a man. Women bore children and that set them apart. When a woman cared for a child, she didn't have time for a lot of other things. Men had more economic freedom and a responsibility to care for women. Just as a man leads in a dance, so too must he lead a family. Headship, argued Ludwig, meaning male headship, was "the divine structuration of life." A chaotic collection of individuals couldn't call itself a family because a true family was an orderly hierarchy of blood and social relations. The men started to wear Old Testament beards while the women adorned their heads with scarves. This head covering symbolized that it was a man's place to lead and protect a family. Hutterites and Mennonites and Amish do the same.

The transition to community life wasn't easy for the Boonstras or the Ludwigs. Mamie learned "I didn't have to be involved in church meetings and driving kids to violin lessons." Harmony struggled with her selfishness. Lois balked at the idea of headship and wanted to set her own agenda. Richard battled his laziness, and Ludwig himself struggled with his caustic tongue and his impatience. But, day by day, the families moved closer to Christ by accepting His authority in their lives.

Every church must have discipline, and Trickle Creek looked to Biblical precedents, including excommunication and head-shaving. Ludwig believed that society had gone all flabby on punishment. He recognized, like the apostle Paul, that a church must be neither too lax nor too severe. Reconciliation with repenters was also a blessed activity which elicited great sea-like waves of emotion. As Ludwig used to say, "Oh, the reunions!"

Every adult was disciplined at Trickle Creek, including Ludwig. It wasn't as simple as some people made it out to be or as harsh as some relatives and reporters later portrayed. Harmony, for example, once shaved Ludwig's head for his failings as a father. Lois Boonstra twice arrived at her brother's house in New Jersey bald as a billiard ball, with a letter from Richard attesting to her sinfulness and rebelliousness. "I'm not saying those were nice experiences," she says, "but they did bear fruit in my life." Mamie made a similar startling visit to her parents in Iowa in 1988.

At first the community of Hythe, 12 kilometres southeast of the farm, didn't take much interest in Trickle Creek. Hythe, which sits on the edge of the forest, is a taciturn collection of 600 souls. It's the kind of small town where everyone knows that Mayor Frank Webb went to the Philippines to find an agreeable wife, where newcomers are still newcomers after 15 years, and where the United Church might never be ready for a gay minister. Hythites thought it odd that the Trickle Creek children didn't attend school or play at the hockey rink, but oddness has never been against the law in the Peace. The owner of the Bigway, Hythe's grocery store, occasionally spotted Mamie shopping with a shaved head and concluded it was a ritual associated with pregnancy. Others gratefully bought the community's fresh goat's milk and organic eggs. Neighbouring farmers commented on the strength, courtesy, and honesty of Ludwig's sons. Some considered Ludwig a typical Dutchman: "Wooden shoes, wooden hat, wooden listen."

For the most part no one paid much attention to the Church of Our Shepherd King. It was live and let live in the Peace. The school board once knocked on the door at Trickle Creek but, on learning that Ludwig and Mamie were both trained schoolteachers, left. Social services conducted an investigation into the Boonstras because some of their American relatives feared their nieces had been kidnapped. "They visited for a while and let it be," said Ludwig. The Boonstras sent shit-smeared letters to Michigan to convince their relatives to leave them alone. One day Ludwig shot at a pit bull in a neighbour's yard, but the story got all "twisted" in the local gossip mill. Ludwig says he merely fired towards the charging dog to scare it off, and the dog was unharmed. Nobody particularly liked the aggressive animal, and Mamie took a turkey to the McCallisters to smooth things over.

Jake Janzen, a beekeeper who lives north of Beaverlodge on a farm as neat as a pin, had an odd sort of run-in with the reverend. Ludwig ordered a package of bees one spring but failed to pick them up in time. As a result all 8,000 bees died. Ludwig sent him a nasty letter, even visited his house one day without taking off his muddy boots. Mamie, Richard, and Lois also came along and chastised Janzen and his wife, Kit, for treating Ludwig rudely. Janzen ordered them out, saying Ludwig reminded him of the Pharisees: "Yapping all the time with no substance to it." Janzen still can't make head nor tail of it.

Now and then Ludwig felt the prophetic burden of speaking directly to people around Hythe and Beaverlodge. One day he encountered Gisela Everton, their closest neighbour, who was raising money for a playschool and kindergarten. "Don't you know the school system is ruining our children?" he began. Everton, the mother of three, didn't know what to say. And when he encountered single moms working as waitresses at the BMI restaurant in Beaverlodge, he asked them the question so many working mothers secretly fretted about: "Don't your children miss you?" The restaurant eventually banned him.

Ludwig also had a tussle with the City of Grande Prairie. When one of his competitors complained that he was operating without a business licence, the city took him to court. Other communities where he worked didn't charge him or his boys $400 a year for working there. Nor did the Ludwigs have an office in the city. The court case lasted several weeks and cost the city nearly $25,000. When Ben Ludwig showed up with a crewcut and shackles on his hands to symbolize the city's shameful pigheadedness, the judge looked dumbfounded. He eventually threw the matter out of court. The family moved most of its drywalling business to Dawson Creek and Fort St. John, across the border in British Columbia. The complainant later shot himself in the very garage Ludwig had finished for him.

In one departure from community building, Ludwig, Mamie, and Richard Boonstra travelled down to Sioux City, Iowa, spiritual home of the Christian Reformed Church and the home of Mamie's parents. Ludwig thought the church needed a wake-up call and felt the Devil had entered its doors. Ludwig had sent copies of 22 sermons to his in-laws, requesting that they dissociate themselves from it. Shortly afterwards Ludwig felt they needed a "visual aid," believing that people don't read the way they used to.

To dramatize their message, Ludwig and Boonstra dressed in sackcloth and stood bald, with ashes on their scalps, on a downtown street in Sioux City. Mamie dressed in black. Ludwig wore a sign quoting the weeping prophet Jeremiah: "How the gold has grown dim." The sun was so hot that the two bald protesters burned their heads, but Ludwig wanted to show the centre of the Christian Reformed Church that it had sold the denomination down the river. After contemplating a similar protest at the very church Mamie's parents attended, the three Protestants returned home to the Peace.

Our Shepherd King wasn't the first breakaway church to settle in the Peace or challenge the status quo. The Bull Outfit, a group of dissenting Methodists, had wanted, like Ludwig, to restart their lives and find truth in the wilderness. In 1893 the Methodist Church of Ontario expelled five pastors for questioning church dogma. Led by Nelson Burns, a fellow as well bearded and outspoken as Ludwig, the Burnites believed that hell was a bad conscience; that the Bible was a decent work of history; that the immaculate conception of Christ was hokum; and that a man could be as good as Jesus. Burns didn't think you needed a Methodist pastor to commune with the Holy Spirit. He called his group the Christian Association.

A Methodist court solemnly condemned the association as heretical, ruling that it was "dangerous to surrender all to God without the intervention of an ecclesiastic." One of the castoffs, Elias Smith, received word from God to go west. Along with five other families, Smith and his family abandoned Toronto in 1909. In Edmonton the 31 pilgrims acquired 36 oxen, loaded 14 wagons, and placed the women and children in a small red streetcar. A politician advised them to go to the Mighty Peace, and in particular "the Beaver Lodge valley."

After selling the mud-sucking streetcar to a trapper, the Bull Outfit struggled through frozen mud, su⁻ly rivers, dense bush, and clouds of mosquitoes. Four months later the congregation arrived in the Beaverlodge valley to find the grass waist-high. They fanned out across the open prairie and prospered. When the Bull Outfit opened the area, a good suit of clothes cost as much as a milk cow, trains often ground to a halt when muskeg swallowed sections of track, and loggers, asked where they had cut trees before, cheekily replied, "The Sahara." For a short while the prairie south of the forest sported some of the country's finest wheat crops. The region even thought of seceding from Canada. But bad weather and poor soils made wheat an unreliable liberator from distant governments.

One of the Bull Outfit's apostles was Donald Albright, a man of Pennsylvania Dutch stock. He grew the first alfalfa and apples in the Peace and published a weekly paper called *Timely Hints*. The region's harsh winters and unpredictable rainfall (usually either too much or not enough) taught Albright that there is no better science "than the science of doing without." He believed that the continent's most northerly agricultural frontier required at least six men in a row telling hard-luck stories "to keep each other cheered up."

In the wake of the Bull Outfit, a party of Norwegian Lutherans hopefully founded Valhalla, about 25 kilometres north of Beaverlodge. Buffalo ranchers now live around Valhalla (officially called Valhalla Centre) because not much else will thrive there. British and Norwegian settlers later established Hythe, "the town of flowing wells." German Roman Catholics created Fairview, and Ukrainians and Poles nabbed the best wheat-growing land around Sexsmith.

As the Peace filled with Europeans, those Beaver Indians fortunate enough to have survived the smallpox epidemics quietly faded into the boreal forest. These Dunnaz, or "real people," had roamed the Peace for 10,000 years; they looked and talked like Apaches and believed that frogs enjoyed gambling in ponds. A hunt chief, or dreamer, led every tribe by keeping a dream map. These maps showed where to pick berries, hunt buffalo, and fish trout. By the time the Bull Outfit had established itself, all the chiefs' maps pointed north or west to the Rockies.

Without the Bull Outfit there never would have been a Beaverlodge. Without Beaverlodge the people in Hythe would never have had a rival for the region's schools and hospitals. When not sitting around uncharitably criticizing each other's sins, members of the Christian Association built the town's first store, first butcher shop, and first school. Although the association finally scolded itself out of existence, its descendants still own businesses in the Peace. The Ludwigs traded with the sons and daughters of the Outfitters without ever knowing it.

By the end of the 1980s the community's struggles at Trickle Creek had borne fruit and lost something of their intensity. Those who made up Our Shepherd King now knew, as the Psalmists say, "how good and how pleasant it is for brethren to dwell together in unity." Each member of the community had a special job, from goat-rearing to beekeeping, that provided the church with sustenance and pleasures as flavourful as high-bush-cranberry wine. The families held daily devotions and ate communally from cellars stocked with jars of pickles and sacks of potatoes. The women took weekly turns preparing meals, with one or two assigned helpers. The community purchased a second quarter-section, just across the county road.

One day the subject of marriage came up. Ludwig looked at the three Boonstra girls and his three oldest boys. "This is what we have here. You should look at the possibilities." Ben married Kara, then Fritz married Dania. A year or two later, in a double ceremony, Bo would marry Renée and Trevor Schilthuis would wed Harmony. Trevor, a friend from Harmony's childhood in Goderich, had come at Ludwig's invitation for a look-see and stayed on.

Before long grandchildren frolicked around Trickle Creek, and the community eventually built more houses for some of the newly-weds. By 1990, Reverend Wiebo Ludwig, now a proud 49-year-old grandfather, could fairly claim that his church was rich with children, deeply united, and righteous with God.

Chapter 2

The Woes

The woes, as Ludwig calls them, began with a phone call early in 1990. That's when Phil Prefontaine, a 29-year-old Calgary landman, gave Ben Ludwig some bad news. Ranchmen's Resources Ltd., a medium-sized Calgary oil firm, had mineral rights to the family's property. A survey would spell out the exact location and surface area that the company required for a well site – about two acres plus road access, said Prefontaine. He explained that it was a landman's job to work out a deal for the survey and for future transactions between the oil company and the landowner.

Ben had built a cabin for his family across the county road from the community's homestead. His dugout – an excavated pond – sat behind the house, watered his animals, and was home to some trout. Kara often played with their newborn there. A well site? Ben told Prefontaine his dad would get back to him.

Ludwig phoned Prefontaine and asked for more information. Prefontaine explained that every piece of land in Alberta has two titles and two rights. The landowner owns the surface and the right to work it. Mineral title gives oil and gas companies the right to explore and extract what's underneath it. In 1930 the Alberta government had acquired mineral rights to 80 percent of Alberta, including Trickle Creek and indeed most of the Peace, from the federal government. Alberta leases these rights to exploration companies, which pay Alberta good money for the right to get at the oil and gas. "I appreciate it's difficult and hard to swallow," said Prefontaine, "but it's considered to be in the public good." About a third of the Alberta government's revenue comes from oil and gas royalties. The landman calculated that the well might go in close to Ben's house, but only the survey could tell. Ranchmen's wanted Ludwig's permission to do the survey.

Ludwig said the family wasn't interested. Goodbye.

A particularly large and deep gas formation called the Peace River Arch had precipitated the industry's interest in Ludwig's land. The discovery of this ancient subterranean coral reef, which time and pressure had turned into natural gas, had brought industry to the Peace in fits and starts since the 1960s. Some failing wheat farmers hailed the new colonizer as their financial saviour. A gas well in the middle of a wheat field looked like hell, but the rent often paid the bills, even kept a farm going. The industry also provided lots of off-farm jobs and paved most of the roads.

By the time Prefontaine came calling at Trickle Creek, the industry employed about 70 percent of Hythe's inhabitants full- or part-time and had already left an enormous footprint on the neighbouring forest. To find gas and transport it, mostly to American consumers, scores of companies had put down 17,826 kilometres of pipeline, built dozens of gas-processing plants, created 15,000 kilometres of new roads, and drilled more than 18,000 wells in the Peace. In the process, they had removed a forest the size of Banff National Park. Half the timber was left to rot by an industry always in a hurry. Oil patchers have a snappy saying: "Rome wasn't built in a day because an oil company didn't have the contract."

One of the first gas plants to go up around Hythe had met with considerable resistance. In 1980, Chieftain Oil expected a two-day, rubber-stamp hearing, but locals forced a two-week examination of its gas-processing technology. Farmers and ranchers argued that emissions from the plant would acidify soils, threaten trumpeter swans, devalue property, and expose everyone to the risk of poisonous gases from pipeline leaks or plant breakdowns. One rancher demanded 100 percent emission control. "If I must receive your 3 percent or whatever of emission against my will, then I feel it would be fair to give you 3 percent of the emissions from my 300-plus cattle." Gas plants, which resemble noisy chemical factories, now dot most of the Peace.

Prefontaine's call to the Ludwigs marked the beginning of a new wave of industrial activity in the Peace. Canadian companies weren't making enough profit on their gas and so decided to export as much as possible to make up in volume what they weren't getting in price. The American electricity industry had also become dependent on Canada's cheap gas. As a consequence, in the early 1990s the industry was drilling an average of 800 wells a year around Grande Prairie, twice as many as in the 1980s.

Landmen are paid to be persistent. In subsequent calls to Ludwig that spring, Prefontaine explained that Ranchmen's didn't actually need consent to survey the family's land and quoted from the Surface Rights Act, which gives the mineral rights holder the authority to proceed without a landowner's blessing. He pointed out that oil companies don't make the laws, they just follow them.

Ludwig, his eldest son, Ben, and Richard Boonstra talked over the unwelcome intrusion. This unexpected business about mineral rights perturbed them. Giving landowners rights only to six inches of topsoil, with everything underneath granted to mineral rights holders, seemed like a perverse Biblical formula for conflict. It was like having two husbands in one house, two captains on a ship. The men weren't sure how to make a stand but felt that certain fundamental rights had been trampled on. "Is a man not even master in his own house, let alone his own land, on matters like these?" asked Ludwig. After years of building a community, the last thing they needed was a clamorous invasion of profane drilling crews. They agreed on what they wanted: no well, or a land buyout.

In March 1990, Prefontaine flew up to meet Ludwig at the law offices of Darryl Carter in Grande Prairie. Ludwig, despite his distrust of lawyers, needed legal advice. Carter has a fearsome reputation in the oil patch. For years he has negotiated higher rents for landowners faced with unwanted oil or gas wells in their wheat fields. Indeed, the oil patch refers to the Peace as "Carter Country." Carter declined to take on Ludwig's case (for reasons he says he cannot disclose) but gave Prefontaine and the family a room to meet and talk. The two sides could agree only to disagree.

In the oil patch everyone assumes that a landowner's objection to a well or a pipeline is a negotiating ploy to gain higher compensation. Prefontaine tried to convince Ludwig that a survey would help pinpoint the family's concerns. Oil companies had an obligation to deal with landowners fairly, and there were a dozen things Ranchmen's could do to lessen the impact of the well: oiling the access road to keep the dust down, planting trees around the well site, installing cattle guards, and so forth. Ludwig said he wasn't interested. Nor did he want "hush money" – $3,000 or more, depending on the landowner's negotiating skills – or annual rent. He didn't want a well, and that was that. To Prefontaine he sounded like the No Man in the Dr. Seuss book *Green Eggs and Ham.* And to Ludwig, Prefontaine increasingly sounded like the Egg Seller.

When Ranchmen's surveyors showed up early one spring morning, the boys roused Ludwig from bed and told him about the strangers near Ben's house. Ludwig dressed and nonchalantly greeted the surveyors with a 30-30 in hand. He politely refused them entry onto the land and the men left.

When Prefontaine learned about the ejection of the crew, he phoned the RCMP in Beaverlodge. The company had a right to survey. The officer on duty said the Mounties weren't in the business of enforcing the Surface Rights Act and suggested Ranchmen's get a court order. Prefontaine did so – the only time he's ever had to get a court order for a survey.

Ludwig, meanwhile, researched the rules and regulations that govern drilling. These were overseen by the Energy Resources Conservation Board (ERCB), an agency that had regulated the oil and gas industry since 1938. The rules permit landowners to raise questions, challenge developments, even force public hearings. William Aberhart, the evangelical Social Credit premier of the day, set up the board partly to stop the wasteful flaring of gas by oil companies in the Turner Valley, south of Calgary. At the time companies burned off enough gas to heat the entire nation for several winters just to get access to oil reserves underneath the gas. Over time the ERCB, largely financed by the industry itself, became a sizable bureaucracy staffed by engineers or farm boys who had worked in the oil patch. It had an eight-man office in Grande Prairie to cover the Peace.

As an independent, quasi-judicial agency, the board approves or turns down applications to drill wells, install pipelines, or start up gas-processing plants. Part of its mandate is to govern energy resources in the interests of the people of Alberta, which it generally interprets to mean bringing in government revenue. Ludwig read up on the board and concluded it has a "structural bias" and lives by the maxim "Don't bite the hand that feeds you." Nevertheless he filed an objection to the well. An ERCB employee assured him that Ranchmen's couldn't proceed or get a licence without a hearing. Trickle Creek was "flagged" by the regulator and then forgotten.

In May 1990 Prefontaine again flew to Grande Prairie and rented a car to drive out and serve the court order for the survey. By law the papers weren't valid unless Ludwig touched them. For weeks Ludwig had been refusing all registered mail from the company, including information letters on natural gas. Ludwig invited Prefontaine in and asked what was on his mind. Prefontaine explained that he had some documents to deliver.

Ludwig said he wasn't interested in the reading material or in dealing with Ranchmen's. Prefontaine took the papers out of his briefcase and set them down.

"Now take those papers off the table," said Ludwig.

"No, I'm going to leave them here."

Angered by the landman's obstinacy, Ludwig grabbed the papers and put them back in Prefontaine's case. "Now listen. You are in my house and I've told you I'm not interested in your material." He walked out the door and threw the briefcase in the back of Prefontaine's car. "Get in. That's enough."

Just about everyone in the Ludwig community has heard this story a dozen times; it's the Genesis of the Ludwig saga. Prefontaine never came back. He later filed an affidavit with the Surface Rights Board that a notice of right of entry had been served. Prefontaine has dealt with hundreds of landowners over the years, including one who nearly strangled him on the hood of a car. "But I have never run into anyone so absolutely strong in their conviction as Ludwig. If I said the sky was blue and Wiebo felt it was black, I couldn't have dissuaded him of that."

In the end the court order wasn't needed. Ranchmen's chief operating officer, Terry Brooker, became alarmed and decided to bypass the Ludwigs altogether. He understood that a family retreating from civilization objected strongly to the well. It wasn't uncommon to find groups like that in northern Alberta. So Ranchmen's applied to drill south of Ludwig's fenceline and secured a surface lease from an absentee neighbour. Everyone, including the ERCB, assumed that the move would dampen Ludwig's opposition and that he would forget his overlooked request for a hearing.

Ludwig, however, wasn't mollified. A piece of Trickle Creek now fell within an exclusion zone; by law, Ludwig could not build on his own land within 100 metres of the well (nor could Ranchmen's drill within 100 metres of any existing residence). He was also outraged that Ranchmen's and the ERCB had ignored his objection. He told them they couldn't write off Trickle Creek by plopping a well against the corner of his property rather than in the middle of it.

To Ludwig's dismay, a drilling crew arrived that summer. So did 25 semi-trailers full of casing pipes, compressors, and rig gear. The drillers informed the family that it cost as much as half a million to look for gas. When Ludwig asked why they worked on Sundays, the workers said they had to take advantage of the weather; besides, it wasn't safe to stop drilling for a day. Their willingness to offend the King of Kings struck the residents of Trickle Creek as sacrilege.

Like most of the 30-odd companies operating in the Peace, Ranchmen's was hunting for sour gas. Initial exploration in the area in the

1970s and 1980s had found lots of gas in shallow formations quaintly named after local towns: Bluesky, Dunvegan, Pouce Coupe. Now Ranchmen's was looking for gas in the Halfway, a Triassic basement some 2,000 metres below the surface. The company suspected the gas could be anywhere between 2 and 6 percent sour.

Sour gas contains sulphur or hydrogen sulphide (H_2S) and is found at hellish depths up and down the Rockies. Nearly 40 percent of Alberta's gas is sour, and the rest is called sweet gas. Before the foul-smelling sour gas can be piped to anyone's home furnace, gas plants must remove at least 97 percent of the sulphur. Gas containing H_2S is as poisonous as cyanide. A gas deposit doesn't have to contain much H_2S to be lethal. Just 0.06 of 1 percent, or 600 parts per million (ppm), can kill a man. A lot of gas deposits are 35 percent sour, meaning they have H_2S concentrations of 350,000 ppm.

More than 70 industries, including hog farms, cellophane makers, herring oil factories, and pulp mills, also spew hydrogen sulphide into the air as a waste byproduct. The colourless substance stinks like rotten eggs and acts like brimstone. Hydrogen sulphide kills by starving cells of oxygen. It attacks the brain first and then paralyzes the lungs. Breathing a good whiff of sour gas is like being winded and hit with hammers on both temples at the same time. Workers who have been knocked unconscious for more than five minutes by sour gas rarely lead a normal life. The gas can steal a man's memory, cripple his lungs, leave him blind, erase his sense of smell, give him the shakes, weaken his heart, and induce psychotic nightmares. Men who have worked Alberta's sour gas fields tend to age rapidly and look old before their time. Like Gulf War veterans, they are plagued by a host of health problems doctors don't understand.

Yet physicians have understood the killing efficiency of sour gas for hundreds of years. In the 17th century, Italian cesspit and privy cleaners routinely complained of inflamed eyes, burning throats, clogged lungs, and splitting headaches after a day's labour. During the 1920s oil workers in west Texas experienced the same symptoms while drilling sour gas wells. In 1929 alone sour gas leaks killed

30 workers. The deaths horrified one Houston physician. "It is quite a surprise to find that the old rotten egg gas of our laboratory days is as toxic as hydrocyanic acid and that it is coming from nature's laboratory three thousand feet underground in such concentrations." In 1951 a Swedish physician reported that 79 percent of some 400 oil shale workers suffered from fatigue, irritability, headaches, loss of appetite, poor memory, and other neurological symptoms due to H_2S exposure. The next year a sour gas leak at a Mexican refinery near Ponza Rica killed 22 people and left another 47 brain-damaged.

Hydrogen sulphide can also interfere with reproduction. Finnish public health workers studying child-bearing women exposed to pulp mill pollution (sulphur dioxide, hydrogen sulphide, and carbon disulphide) found in 1982 that H_2S concentrations of less than 1 ppm could cause spontaneous abortions. Seven years later University of Calgary researchers found that rats experienced all kinds of birthing problems when exposed to H_2S. Small amounts can starve the fetus of a cow or horse, too.

When Albertans started drilling their sour gas fields in the 1930s, workers called H_2S "skunk oil" or "the smell of money." Many workers falsely assumed that the more often you got "knocked down" by sour gas, the more resistant you became. To convince people just how deadly the gas could be, safety experts went around the province with a travelling show of white rats. After knocking out a rat with a snootful of H_2S, the showmen revived the seemingly dead animal with oxygen. Sometimes the rat didn't wake up.

The demonstration took a while to make an impact. Between 1977 and 1987, sour gas knocked down hundreds of workers, killing 21 of them. The fatality reports all told the same sad story. In 1977, five workers sent fluids down a newly completed well to open it for a cleaner gas flow, then pumped the fluids back into a tank. While checking the fluid level of the tank, one worker opened the hatch, fell in, and was overcome. Another tried to rescue his co-worker and also died. A third was similarly dispatched. The fourth worker entered next and was also struck down and died. The Good Samaritan instinct can be a worker's deadliest friend in a sour gas field. "I have never believed in the dog-eat-dog attitude or 'Fuck you, Jack, I'm all right' approach," said one rig worker. "But under H_2S conditions, it must be the attitude you take. If your best friend is lying out there, you do not go and assist until you have masked up."

Training and safety gear for oil-field workers in Alberta have generally improved. But both industry and government argue that no conclusive body of scientific evidence supports the claim that small doses of H_2S are harmful. Big Oil seems to be today where Big Tobacco was 15 years ago: deny, deflect, dismiss. Ranchmen's information letters to Ludwig omitted most of the frightening history of deaths and accidents, as well as the research on spontaneous abortions. The letters told Ludwig that a man can smell sour gas at 1 part per million, happily breathe it at 10 ppm, lose his sense of smell at 100 ppm, and start choking at 200 ppm. At 500 ppm sour gas robs a man of his reasoning, balance, and lung power. After 700 ppm a person is unconscious and pretty well dead or brain-damaged. But concentrations this high "are unlikely to be encountered in an accidental release."

Ranchmen's also explained that every sour gas well had to have an Emergency Response Plan. In the event of a sour gas release, the ERP spells out evacuation routes and the dimensions of the danger zone where residents might be affected by H_2S. Using dispersion modelling and other formulas, an ERP calculates the maximum amount of H_2S that might assault a downwinder, given the sourness of the well and the lay of the land. In Ludwig's case, it was 100 ppm, or enough sour gas to kill any sense of smell, induce miscarriages, cause minor brain damage, and burn eyes and throats. "Every precaution will be taken to ensure your safety," concluded one letter.

Ludwig did not delight in this information. As the drillers bore down 2,000 metres, he and his sons put up the first of several public billboards, or visual aids. The sign appeared at the south edge of Ludwig's property, where Ranchmen's drilling crews turned west off the county road. The sign, which came with its own shingled roof, said that neighbouring residents didn't like oil and gas activity for the following reasons: "the ruthless interruption and cessation" of privacy, "the relentless greedy grabbing of Creational resources," "the caloused [sic] disregard for the sanctity of the Lord's Day," the legislation of land and mineral ownership policy "that does violence to the God-given 'right to property,'" and the establishment of arbitration boards funded by oil interests. Ludwig later presented Ranchmen's with a bill of $600 for the sign's construction. The company, of course, refused to pay for something it said wasn't necessary.

At the end of August 1990, after the well had been drilled and secured, Ludwig met with Ron Paulson, supervisor of the ERCB's well licensing section in Grande Prairie. Paulson noted that Ranchmen's was willing to reroute the access road and even attempt Sabbath Day observance. Ludwig said he wasn't interested in mitigation and explained that oil and godly pursuits did not mix. He requested a buffer zone to protect his community and a public hearing so his views could be aired. He also wanted all rig activity to stop on the site. Ranchmen's had the right to proceed to production but it suspended work for two weeks in September, so that the Ludwigs could produce the necessary paperwork for a hearing.

In all, the ERCB held 20 public hearings in 1990. A hearing, by design, tends to be an antagonistic and quasi-legal affair. Each side comes armed with a lawyer – or, in the case of some oil companies, several lawyers. Whether mediating disputes between oil companies and landowners, between oil companies and oil companies, or between electricity companies and the government, the board has to pick a winner on the basis of what's in the public interest. Given that the board has a mandate to develop oil and gas reserves for maximum public royalties, landowners are rarely winners.

Just before Ludwig's hearing, a routine case neatly illustrated the ERCB's bias. Corvair, a Calgary firm, wanted to drill five additional oil and gas wells and expand a storage and processing facility near a subdivision west of Edmonton. Bruce Cook, a local landowner, objected strongly. He applied to have Corvair's existing licences for three wells cancelled. Their collective odours, H_2S emissions, and vehicle traffic had, after 13 years (three more than the well's predicted longevity), outworn their welcome. Cook recognized that the

ERCB "must consider whether the rights of the surface owner and the mineral owner can both be met without unacceptable impacts being imposed on the other" but argued that the addition of five new wells wasn't harmonious with suburban living. The ERCB ruled that cancelling wells wasn't in the public interest and that five more wells could "easily be developed with acceptable levels of impact on local residents and property owners." Such decisions haven't made the board a lot of friends in rural Alberta.

Other hearings in the early 1990s involved scores of aggrieved landowners around the province. The ERCB told a group of ranchers in Provost that their concern about soil erosion, burning of waste gas, and groundwater contamination from existing facilities wasn't the board's problem and approved another well. It told a group of angry ranchers in Waterton that Shell, whose sour gas plant had affected hundreds of locals, was a good citizen and deserved another sour gas pipeline. It informed a resident near Leduc that moving a loud compressor station with high-intensity lighting away from his house "would simply transfer the impact to other residents without measurable benefits to the public." When a rancher named Roy Hanson challenged another pipeline around Provost by questioning whether the board had the agricultural and environmental expertise to address the industry's heavy footprint on the land, the board said he hadn't presented "any specific evidence in opposition." When he appeared before another board hearing, friends had to persuade him to keep his shotgun at home.

At Ludwig's hearing, on September 27, 1990, in the ERCB offices in a strip mall on the edge of Grande Prairie, each side presented its case before a professional engineer, E.J. Morin. Ranchmen's argued that when it became aware of Ludwig's opposition to its well, it chose to drill on the other side of his fence. It had secured a surface lease and well licence and had done the emergency planning. It was prepared to relocate the access road, fence off the well site, and take other mitigative measures. After determining the character of the well, the company would do the customary thing: abandon, suspend, or produce it. If all went according to plan, a pipeline would connect the well to a gas plant for processing. In short, said Ranchmen's, it had operated with good oil-field practice.

Ludwig argued that drilling on the other side of the fence didn't alleviate his concerns about sour gas and "industrial intrusion." He objected to the traffic, dust, and noise and to the effects of industrialization on the family's attempt to build a Christian community "without social, industrial or political intervention." He compared the construction of a sour gas well in one's front yard to having a nuclear bomb in the basement. He didn't want precautions or people saying how safe it was to have a bomb in the basement. He simply didn't want the bomb anywhere near him.

A month later the ERCB issued a four-page report that summarized Ranchmen's and Ludwig's views with mechanical prose. "As holder of the mineral rights to section 19-74-11 W6M, Ranchmen's submitted it had a need for the well to capture any reserves." The board said that the "interveners had a fundamental objection to what they considered to be an industrial intrusion." The board recommended that "the completion and testing be allowed to proceed" with one condition: that another hearing take place if the well went into production.

In December 1990, the drilling crew arrived to finish what it had postponed in September. The day the crew showed up, Ludwig gave them a letter ordering them to stop preparations for testing while his community appealed the matter to Premier Don Getty and procured legal counsel. It was a bluff and nobody paid much attention.

Terry Brooker had instructed his crew to dot every i and cross every t since they were dealing with a neighbour who was watching their every move. "Danger" signs popped up all over the site, and the crew regularly held H_2S safety meetings, or what the rig hands called "indoctrination" meetings. Three H_2S monitors gave base readings on the site. The crew also informed the RCMP, the ERCB, and the Ludwigs of their plans.

When Ludwig visited the site on December 6, he met a man from Occupational Health and Safety who told him he shouldn't complain about the sour gas industry. "You use a lot of gas in your vehicles." This argument has been repeated a thousand times in every coffee shop in Peace River country as a sort of born-again petroleum truth. Ludwig said he was looking for alternatives, and the next year Ben designed and installed a windmill to power the farm.

Testing a gas well demands labour and language seemingly suited to ancient mariners. The daily rig reports for 7-19-74-11 W6M read to a layman like a strange captain's log. Seal assemblies were run in and nitrogen was flared off. The crew pressured up lines to the separator and rigged up to the swab. The men rigged in bonnets and latched back onto "fish" thousands of metres underground. They jarred until dogs peeled off. Every night the crew secured the well and monitored pressure like watchmen on deck in the Sargasso Sea. They set collars and ran pull plugs, rigged down wire lines and pumped methanol. In the midst of all of this work (which cost about $15,000 a day), they reported "shutting down for the Lord's Day as per offsetting landowner's request."

Late in December the crew quit for Christmas and promised to return in the New Year. Almost daily in January they flared off gas, monitoring the pressure to test how much gas the well contained.

The industry flares a lot of gas in the Peace and throughout Alberta. Oil wells flare to burn off gas that doesn't warrant the cost of a pipeline. Gas plants flare to convert H_2S into water and less-toxic sulphur dioxide. Both wells and plants often flare during routine cleanups or emergency burn-offs of gas, called "upsets." All in all the province flared enough gas in 1990 to heat the city of Calgary for a year.

Most flares look like giant candles and roar like jet engines. Some burn off gases at ground level; others come with high flare stacks that tower above the trees. Oil workers assured Ludwig and other farmers that flaring was just a safe and handy way to get rid of unwanted gas. Most downwinders, however, detested the practice and compared living near flares to sucking on the end of a car muffler.

On January 13, a low-pressure separator gauge glass burst at the Ranchmen's site. About 59 cubic metres of raw gas was released into the air. An H_2S monitor picked up 8 ppm 200 metres east of the rig.

The crew shut down the well in three minutes, held a safety meeting, and repaired the separator glass. "The volume emitted was extremely small, and normally a site glass break is a non-event," says Terry Brooker. "We felt they could not smell it at their house."

Ludwig didn't learn about the accident until two years later, but he did smell the gas at the time. Indeed, he reported unusual odours to the ERCB's Grande Prairie office. A functionary there assured him there was nothing to worry about. The industry flared all the time and it was completely safe. The community smelled lots of rotten odours through January but, reassured by the ERCB, Ludwig concluded "it was probably a case of nasal neurosis."

That spring Harmony, the shepherdess, noticed reproductive problems in her flock. In her five years as a shepherdess she had seen only two abortions. In the spring of 1990 many of her ewes either aborted or delivered stillborns. At first she thought the newborn lambs couldn't breathe, so she gave them mouth-to-mouth. She quickly discovered that they were stone dead. More than 20 of 55 lambs born at Trickle Creek that spring died the same way. She gathered their ungainly white bodies in a wheelbarrow and burned them on a wood pyre.

The goats also aborted like crazy – a phenomenon the family hadn't experienced before in the Peace. The goats and sheep grazed on the field downwind from the well, but nobody made the connection to sour gas at the time. Ludwig even rebuked Harmony for getting upset about the unusual die-off.

That same spring Mamie Ludwig had a miscarriage in her first trimester. Mamie, who at age 45 showed no signs of menopause, had had 11 healthy pregnancies and no previous miscarriages.

Ludwig didn't know that similar livestock fatalities and human health problems had been occurring throughout rural Alberta for nearly 40 years. Although industry recognized that sour gas could be a killer at high levels, it persistently denied that chronic low-level emissions could cause trouble for people or animals. Since the construction of the first sour gas plants in the 1920s, industry has routinely described H_2S emissions as "harmlessly unpleasant." In the 1960s the Canadian Association of Petroleum Producers told farmers, "The problem is mainly a psychological rather than a physiological one."

People downwind from gas plants challenged industry's claim but with little success. In central Alberta, farmers readily noticed the invasion of three sour gas plants because of "black streaks of smoke in the sky." When they wrote letters to the government about foul odours, "cow asthma," dead calves, and retarded tree growth in the 1960s, the government promised to study "possible air pollution problems." One farm woman wrote, "Don't talk and study. Do something about pollution." Another got so totally disgusted with the runaround in 1968 that she scolded one official: "'Detailed investigations' are largely confined to telling us there is no pollution problem yet no explanation is given for the unprecedented incidence of emphysema and deformed feet in cattle, loss of pigs, dying trees and rusted metal. The fact that some farmers have been reimbursed by the company admits at least some damage. Then why not work on the assumption there is pollution damage?... We live here and know there is a definite problem."

When an Olds-area farmer lost 11 cattle grazing in a river-bottom pasture (H_2S is heavier than air and settles in low areas), the government reported that "no excessive amounts of air contaminants have been indicated." The company, of course, said there was no evidence that H_2S could kill cows, as companies had been saying for decades.

The people of Pincher Creek, west of Lethbridge, who lived downwind from two of the province's largest sour gas plants, experienced similar woes. The plants emitted 300 tonnes of H_2S a day into the air. Its corrosive properties (H_2S can eat away high-strength steel) also ensured that the plants leaked like a sieve at first. The resulting pollution killed pigs, rusted fences, peeled paint off houses, and caused reproductive problems in cattle. Whenever the plants flared and sputtered at night, the H_2S settled in coulees and river valleys, where many ranchers had their homes. The poison then crept indoors. To revive unconscious children bleeding from the nose, ranchers had to bundle them up and drive as quickly as possible out of the plume. Rather than suffer weekly insults of watering eyes, coughing, and diarrhea, one mother, Janet Main, raised her children in a tent on a corner of her property unaffected by Shell's pollution. It wasn't unusual for many downwinders to find clothes hung up to dry peppered with holes from clouds of H_2S. Government and industry called it all a "riddle." Gulf and Shell steadfastly denied any connection between ill health and sour gas emissions.

To document their claims, many ranchers kept detailed diaries in the 1960s and 1970s. Health effects on children and cattle almost always corresponded with flaring or upsets at the plants. Fifteen families eventually sued Shell for millions in damages. At the insistence of the Queen of the Netherlands (Shell was Dutch-owned), the company settled out of court and bought the land of each complainant. The company then placed a "caveat in running" on their lands for 99 years. No matter how many times the properties change hands, each new owner must sign a 25-page waiver holding Shell blameless for pollution.

In the early 1970s another rancher, Zahava Hanan, battled the Quirk Creek sour gas plant owned by Esso. The Energy Resources Conservation Board didn't take Hanan's health concerns seriously and called her "dearie." She accused the government of performing an "Emperor's clothes act" on the nightmarish qualities of sour gas, in which "the oil companies were the judge, jury, the trial and all." For her outspokenness, friends stopped visiting her. It wasn't proper to question Big Oil, the source of Alberta's considerable wealth. After pink and green fumes turned Hanan's extremities numb, she sold her ranch. "How do the down-winders convey to those who have windows that do not open what it is like to have their pollutants invade one's being?" she asked.

In 1982 sour gas again made headlines in Alberta when a well near Lodgepole blew up and killed two workers. For 67 days it spewed poisonous gases on cattle and farmers downwind, all the way to Edmonton. Downwinders reported the same symptoms as had the sewer workers, shale oil miners, and Texas drillers: watering eyes, nosebleeds, memory loss, gastrointestinal ailments. Cliff Whitelock, a local rancher, noted that calves born before the blowout weighed 630 pounds before being weaned in the fall. Calves born during the blowout reached only 430 pounds. His next crop of calves had no immune systems and walked on their ankles. Many died of pneumonia. Whitelock has never had such problems since. Company air monitors showed that his cattle were breathing just 5 ppm of H_2S. Despite such stories both industry and government maintained that the farmers and their animals were suffering a form of "social contagion." Because nobody liked the smell of H_2S, suggested industry experts, people and animals made themselves sick when they smelled it.

At a 1986 forum on the "effects of acid-forming emissions on livestock," several scientists dismissed industry's notion of psychosomatic symptoms. They argued that the Lodgepole incident turned local people and animals into sensitive biological assays. "If we were rats in an exposure chamber being examined by scientists, we would have been diagnosed as being poisoned by the blowout emissions, a full-scale chemical disaster," said one veterinarian. The forum recommended more studies, better regulations, and improved air monitoring. "The onus is almost exclusively on the livestock producer to prove that sour gas and acid-forming emissions have an effect on the health of animals and human beings. The government of Alberta needs to take responsibility for safeguarding environmental health." The government didn't publish the forum's proceedings for five years; the onus has never changed.

By the time Ranchmen's came knocking on Ludwig's door, Alberta scientists had become the world's top researchers on hydrogen sulphide. In 1990 they knew that H_2S, at low levels, altered the growth patterns of cells in a rat's brain responsible for learning and fine motor control. Eight-hour exposures of 1 ppm could cause bronchial hyperreactivity in guinea pigs. Hydrogen sulphide could also prevent coughing and wheezing in an animal, freezing its defence mechanisms and allowing it to stay in areas it would normally flee. After these studies were shared at an international forum on H_2S, funding for research dried up in Alberta.

Because of poor gas prices, Ranchmen's sat on its sour gas well for more than a year but geared up for production in 1993. By then,

Trickle Creek, like much of Peace River country, had come under full-scale assault. For starters, the Louisiana Pacific Wafer Board Plant in Dawson Creek clear-cut about 200 acres south, east, and southeast of Ludwig's property without warning. It gave the forest a crewcut and left piles of uneconomic trees strewn across the land. "Surely this can't be going on everywhere?" wrote Ludwig to the ERCB. "But we've noticed that it is going on, everywhere. The Louisiana Pacific Plant seems to have an insatiable appetite for trees, trees and more trees." Ludwig also noted that Gulf Canada had bulldozed the land that hugged the northeast corner of Trickle Creek.

Overwhelmed by these "intrusions," Ludwig requested that the ERCB give him the promised second hearing, and this time before a full seven-man board. He also repeated that he wanted the ERCB either to negotiate abandonment of the Ranchmen's well or to compensate his clan for the inconvenience of moving away. "In truth there is less room for us to develop there as we had hoped, particularly if this well with its lethal potential is permitted to be reopened and put under production. In anticipation of this scenario, we have in fact already purchased and paid for land elsewhere. Land that is not subject to these kinds of intrusions." The land in question was a verdant 120 acres in southern Costa Rica.

This letter was accompanied by testimony from the heads of households. Ben Ludwig asked, "What good is etiquette or respect for a quiet, wholesome, God-fearing lifestyle, when in the end it receives nothing, even when it should receive the most?" Fritz Ludwig wrote that he hoped his children, grandchildren, and great-grandchildren would live close by, and so "this sour gas well is also a family concern to me." Trevor Schilthuis said he had left "the jungle of our society's school system" two years ago to live a simple God-fearing life with people who cared about Creation: "I distaste the thought of our night sky artificially lit by flames." Bo Ludwig said that the idea of living in an emergency response zone made him feel like "we are in Bosnia, Herzegovena or some other war torn country." Copies went to Alberta energy minister Pat Black, Premier Ralph Klein, and more than 20 other dignitaries. By now Ludwig had written nearly 50 letters on the matter.

The weight of this discourse appeared to have an impact: in September 1993, against Ranchmen's objections, the ERCB granted Ludwig another hearing on the well.

Richard and Lois Boonstra never made it to the second hearing. Bad feelings had been festering for months at Trickle Creek. Lois says she and her husband weren't obeying certain Scriptural commandments, and the whole community was suffering from their backsliding. Their most adamant critics had been their own daughters. One day the couple left without telling anyone where they were going. They eventually settled in Vernon, B.C. They thought they might be away for only a week but ended up staying six years. Richard painted homes and watched just about every movie ever produced by Hollywood. Lois worked in the office of a local lawyer. On the shores of Lake Okanagan they lived pretty much alone with their thoughts.

While the Boonstras undertook this new life, Ludwig prepared for another battle with the ERCB. A newspaper story he had read made him cautiously optimistic. Simon and Michael Skinner, brothers and dairy farmers near Provost, had called in the ERCB after enduring nearly four years of chronic pollution. Their property was shared with 40 wells and a battery – equipment that separates water, H_2S, and other impurities from oil or gas – next to the milking barn. Amax Petroleum, an American firm, had installed 22 of the wells and the battery, which flared off raw gas just 35 metres from the cow paddock. The hearing had lasted four months in 1992 and cost all parties nearly $1.5 million. The ERCB heard some fairly dramatic evidence.

The Skinners' dairy herd breathed the foul emissions for years. Dairy farmers keep impeccable records, and the Skinners soon found a direct correspondence between heavy emissions and the incidence of pink eye, abortion, and respiratory distress in their herd. They also noted a decline in milk production by 35 percent. In addition the Skinners documented three grass fires caused by sparking oil-well equipment; 71 incidents of "fugitive" emissions of H_2S in 1991 alone; numerous saltwater spills from pipeline ruptures; a rain of oil on 23 acres of land; and the dumping of oil-field waste near a pond.

Amax argued that it had done no wrong and that emissions from its battery were below provincial standards. The company hypothesized that much of the H_2S was coming from the Skinners' manure lagoon – an argument the board dismissed. Amax also argued that the suggestion that H_2S and other sulphurous compounds could poison cattle "was at best speculation."

The board had never dealt with a landowner as well prepared and represented as the Skinners. After much reflection it released a carefully worded 60-page decision. The board couldn't admit that oil-field emissions were poisoning cattle, having already taken the position that "there is no evidence to date that demonstrates that sulphur emissions from the sour gas industry have had a deleterious effect on local health or the environment." So it called the Skinner experience "a very unusual situation" and ordered Amax to clean up its operations, remove nine sour gas wells, and change the site of the battery. Amax had interfered "significantly with the Skinners' quality of life and their emotional well being and therefore may impinge on their ability to earn their livelihood from the dairy."

The story Ludwig read didn't give all the details; it merely said a farmer and his family had beaten off one company's push to build more wells near their farm. Ludwig hoped to do the same. What he lacked in scientific evidence he hoped to make up for in conviction, showmanship, and passion.

Ludwig's second hearing took place on October 6, 1993, at the Golden Inn in Grande Prairie, which caters mostly to drilling crews and other petroleum people. Three members of the board – Phil Prince, an economist, and Norm Berndtsson and Bill Remmer, both engineers – were on hand to hear the facts. Ranchmen's was represented by a lawyer and two engineers, including Terry Brooker. The Ludwigs represented themselves.

As is customary, the well applicant spoke first. Terry Brooker explained that Ranchmen's was a publicly owned company with a market value of $100 million that operated nearly 500 oil and gas wells. He said the company recognized the industry's impact on surface rights holders and was working hard to address their concerns. The well under discussion was pretty important. The company had a $1.4-million investment in it and planned to spend another $650,000 on pipelines and such. He estimated the total value of natural gas from the well to be $4 million and emphasized that the province stood to gain $750,000 in Crown royalties. He said Ranchmen's had tried hard to work with the interveners. "Unfortunately they have refused to accept our registered letters, and they have not responded to our offers to meet with them to the point of accusing us of harassing them." Another engineer explained how the well would be completed and gas would be piped to the Hythe Brainard plant, 10 kilometres west of Trickle Creek, off Highway 43.

Then came Ludwig's turn. He expressed misgivings about the board's "structural biases" and related some family history. He talked about the importance of protecting privacy, private property, and extended family life. He noted that four grandchildren had been born since the summer of 1990, when the well was first spudded. He wondered just where the family would find more land to pursue legitimate goals. He said his family had tried not to isolate themselves from corrupting forces but to insulate themselves against them. When he had finished his speechifying, Ludwig wryly introduced members of his family as the board members sat transfixed.

"If Harmony, my oldest daughter, would stand up a minute, and her child Mercy. And my wife, I shouldn't forget her. She has been giving me all these problems [children]. A single man I could have gone where I wanted to, well or no well. Would you stand up, Mamie, Mamie Lou Ludwig." Mamie stood and smiled and sat down again. "And then Joshua, one of my sons who is very interested in farming, taken to the soil. Mamie, Mamie Lucinda, who works with the animals quite a bit, makes cheese, a few things like that. And where is Salome? Salome Katelynn has grown about six inches this year and assists Mamie in a lot of her work."

On and on went the introductions. When he finished, individual families made their own statements. Ben expressed concern about the health of cattle grazing in the field adjacent to the Ranchmen's well. His wife, Kara, the mother of three children, said that "if they had put it originally where they wanted to, we would have had to wear gas masks in our house." Fritz, Ludwig's second son, said he couldn't see a need for the well. His wife, Dania, described the premature birth of a boy after the well was tested. The third son, Bo, said that roughnecks had told him "they would not like to live where we live, knowing about the sour gas." Ludwig's fourth son, Josh, noted that Occupational Health and Safety records showed that sour gas had killed 30 oil and gas workers between 1976 and 1991. Harmony described in vivid detail the tragedy of the sheep. Renée, Bo's wife, followed with a description of the goats and their woes. Mamie Ludwig asked a sensible maternal question: "Why place a well right so closely to a family, a growing family, with all those potential dangers?"

After the presentations the board chairman, Phil Prince, asked what Ludwig had done before he located his family in a gas-rich region like the Peace. Ludwig said they were vagabonds then, looking for a place to settle in for the winter. When they found a quarter-section with a little log cabin in the woods, they thought it looked pristine. He knew there were a few oil and gas installations around but he didn't realize how many until years later, when he looked at an ERCB map. "When I saw all the little red pins in our district I was quite shocked. I wish I would have known that before I came here."

A lawyer for the board asked what would happen if the board approved the well. Could the family coexist with such development? "I can coexist with a Nazi camp supervisor if I am a captive," replied Ludwig. "What does it mean, coexistence? I thought we had more than that in this country as a possibility." Ludwig said the family would either leave or make appeals elsewhere. "I don't think you have to worry about violence unless we can somehow defuse the well without doing anybody harm, but we are not going to try it, you know."

At the end of the hearing Ludwig pleaded his case by telling the board no one could guarantee the safety of a sour gas well. "It's not so much your ability to put into place safety measures. It's more that the stuff is very lethal, and human errors do get made, and why not understand that lethal things like that are not desirable close to residences such as ours?

"We get so greedy and pushy and [we] shove, it's sad. It's part of our materialistic, poverty-stricken assessment of what it is all about, and then we run over the neighbours. We say, How come you can't be a good neighbour about this? Why don't you communicate with us? Well, you are running over top of your neighbour. Your neighbour has a reason to object.

"The other thing that has come up repeatedly is: Trust us, we know. This is what I keep hearing from the ERCB and from Ranchmen's. Why can't you trust us. Talk to us. We will convince you it's okay. It's all part of the same play that is going on all over the place in our society.

"I would like a little integrity in this decision, a little genuine integrity rather than, Well, we will just go with the flow. That's the way it's been going, we have done this before, let's do it again. If the board should decide just to ignore everything we have said, especially when it comes to that fundamental question of the lethal possibilities, I would say you have some answering to do somewhere along the line, some serious answering."

Ludwig's eloquence impressed the board members and Ranchmen's. The family also charmed them. "It was a masterful performance," says Terry Brooker. Nonetheless, the following month the board issued Decision D 93-8, nine pages of stilted prose. The board concluded that "coexistence is possible through the use of effective planning, compliance with applicable regulations and effective communication." It said there was no evidence to link livestock problems with oil-field-related operations. It encouraged all sides to "dialogue" and downplayed any safety risk from H_2S: "In the unlikely event of a release occurring, it will have minimal impact on the interveners and will not be life threatening to their residence and evacuation need not occur." In sum, the board ruled that "the well can continue to operate."

The ERCB ruling flabbergasted and aggrieved Ludwig, as his three-page reply made clear. In it he described Prince, the regulator's 300-pound vice-chairman and a veteran of countless hearings, as a corpulent fool. "Yes, your own belly betrays your hypocrisy, Dr. Prince. Moreover, because justice will have its way regardless, you are compelled to stuff yourself to fill the perpetual emptiness you will feel while you continue to set yourself against the demands of justice and slavishly support the wicked and the greedy who deceive the unwary, buy out the needy and run roughshod over the weak and the defenseless."

Ludwig equated the board decision's with being told to go to hell. He terminated dealings with the ERCB. "It is not the part of wisdom to seek justice from those who have not the stomach for it due to their own unfortunate religious disposition. We tell you we cannot continue constructive communication with men who insist on being spiritually mad and therefore truly insensitive and unable to give of themselves to the critical spiritual goods of justice and mercy and peace that are in truth born of love for God and neighbor."

Ludwig said he wanted to leave the board with one final visual aid, a picture of Ben's house. The cabin, once 758 metres from the well, now appeared to be only 95 metres away. Ludwig offered no explanation for this mystery but enclosed a picture of the house, now uninhabited, bedecked with a "Home Sour Home" sign. "Visual aids are meant as a help to those who do not listen well." He ended by calling the ERCB a squatter on the land, one that would be permanently evicted unless it repented of its bad ways. "I remain ... cordially yours."

Prince felt Ludwig had spoken with sobriety and passion at the hearing. But no one had called him a fat pig before. "It wasn't the kind of letter you responded to," Prince said later. "I took it as an indication that some of the candour we thought we heard during the hearing wasn't candour. He did himself a disservice." After the personal attack Prince withdrew from Ludwig's case.

Shortly after the release of the decision, an Edmonton television station ran a story about the family's opposition to the well. The report showed the house adjacent to the Ranchmen's well, in contravention of the ERCB's guidelines. Using log skids, the family had moved the cabin 700 metres across their land to within the 100-metre H_2S exclusion zone. It clearly looked as though Ranchmen's had broken the law and the ERCB had failed to uphold it. Bent-over human dummies decorated the porch, as though they had been overcome by sour gas. All in all it was a well-staged media event.

Three months after Ben's old cabin migrated across the quarter-section to the fenceline, the residents of Trickle Creek were gassed with hydrogen sulphide. Everything the company and the ERCB had assured Ludwig couldn't happen, did. "It was disturbing that something like that would happen after we had been involved," admitted Prince. "The world is full of people and mistakes are made."

On December 12, 1993, while testing gas in the Jurassic zone, Wayne Lawrence, the Ranchmen's well-site supervisor, released some gas without renting a flare stack. In order to measure the volume of gas down below, he simply vented 1,694 cubic metres of gas containing up to 3.2 percent H_2S into the air. He had orders not to vent but didn't follow them. "The guy screwed up and made a mistake and should not have done it," says Terry Brooker. "In a remote area, when you can't get a flare stack, you do it. But in a populated area with a known resident like Ludwig just half a mile away, you don't." When Brooker heard about the 20-minute venting, he slumped in his chair and muttered, "Oh, Jesus."

It didn't take the Ludwigs long to smell rotten eggs. The stench was so bad that the family thought the well had popped a leak. By the time the mothers had packed up the children and grandchildren, just about everyone was nauseated, vomiting, or suffering from throbbing headaches. Ranchmen's later estimated that the family probably breathed between 2 and 4 ppm of H_2S that day. Ludwig phoned the ERCB and made an angry complaint. Within 15 minutes of the venting, all 24 members of Trickle Creek were on their way to the Hythe Motor Inn. They later re-enacted the chaotic scene for a video they produced about the woes, complete with folks running to the toilet and throwing up.

Two men from the ERCB showed up at noon and shut down the well. The next day Ranchmen's, the ERCB, and the Ludwigs had an hour-long conference call. Kerry Sully, Ranchmen's president and CEO, personally apologized and admitted the company had screwed up. Even the ERCB people sounded contrite. Everyone dripped apologies like a leaky faucet. Ludwig basked in their remorse and pointed out that he had been right all along. He repeated that he wanted Ranchmen's to abandon the well or buy him out. A quickie board report concluded that the release of H₂S was "a serious matter" and that the board was "extremely disappointed with Ranchmen's performance."

Not long after the gassing, Ludwig sold all his animals, shut up the property, packed his family into their school bus, and left for Costa Rica. Several years earlier he had bought the 120 acres on the Osa peninsula near Panama just in case Big Oil got too intrusive. Now he wanted to show his family the possibilities of a new start in Central America without sour gas.

All went well until they arrived in Mexico. In Chiapas the family got caught in the middle of the Zapatista rebellion. Heavily armed soldiers patrolled all the roads and Mexico's heat, dust, and poverty gradually eroded the family's pioneering spirits. What was to have been a vacation from Ranchmen's became a tropical ordeal. While waiting on the bridge to cross into Guatemala, the family decided to return home to Alberta.

The bridge allowed traffic to flow one way each day. Ludwig was stuck in a line heading south. He didn't see the sense of fainting in the heat waiting to enter Guatemala, only to turn around. So he parked the bus sideways, stopping all traffic on the bridge. Ludwig marched to the nearby Mexican consulate on the Guatemalan side and demanded a visa back to Mexico. When he got uninterested stares, he banged his fist on the table and yelled in Frisian, "Pot verdikke!" meaning, "Holy cow, how can you do this?" After a couple of nervous guards checked with the consular official, Ludwig got his special visa. He went back to the bus and pointed it northward; it was the only vehicle allowed back into Mexico that day.

The next day the family met a mysterious Mexican stranger named Joseph, who wore a fancy linen suit and helped them with more paperwork. Ludwig had several spiritual conversations with Joseph that yielded healthy tears. "Don't worry," Joseph told the family. "The Lord has things for you to finish in Canada."

That spring Kerry Sully and Terry Brooker of Ranchmen's visited Ludwig at Trickle Creek. After the entire congregation had said grace, Ludwig raised a glass of one of the community's fine homemade wines for a toast: "Now, Mr. Sully," began Ludwig. "Just as you have poisoned the air we breathe, we have poisoned the wine you are about to drink."

Sully blinked. "I don't think you would do that kind of thing," he replied. "Let's drink to the health of your community."

So began a wide-ranging, six-hour conversation. Sully apologized for the venting. He said completion of the well was now under his personal supervision. The oilmen and the Ludwigs talked about Ludwig's vision for a Christian community, his days as a navy diver, the relentless nature of industrial intrusions. They spoke of H_2S monitors (which Ludwig initially refused), Biblical tales, and the oil and gas industry. Ludwig again asked Ranchmen's to buy the farm or help him sell it. Sully said Ranchmen's wasn't in the business of buying farm or ranch land but assured Ludwig that the family could continue to live safely on the land and enjoy its many fruits. Ludwig indicated that he was considering litigation.

Towards the end of the dinner, Ludwig told Sully about David and Goliath. After hearing the Biblical tale, Sully and Brooker asked how the family could ever hope to resist all oil and gas developments coming into the Peace – the Ranchmen's well certainly wouldn't be the last on their doorstep. "The war is won before it is fought," explained Ludwig calmly. The story of David showed that the scale of a righteous army has no bearing on the outcome of a battle. "It's not size. It's whether a man is right or not. The fight is won on principle."

Sully and Brooker left Trickle Creek with a couple of bottles of homemade wine and the certainty that the two sides were polarized. Ludwig wanted a buffer zone. Ranchmen's couldn't provide it. Nor could Sully imagine what the solution might be. "I could see where he was coming from and could understand the dream and vision he was trying to accomplish," he recalls. The place, with its barns and houses and neat gardens, reminded him of some noble 19th-century Utopian experiment. "Unfortunately he was just in the wrong place at the wrong time."

Before long, another oil and gas outfit, Alberta Energy Company, took over the well's operation, and Ranchmen's presence near Trickle Creek ended. The following year Sully sold Ranchmen's to Crestar

Energy of Calgary, and eventually he moved to Vancouver. Ludwig later suggested that Sully had resigned from the oil patch because he felt morally sick about the venting. That wasn't so. Sully, who owns an eco-friendly resort on the Pacific, now has interests in two oil and gas companies with offshore projects in South America: "There are fewer issues offshore."

The Ludwigs, meanwhile, retreated to their drywalling and animal husbandry and community making, and slipped back into the forest. But the forest was shrinking, and Goliath wasn't dead.

Chapter 3

Rumours of War

One day in 1995 Ludwig got a call from another landman. Jack Evans had been negotiating with landowners for 20 years and had dealt with all kinds of characters, from ranchers with Uzis to sheep men who threatened to blow his kneecaps off. In most cases he quieted angry citizens simply by listening to their concerns. A tall, friendly fellow with a moustache and sandy hair, Evans enjoyed chatting and negotiating. He had learned that southern Albertans were easier to deal with than northerners, and that people in British Columbia were "just one notch higher on the difficult scale."

Evans was calling Ludwig on behalf of Suncor, a multibillion-dollar Calgary-based company. Suncor owned lots of sour gas wells in the Peace and had acquired the mineral rights around Ludwig's place. Evans wanted to sound Ludwig out about his feelings on seismic activity, gas wells, and pipelines.

Ludwig explained that his sheep had aborted and his wife had miscarried after an exposure to hydrogen sulphide. Kara, Ben's wife, had just suffered the same horror after Rigel Oil and Gas burned 787,000 cubic metres of gas just east of the farm, in eight flare-offs during the first three months of her pregnancy. After the "fumigation" she had suffered headaches, light-headedness, and nausea before losing the baby. One goat and one sheep spontaneously aborted at the same time. Ben had written to the ERCB ("I want you to take seriously the effects of your greed") but the board had passed the buck. Coexistence with industry wasn't possible, Ludwig told Evans. Executives in Calgary didn't give a damn about people who lived off the land, because they were strangers to the Peace and weren't married to anything but money. Yet these men made decisions that devastated livelihoods and lives.

Evans heard the man out. He knew most problems in the oil patch were caused by arrogant men who didn't listen. After an hour, though, he saw that no amount of wheeling or dealing would satisfy Ludwig. The man simply didn't want his pioneering Christian homestead industrialized further. Every now and then industry came up against individuals who actually stood for what they stood on. Fortunately, there weren't too many of them. And the man had already been radicalized by sour gas exposure. Evans never relished dealing with such people. Once the industry had broken a trust, it rarely won it back.

Evans told his employers at Suncor that Ludwig was against development, pure and simple. He strongly recommended that the company give up the idea of exploring around his place: "Unless Trickle Creek is the very last lease the company owns in North America, you could save yourself a lot of grief and more money than you can imagine by exploring and drilling elsewhere."

Suncor agreed and backed off.

A year or so later, in July 1996, two oil and gas surveyors arrived at Trickle Creek one Sunday morning. That was their first mistake. The second was not reading the big sign out front, the one that railed against the "ruthless interruption and cessation" of privacy. When approached by one of the Ludwig boys, the men innocently announced that they were marking a grid to do seismic tests every 23 metres along the county road.

A seismic test involves drilling holes about 12 metres deep and exploding dynamite in them. Technicians in trucks or helicopters measure the shock waves from the explosions to gauge the depth of gas or oil pools underneath. To do seismic work in the bush, a crew will cut a five- to eight-metre-wide swath through the forest. The industry has cut more than 350,000 kilometres of "seismic" in the Peace, lines that added together would stretch to the moon.

Ludwig knew that a seismic crew was the vanguard of what environmentalists called "the rape, ruin, and run boys" and went out to meet the men. One of his sons carried a rifle, and Ludwig wore a Costa Rican machete, which swung like a sword from his belt. An RCMP report, the first of scores that year, says that Ludwig "expressed his dislike for the oil companies and the manner in which they operate."

The surveyors showed Ludwig a map with his two quarter-sections blacked out. The black parts meant a no-go for seismic testing. But the county road was public, and they were going to test along its right-of-way.

Ludwig explained that Trickle Creek's aquifer was too close to the road for that kind of testing. Seismic activity could fracture an aquifer and cause gas to mix with the water in his household taps.

The surveyors asked if they should leave. "Definitely," said Ludwig. He shook the young men's hands because they didn't know better. On their way out the surveyors made a point of reading the anti-oil billboard, then reported their run-in to the RCMP.

Ludwig called up the ERCB, which had changed its name to the Energy and Utilities Board (EUB). He told one functionary in Grande Prairie that he didn't want more surveyors around his place. He said he'd have to start some kind of action if the oil and gas developments didn't stop. "This is a warning," he added. "Not a threat."

The surveyors worked for Absolute Seismic, which had been hired by Aguila Exploration, which in turn had been contracted by the Alberta Energy Company. AEC had an unusual pedigree. Premier

Peter Lougheed created it in 1974 as a Crown agency so the province and its citizens would have a say in their own oil patch. At the time, American multinationals such as Gulf and Imperial dominated oil and gas exploration. To challenge their stranglehold on the province's resources, the government kept half of AEC's shares and sold the remainder. The province then gave the company some of the best oil and gas leases around, including the Suffield natural gas field and a big share of the tar sands. AEC quickly became a cash cow.

The Crown company also had a growth mandate and soon had interests in petrochemicals and sawmills. But AEC's comfortable life as a hybrid Crown corporation came to an abrupt end in 1994 when Premier Ralph Klein sold it. The populist premier needed cash to cover huge government debt. Without public consultation Klein sold the government's shares for half a billion dollars. AEC's directors and Tory investors hailed the deal. Just two years after the sale, the value of AEC had shot up to $6 billion. By the time it ran into Ludwig, it was one of Canada's biggest gas producers, right up there with Talisman and Anderson Exploration.

One of the firm's most aggressive business units was AEC West, which operated two sour gas plants – the Hythe Brainard plant and another near Sexsmith – and three sour oil batteries in the Grande Prairie area. About 200 wells kept these plants huffing and puffing, thanks to 400 kilometres of pipeline that cut through farmers' fields. AEC West had pioneered the exploitation of sour gas in the Montney formation throughout the Peace and was again in expansion mode. Other companies such as Suncor, Norcen, and Talisman had bid for leases near Trickle Creek because Hythe had become a hot exploration area. In all, more than 200 wells were drilled in the area in 1996 alone.

The company's reputation among landowners was mixed. AEC didn't cut environmental corners like Amoco, but it had a history of taking landowners to the Surface Rights Board whenever they raised too many objections. Like a lot of firms, AEC operated by a simple code: if the landowner was cooperative, AEC worked with him. If he was obstreperous, the company would fight him tooth and nail. A lot of AEC executives had worked for Dome Petroleum, and that had been Dome's style, too. In the 1980s Dome had bossed landowners around in the Peace as though they were Guatemalan peasants.

When AEC West took over the mineral rights to Ludwig's home quarter-section for $50,000 in 1996, it suspected that at least $5 million worth of gas lay beneath it, an average find for the region. And it wanted to get that money flowing before another competing firm tapped into the gas from an adjoining lease. But it needed seismic data first.

Ludwig didn't know AEC had acquired mineral rights to his land until years later but suspected that AEC's seismic crews spoke of a looming industrial invasion. He erected another sign on a four-by-eight-foot sheet of plywood. It went up on the east side of the county road at the south boundary of the farm: "BEWARE of the mounting anger of the local residents! ABANDON any thought of further gas & oil exploration in this area! Laissez-Faire." The family also posted a 20-kilometre-per-hour speed limit on the road.

Ludwig's growing intransigence that summer owed much to Ken Saro-Wiwa, a jaunty, pipe-smoking Nigerian journalist. For nearly a decade the non-violent activist battled Shell in the Niger Delta. The multinational oil company, aided by a corrupt military government, had turned a 1,000-square-kilometre region into an industrial wasteland. Oil roads blocked rivers; pipelines severed rich farmland. Shell flared so much gas that the fumes shrank guava and orange trees and turned the night sky into a ghoulish painting. Because of the incessant burning, downwinders – such as Saro-Wiwa's Ogoni tribe – suffered Nigeria's highest rates of cancer, asthma, bronchitis, skin diseases, and miscarriages. The Ogoni leader repeatedly condemned Shell's ravages and demanded compensation. He wrote poems about flaring:

> The flares of Shell are flames of hell
> We bake beneath their light
> Nought for us save the blight
> Of cursed neglect and cursed Shell.

As a consequence of his outspokenness, Saro-Wiwa spent much time in jail. When the Nigerian government hanged him and eight other troublesome Ogonis in 1995, Saro-Wiwa cried, "Lord, take my soul, but the struggle continues."

Ludwig put up a poster of the black martyr in Trickle Creek's main cabin, one of the few adornments of any kind in the austere household. It quoted Saro-Wiwa: "The environment is man's first right. Without a clean environment man cannot exist to claim other rights be they political, social or economic." Meanwhile, the wheels of industry rolled on around the farm. The road to Trickle Creek was no longer a dead end; oil companies had punched in trails at the north end of Ludwig's property with the result that traffic on the dusty county road had become continuous. When oil vehicles sped by Ludwig's new sign too fast to read it, Ludwig stopped the drivers to ask why they had to chase life down instead of just living it. The oilmen normally replied that they had deadlines to meet and were in a hurry. But in one three-day period eight truckers actually stopped to read the sign; some even turned around.

Ludwig started calling anyone associated with AEC or its contractors. He told Jim King, who supervised Aguila Exploration's seismic crews, that lives were at stake and that a man needed to consider the fact that you can drink water but not oil. When King said he needed his paycheque, Ludwig rebuked him for being a slave to the almighty dollar. King said AEC had legally acquired the lease from the government and that the road was not Ludwig's land. Just because something was legal, said Ludwig, didn't make it right. Abortion and homosexuality made a mockery out of that argument.

Ludwig talked to an AEC geologist, suggesting that AEC should get the Alberta government to reimburse it for the mineral rights. Anyone with half a brain could realize that his farm just wasn't suitable for exploration. Didn't the creation of a Christian community have any value in this world? The geologist didn't say much, but he couldn't understand why anyone would buy cheap land downwind from the Hythe Brainard plant (or any sour facility, for that matter).

Next, Ludwig spoke to Mike Duckett, another AEC manager.

Duckett insisted that Ranchmen's sour gas booboos were not AEC's problem. Ludwig said that all the oil companies worshipped the same god – money – and warned Duckett not to proceed, saying people can be pushed only so far. "Unlike Nigeria, where you face the noose or the gun, companies here smile at you like prostitutes while they take what they want."

"I don't know if I can appreciate the analogy," replied Duckett.

"You don't have to," said Ludwig. "You are the analogy."

In early August two civil servants from Alberta's Environmental Protection Branch showed up at Trickle Creek. Ludwig had invited them to discuss his latest plan: a proposal to seal off the county road from all seismic activity. He insisted the men go back out and read the signs he'd erected. The civil servants obliged and came back to the farm, where family members introduced themselves.

The women had laid out a spread of homemade goodies. Their handiwork lay under a pretty veil. A large platter with a white covering sat in the middle of the table. Ludwig removed the veil. "We have a community interested in these kinds of things," he said, pointing to a splendid array of cheeses, preserves, jams, wild cranberry wine, and a jar of fresh water from one of the farm's cold-flowing wells. "But instead we get this on our plate." He unmasked the central dish: "Death."

The sight of a bleached horse's skull left the two men speechless. Ludwig said he'd retrieved the skull from a neighbour's field. A flaring well had probably killed the horse with H_2S. Ludwig assured them that they had nothing to be afraid of: "It's just a symbol of all the death we've had around here." The men left with an unfinished bottle of cranberry wine and a promise to get back to Ludwig. Their superior later informed him that if he wanted to block a public road, he'd have to take that up with the County of Grande Prairie.

On August 29 an AEC crew started to test-flare a sour gas well a kilometre east of the main cabin. The roaring flame grew larger and larger. It finally got so loud that Salome's ears rang when she went out to collect the sheep.

The next day everyone smelled sour gas. The women closed the windows, to no avail. A canary acquired from a local trapper went crazy in its cage, jumping frantically from one end to the other and trying to stick its head through the bars.

On their way to a drywall job in Dawson Creek that morning, the boys made a short detour to stop at the well site. A worker reeking of sour gas told them that in addition to the flaring, there had been a leak. The company later reported that it had also spilled five gallons of sour crude, a substance rich in odorous mercaptans. The rotten egg smell intensified all morning. When Harmony and Dania felt nauseated to the point of throwing up, the family packed up and went to Bud Farnham's place. Farnham lived two kilometres south of Trickle Creek. A former oil worker who had been knocked down by sour gas, he welcomed the family. Ludwig repeatedly phoned the EUB that day to register his disgust. "Why don't you shut companies down that spill all over people?"

The following day Ludwig and Bo went out to inspect the well. There was nobody there. AEC's completion crew had finished the testing. Father and son found the door to the control shack ajar. As the family's diary noted, "The place was completely unattended and there was free access to all the delicate controlling equipment and monitors. Even a wild animal could have walked right in and done damage. Very irresponsible behavior on their part."

Ludwig himself got knocked down one day as he was checking his eastern fields near the AEC well. All of a sudden he felt faint. "I started to feel really crazy." He didn't know whether to drop or flee, then felt a compulsion to get out of the H_2S plume. For months afterwards he had dizzy spells and coughed up huge gobs of mucus.

On September 1 he registered a formal complaint about the AEC fumigation with RCMP Corporal Cal Mosher at the Beaverlodge detachment. Early in his career Mosher had been ambushed by a pair of Bonnie and Clyde wannabes in Florenceville, New Brunswick, while working the night shift. He took a shotgun blast "and it fixed me pretty good," as he said. Ever since then he had been gun-shy and apprehensive about working the night shift.

Mosher told Ludwig that he didn't think the RCMP could charge a company with polluting the air or assaulting a family, but he'd enter the complaint into the computer. Ludwig said he wanted it documented in case he ever had to prove in court that the RCMP didn't protect people from dangers like toxic gas. Mosher promised to double-check on the force's responsibilities. He phoned the EUB, where a functionary reported that the leak had been fixed. Mosher later told Ludwig that anything related to oil and gas was really the EUB's jurisdiction.

A couple of weeks later Mosher drove out to Trickle Creek to investigate vandalism. A number of oil workers had reported getting nails in their tires on the road to Trickle Creek. Ludwig wasn't home, but Ben said he didn't know anything about flat tires. He told the Mountie, "There've been a lot of rude oil people bombing past our road lately."

Later that morning Ludwig visited Mosher at his office in Beaverlodge. Mamie Lou, Kara, Mamie Jr., and Caleb came along as witnesses. Ludwig told Mosher he wouldn't allow any RCMP on his property unless they called first. Mosher said, "Fair enough," before explaining the nature of his flat-tire investigation. Ludwig said he wouldn't dignify Mosher's inquiries with a response until the RCMP apologized for not investigating the fumigation of his family with sour gas emissions. "When somebody gets a flat tire, the RCMP are down at our place like a bunch of trained poodles. But when people and animals get sick, nothing happens."

"Well, as policemen we always get caught in the middle of everything."

"You don't have to be in the middle," replied Ludwig. "You should stop pushing with the pushers."

When not writing to his member of the legislature or phoning water experts, Ludwig kept trying the EUB. At one time he dealt with Darrold Banta, a 50-year-old field inspector who'd worked for a drilling company. Ludwig gave the inspector the family's full history, then said he had four questions.

"Could the EUB help Trickle Creek get an environmental review that looked at things like the industry's impact on aquifers?"

Banta said that wasn't his jurisdiction.

"Do oil companies legally have to inform landowners of flaring before it happens?"

Banta said it depended on whether there was an emergency.

"Could the EUB reroute traffic so it doesn't come down our road?"

Banta told Ludwig to check with the county.

"Does an oil company legally have to inform surrounding residents about sour gas leaks?"

Banta said that leaks had to be reported to the EUB but not necessarily to the landowners.

Ludwig asked the field inspector to be a man and do something.

"I can't go beyond my jurisdiction," said Banta. He suggested that Ludwig send in water samples for testing, so he could prove later on if seismic or industry activity had ruined his well. Ludwig said that route smacked of compromise and defeat. "We don't want to wait until our water goes bad. We're trying to prevent that altogether."

In a later meeting with Banta, Ludwig and Mamie wondered what his job was. Banta admitted that the EUB didn't have enough men in the field to review the environmental concerns of landowners. "We only come out after the fact, after some damage has been done." Ludwig rattled off the damage done at Trickle Creek over six years and rebuked the man for not doing his job.

That fall Ludwig got a call from Dymphny Dronyk, an AEC contractor who lived nearby. Her job was to create Emergency Response Plans for sour gas wells in the Peace. For every plan she designed, she kept a list of phone numbers, evacuation routes, and personal health information about the landowners in the potential danger zone. After she invited Wiebo and Mamie over to talk, she explained that she was updating AEC's emergency plans. A 30-year-old widow with three children, she said she disliked flaring (it made her children and her mother deathly ill). The Ludwigs weren't impressed.

Dronyk assured the two skeptics that AEC did care about landowners, and one of her jobs was to document people's concerns. Many local employees strongly believed in good health and safety practices. "You can't paint all oil and gas companies with the same brush."

Ludwig couldn't understand why a smart woman of Dutch ancestry ("She was almost like one of us," said Mamie) would work for the Devil. After a wide-ranging discussion (Ludwig told Dronyk to get rid of her TV), Dronyk showed Ludwig a bluntly worded Emergency Response Plan form that warned pregnant women to consider leaving the area if hydrogen sulphide concentrations reached 10 ppm (in the "highly unlikely" event of a leak). She told the Ludwigs that their home was in several such zones and that they should participate in emergency planning.

That struck Ludwig as another surrender to industry's toxic encroachment. "If one of my family dies because of sour gas, maybe people will listen. In the grand scheme of things, it doesn't matter. What is mortal life to us?" Ludwig later urged Dronyk to quit her job with AEC. Oil money was blood money, he said. She said that money didn't just fall from the sky, and that people deserved careful emergency planning by local contractors who cared.

Late one night, Ludwig visited Dronyk's home and threw a wad of $50s and $100s on the coffee table. He told her that money does indeed fall from the sky if you believe. Dronyk felt uncomfortable and asked him to leave.

As Dronyk drove around to well sites and farms that winter, her truck's tires, like those of every other AEC vehicle, picked up nails like magnets. She also noticed that when AEC workers talked about Ludwig, there was now fear in their eyes.

Ludwig believed that Big Oil was plaguing his household like a bunch of unruly Midianites. Industry had made the growing, gathering, and preparation of food for his family increasingly difficult. Pipelines ran through old berry patches, flaring made outdoor work hazardous, and poisonous emissions settled on his garden.

The Midianites oppressed Israel for years, and it took a good farmer by the name of Gideon to set things right. Ludwig says that Gideon inspired him that fall. Gideon adopted all kinds of ploys to protect his people from the rapacious Midianites. He designed a wine press that also served as a sunken threshing floor so the Midianites couldn't steal his grain. One day he got a call from one of

God's angels to save his people from the invaders. Gideon said he was just a poor man trying to provide for his family. "I am the least in my father's house." But God said He would stand with Gideon and help him "smite the Midianites as one man."

Gideon obeyed God with great resourcefulness and speed. He defeated the far superior Midianite armies with just 300 men. He armed one third with trumpets, one third with pitchers, and one third with lamps. The men surrounded the Midianite camp one night and hollered, "The sword of the Lord and of Gideon," as they blew on the trumpets, smashed the pitchers, and lit their lamps. Gideon's small force sounded and looked like an army of thousands. The clamour terrified the Midianites, who in their confusion killed one another as they fled.

With Gideon as instructor, Ludwig hoped to turn back a $26-billion industry invading his land. Ludwig knew that God called upon individuals when His people were challenged. That moment seemed all the more pressing in November, when Norcen Energy Resources Ltd., another multibillion-dollar oil and gas company, began work for a new well northeast of Trickle Creek. To build a drilling pad for the well, the company had to fill in a slough or pond. A convoy of gravel and construction trucks rumbled past Trickle Creek every day.

One morning the drivers of two trucks found what they described as "an old couple" blocking their way. The couple walked as deliberately as crows and would not let the trucks pass. Every now and then they bent down and appeared to plant something in the snow. After a while they left. Later that day one of the drivers took the other aside and asked, "How many nails do you have in your tires?" After a quick check the dismayed trucker counted 29 roofing nails in his tires. One trucker had two flats; the other had two slow leaks.

Not long after the nail incident, four young men carrying machetes, pepper spray, and walkie-talkies approached the truckers on Norcen's access road. One accused the truckers of raping the earth and not doing God's work. Vigorous shouting ensued.

"They were told where to go and how to get there," recalls one of the truckers. "After that day the violence got going pretty good."

Chapter 4

Saboteurs

Bosnia changed Corporal Robert Bilodeau the way wars change all men. He went to the former Yugoslavia in the spring of 1993 as an idealistic 45-year-old volunteer who had served in the RCMP for 20 years. He was assigned to Srebrenica as that city's first full-time UN civilian police station commander. His job was to keep peace in a demilitarized zone packed with 40,000 Muslim refugees. The Serbs controlled everything outside the zone while Muslims struggled to stay alive inside it. Meanwhile the UN stood around, says Bilodeau, "with its thumb up its ass." In this so-called safe zone, Corporal Bilodeau recorded as many as 2,000 ceasefire violations a day.

In the chaos of Bosnia, Bilodeau's superiors forgot about him. He was abandoned for 115 days in the war zone. Here the affable, fast-talking farm boy supped with a school principal who calmly executed former students. He negotiated with a warlord who drove a Mercedes, strutted about like a peacock, and killed with equanimity. He learned that extreme situations can drive people to do things they wouldn't normally do. At night, just before the fighters came out like bats, he drank brandy with men who are now buried in shallow graves.

Rather than defend the enclave, the UN finally let the Serbs overrun it. Within days the Serbs massacred 7,000 Muslim men and boys. Bilodeau still has nightmares about the people he couldn't save. "If you really want to know what Srebrenica was about, imagine a Serb and a Croat raping a Muslim woman with the UN holding a flashlight."

Bilodeau's tour of duty left him with a common Yugoslavian souvenir: post-traumatic stress disorder. PTSD doesn't diminish a man's power of judgment; it just recycles the pain and trauma until he feels stuck in time, hypervigilant and anxious. After Srebrenica, Bilodeau told friends, he didn't have much of a fantasy life.

In 1996 he was posted to the RCMP's Beaverlodge detachment as a sergeant. The small understaffed unit was responsible for upholding law and order in an industrial frontier nearly as big as Bosnia. Bilodeau had worked in the Peace two decades earlier and knew that Beaverlodge, with its landscape painters and good schools, was a cultural and artsy sort of place – "a jewel of the Peace." He reckoned it would be a quiet place to end his RCMP career. His wife, Donna, liked the area too and looked forward to settling down after years of roving as a cop's wife. The couple even designed a dream house overlooking the Beaverlodge valley. While the builders hammered away, the Bilodeaus camped at the Grande Prairie Motel for six weeks. On a clear day Donna, a social worker, could see the Rockies as she drove to work, where she helped refugees from places like Bosnia. The couple planned on staying forever.

One of Bilodeau's first assignments seemed a minor affair: a string of vandalism incidents on a county road being used by Norcen. Another firm, AEC, had hired private security to protect its seismic crews. The contested road had been blocked with parked vehicles and spiked with sharpened rebar and roofing nails. Hythe's Tire Shop couldn't keep up with the repairs that fall. Even the detachment's GMC Suburban picked up a couple of flats while on patrol.

The name Ludwig came up. Bilodeau asked members of his new detachment what they knew about the man. The constables couldn't offer much other than hearsay. Ludwig was "crazy" and "ran some kind of cult" and had started his own church and didn't like the oil and gas industry.

To Bilodeau these stories sounded much too convenient. He set about filling in his intelligence vacuum. An Interpol search on Ludwig pulled up nothing more than the man's birthdate – December 19, 1941 – and there was nothing on CPIC, the national police computer system. He sent two constables out to interview neighbours, including Dymphny Dronyk, and decided to save Ludwig for himself. He called up the farm and said he wanted to come over and hear their side of the story. Ludwig invited "the tin soldier" down.

The next morning Bilodeau arrived at Trickle Creek for coffee. It was the first and only time anyone from the RCMP heard the man out in civil surroundings. Bilodeau brought Constable Jackie Wheeler along. One of Ludwig's first comments was that Bilodeau "needed a woman to protect him." Bilodeau replied that some women make extremely good warriors and added, "I just want another witness."

The whole family sat around in the living room and observed the conversation, the way other families watch TV. Ben sat on Ludwig's right, Mamie on his left. "It was like the Last Supper," said Bilodeau. "Everyone seemed to be sitting in descending order of power and importance."

It didn't take long for Bilodeau to figure out that Ludwig wasn't the kind of guy who rolls over and plays dead. Ludwig catalogued, with repeated Biblical references, the fumigations, the dead animals, the two miscarriages.

"Ben buried a child," said Ludwig.

"You mean you lost a child?" Bilodeau asked in disbelief. "How old?"

Ludwig explained that Kara had miscarried after three months, but that no one in authority took the miscarriages seriously. To emphasize how fearless he was, Ludwig recounted the family's trip to

Mexico in 1994 and the incident on the international bridge. Bilodeau got Ludwig's intended message: "Don't fuck with me."

"As police we have to work in a neutral position and on a compliance basis with people," said Bilodeau. "I'm a peace officer and I'll do whatever I can to keep the peace, but there are rules to follow and Norcen is not doing anything illegal by drilling its well."

Ludwig said it was criminal and illegal for oil companies to murder children and destroy aquifers. He said he wasn't going to kiss the ass of a corrupt system and Bilodeau should realize "there was trouble brewing here and the legality, as such, could not embrace it."

Bilodeau said he was basically powerless. Maybe Ludwig should put pressure on the EUB or contact Greenpeace or form a citizens' alliance. Ludwig said they had had enough of such merry-go-rounds and asked Bilodeau to let the authorities know "that this situation demanded more than present laws are able to deliver."

Bilodeau, who had worked in the oil patch as a young man, agreed that the industry wasn't angelic. "The industry really rapes the land. They don't have a lot of friends; they are business at its worst. Raping and pillaging the land is what they do best, but they are generating a lot of money, and the government gives them lots of slack because of it." He added that the EUB worked like every other bureaucracy. "It's part of their nature to give you the runaround." The residents of Trickle Creek had never heard a "tin soldier" talk so candidly.

Bilodeau wanted to gauge Ludwig's attitude to violence: he asked what Ludwig would do if someone raped one of his daughters. And did he plan any direct action against Norcen? Ludwig got so emphatic that Constable Wheeler put her hand on her firearm. On the rapist question, Ludwig didn't leave much to the imagination. Norcen was another matter. "Not an act of violence," he said. "Only an act of self-defence, and self-defence is not illegal."

Bilodeau talked about Bosnia. He told Ludwig he had worked in a place where people lost sight of things and took the law into their own hands. He said it "wasn't the fat cats that suffer but the women and children." He said the avenue Ludwig had chosen had pitfalls. "Innocent people get hurt and pay the price. Look, we have to live in the grey of this world and follow the spirit of the law." In essence, he gave Ludwig the gospel according to Bob: peace, love, and sue the bastard's ass off.

Ludwig appealed to the sergeant "to be human, since we share in humanity" and to remember his real and only master, God. The family agreed to take apart the roadblock and perhaps seek a court injunction against Norcen.

Bilodeau left a worried man. He pegged the family not as a cult but as a sincerely religious, highly disciplined group. He had seen the beards and head scarves before in Hutterite and Mennonite communities. The children were well fed and healthy. Mamie looked downtrodden, but then women, thought Bilodeau, always got "the shit sandwich" in evangelical communities.

What worried Bilodeau was Ludwig himself, a man at the end of his tether. He had met fearless and cornered men in Srebrenica. Such men calmly drew lines in the sand that even blood couldn't erase. Ludwig had made it clear that he feared no one except God. He had set his course, and it wasn't keeping the peace. Bilodeau felt as if he had met a Muslim in the boreal forest surrounded by an industrial tribe bent on ethnic cleansing.

On December 1, Ben, Fritz, and Josh walked out to the Norcen site and got into a shouting match with a dozen workers from Big Valley Construction in Hythe. The Hythites were madder than hell about getting flat tires and accused the boys of booby-trapping the road. One worker told them, "We are just following the laws of the land, and if you don't like the laws of the land, you should get the hell out of here." Another said if the Ludwigs wanted to mine the road with crap, "they should go down to Waco, Texas." When Josh tried to say something about the law of God, a worker replied, "Well, we're not God-loving people." The Ludwig diary recalls this comment as "very crass indeed."

That night the Ludwigs brought out a mug of coffee to a cold security guard watching the access road. The guard was grateful for the warmth and chatted a bit. He thought the nails in the road were pretty wild. "Ten to one it's a bunch of kids, pulling pranks."

While the security guard was being entertained, a sour gas well a few kilometres southeast of Trickle Creek was sabotaged. Someone poured acid on the remote-control operation valve, causing a chemical meltdown and setting off the sour gas alarm at the Hythe Brainard plant. An AEC emergency response crew later found boot-prints in the snow that led down the road towards Trickle Creek.

When RCMP Corporal Cal Mosher arrived on the scene, he reported a pickup truck not far from the well with a bunch of Ludwigs milling about. The next day two AEC employees replaced the damaged valve, then left for an hour to locate another part. During that time someone stole the new $6,000 valve.

The next night someone removed a replacement control panel from the AEC well that had "fumigated" the family in August; someone had destroyed a remote telemetry unit there the night before. Saboteurs also busted up a solar panel and electrical board at a neighbouring site owned by Highridge Exploration.

Before Bilodeau could question Ludwig about the mayhem, "Dad and Mom" stormed into his office in Beaverlodge. Ludwig wasn't in a good mood and told Bilodeau why. A neighbour, recovering from heart surgery, had told Ludwig that two constables had questioned him in hospital. They had wanted to know about the Ludwig family's habits, the number of children, their interest in guns, and many other things. Ludwig thought the police had acted wickedly and accused them of trying to create "another Waco situation." He was particularly incensed that the police would want to know if his children were fed well.

After "getting beat up with the Bible," Bilodeau told Ludwig that three wells had been vandalized close to Trickle Creek and that their lives could be in danger. "You don't mess with sour gas," he said. He had worked as a roughneck and seen men go down under a cloud of H_2S faster than a dropped hat. He said a criminal investigation was under way.

"There are a lot of angry people around," Ludwig told him. "I'm not surprised that these kinds of things are happening. Time is running out for the police and all the other organizations who refuse to put a stop to these lethal sour gas wells so close to people's homes." Before leaving, Ludwig told Bilodeau he was going to seek a court injunction. Bilodeau encouraged this route: "The judge is the one with the power to stop the well." Bilodeau felt as though he was in Srebrenica all over again.

Ludwig drove to Grande Prairie, where he walked into the Court of Queen's Bench and gave a clerk at the front desk his documents. When she told him he would need a lawyer to get an injunction, Ludwig said he didn't have time for that nonsense. All the judge had to do was read the papers and make a decision, said Ludwig. She suggested he go upstairs to the legal library, where Ludwig had spent many an hour researching the law. Ludwig said he was out of time. This was an emergency. Finally a superintendent arrived and explained that an administrative office of Queen's Bench couldn't do anything. Ludwig dumped his papers on the table, his attempt to defend his property rights in the courts at an end.

Such a battle would have been problematic. Injunctions aren't easy to obtain under common law and require that a formal lawsuit be initiated. If a court finds that an individual's property rights have been harmed, it can issue a stop-work order or grant damages. But there's a catch. Oil and gas companies operate under the "statutory authority" or the blessing of the EUB and the Alberta government. This makes pollution, traffic, and other inconveniences the products of an approved activity. Nineteenth-century railway barons showed the strength of this government blessing when farmers tried to sue the railway companies for setting their fields ablaze with sparking rail cars. The barons argued that the government had given them the authority to run a railway, that railways were in the public good, and that governments just don't do stupid things. So in authorizing a railway, the government implicitly authorized the sparks that caused fires. Oil executives offer the same defence when accused of polluting. Flaring and venting, after all, are approved and licensed activities.

On the drive back to Trickle Creek, Ludwig decided to check out the wells that Bilodeau had mentioned. He found them damaged and, to his surprise, still unsecured. Even after thousands of dollars' worth of sabotage, no one had bothered to lock them up. He phoned Bilodeau and "bawled out" the sergeant again. "Get those sites secured before somebody does more damage and puts my family in further danger." The saboteurs visited all three wells again that month.

If the night now belonged to the saboteurs, the day stirred Ludwig's caustic tongue and psychological terror tactics. At one often-sabotaged AEC well site southeast of the farm, Ludwig showed up unexpectedly and chewed out the entire four-man crew. He delivered another angry sermon about sour gas, animal deaths, and miscarriages. "Are you Reverend Ludwig?" a frightened worker asked. Ludwig said the vandalism was nothing to be complacent about and warned that industrial terrorists were getting testy. He declared that this well site could become a target and that the terrorists weren't averse to blowing up homes belonging to AEC personnel. He also put the fear of God into an AEC field operator named Keith Gerlack. "For 364 days of the year I'm sane, and then one day a year I go crazy," said Ludwig. "I know where you live." (Ludwig says he never said any such thing.) The sabotage campaign so unnerved Gerlack that he moved five times that year and had an alarm installed in his house.

After weathering this evangelical blast, the crew suggested that Ludwig get together with the company to talk things over. They assured him they could be good neighbours and that everything was "perfectly safe." Ludwig heard none of this and ended his jeremiad by saying he was going to discuss things only with "the chairman of the AEC, until I discover that he's an asshole too. Then I won't bother with him either."

One morning three oil workers called an open-line radio show in Dawson Creek to vent their frustration. They claimed that Trickle Creek was a cult and that Ludwig had eight wives. After getting kicked out of the United States, they said, Ludwig was now "kicking up a fuss here." The workers claimed that the oil companies had videos of Ludwig's grandchildren putting nails on the road and committing other acts of vandalism because "Ludwig makes his kids do the dirty work." The family listened to the entire show: "We got some good laughs out of this gossip," noted their diary.

By then most AEC employees in the area considered Ludwig "the rudest asshole they ever met." Landowners in the Peace could be contentious, even trigger-happy, but no one had ever encountered one as adamant as Ludwig. "He wasn't your run-of-the-mill upset landowner," noted one worker. "He was justifying all the vandalism by saying God told him to do it. How do you deal with a man like that?"

To deal with the man who feared only God, AEC West hired Shel Kelly in November. A former RCMP superintendent, Kelly had once commanded 2,500 men and now worked as a consultant with Security Management Consulting Inc. in Calgary. When the oil patch has a big security problem it wants solved quietly, it hires SMC. Kelly, a lean, hard, old-school cop who loved bull riding, became Ludwig's shadow. He arrived at work with a trench coat, a notebook, and no misconceptions. For the next two months he talked with Bilodeau nearly every day.

On December 18, Ludwig called up Bilodeau and asked if he wanted to attend a meeting with AEC personnel. Bilodeau agreed, and met Ludwig's family for coffee at the Golden Inn the next morning. Along with Mamie, Ben, and a couple of the other boys, Ludwig tramped into the corporation's Grande Prairie office with a solemn grimness. There they met Ken Woldum, vice-president of AEC West, and Mike Weeks, the new plant supervisor for the Hythe Brainard and Sexsmith gas plants. Shel Kelly sat in the background, watching like a lynx.

Ludwig did most of the talking. He launched an angry barrage of accusations at Woldum. Known to his colleagues as "Teddy Bear" because of his genial disposition, Woldum said he couldn't answer most of the questions because he wasn't in charge of day-to-day field operations. Ludwig accused him of sitting "in an ivory tower" and then came to the point of his visit: "We have deep concerns. Coexistence is not possible."

Woldum said that if AEC wanted to put a seismic line up a public road, it would damn well do so.

Ludwig demanded that AEC buy the family out for $750,000 or else change its practices. "I'm here to say that if the wells won't be removed, therefore you must pay to have us removed."

Woldum, angrier by the moment, repeated that AEC was doing everything legally.

"I'm saying the war is on," said Ludwig. "You'll either pay now or pay down the pipe."

Woldum, flabbergasted, repeated that the company was doing everything by the book. He also told Ludwig that whoever was responsible for all the vandalism should be put behind bars.

Weeks, the new plant manager, thought Ludwig was a few bricks short of a load but a man possessed by his cause. Woldum wasn't dismayed by the money figure at all, noted Bilodeau. He just didn't relish the precedent of buying out an adversary as inscrutable as Ludwig.

After Ludwig's war declaration, Bob Bilodeau took statements from Woldum, Weeks, and Kelly. He thought there might be grounds for an extortion charge and consulted Al Munro, a popular and erudite Crown prosecutor in Grande Prairie. Munro said there was nothing there. "It's just a case of Japanese negotiation tactics in a David-and-Goliath struggle against the oil and gas industry," said Munro. "Any charge would get punted out of court."

Ludwig left the meeting thinking he had made his position as plain as split wood: buy me out or it's war. He felt the same calm he had experienced while serving on HMCS *Iroquois* in 1960, when he had his spiritual awakening. Ludwig had joined the Canadian navy at the age of 17 to see the world, training as a frogman and mine expert. One night the warship entered a storm in the Bermuda Triangle. That tempest tore off most of the life rafts and nearly capsized the ship. Ludwig, on the midnight watch, stood on the upper deck through it all. As the salt wind blasted his face to the point of tears, he felt an awe and joy beyond words. The next day he couldn't explain to his officers why he had felt so calm and exhilarated. "While everyone seemed to be either scared to death or vomiting or both, I felt entirely at peace and entertained."

Soon after the meeting with AEC, Ludwig wrote a short letter to the EUB in Calgary, warning of the storm ahead. He strongly advised the agency's "bureaucratic terrorists" to "get your asses in gear and deal with the situation. Cut the bureaucratic crap since you are ill-prepared for the worst. Murder has been committed here and our patience with you has ended."

Norcen got a similar letter.

Three days after Ludwig's declaration of war, Corporal Mosher inspected another vandalized AEC well site near Trickle Creek. He found two propane tanks on a window ledge in a sour gas well shack. Inside the hut he found a guttered candle. A bullet had torn a hole through one of the tanks. A punctured propane tank has a 50-50 chance of exploding. When Bilodeau heard about the failed attempt to blow up a well containing one of the deadliest poisons known to man, he drew a deep breath. "That's when I knew a line had been crossed."

He instructed Mosher to send an urgent note to Superintendent Al Bunn in Peace River. The note described the Church of Our Shepherd King as a "compound" and detailed the vandalism to date. It concluded that "Ludwig is apparently convinced that he is right and everyone else is wrong and there is to date no reasoning with him or middle ground found. There is no reason to believe that the suspected criminal activity of sect members towards oil gas and seismic workers will cease given the present situation." Bilodeau made sure Criminal Operations in Edmonton got a copy, too.

Several nights later AEC workers at another well site in the area found electrical cables cut and solar panels damaged beyond repair. Every day, it seemed, a facility was being sabotaged. Some days the police found Ludwigs at crime scenes, shouting, "You're poisoning us!" The two constables on day shift could no longer handle the Ludwig file, let alone their other duties. Donna Bilodeau, who rarely asked about police business, didn't see much of her husband that Christmas. He merely told her, "There's stuff going on in the detachment."

Through December middle management at AEC West called Bilodeau for updates. They were spending $5,000 a day on private security and not getting a hell of a lot of protection. Time and money is everything in the oil patch, and Ludwig was costing them on both fronts. "What are you going to do to stop all this?" they asked. Bilodeau said, "We'll call in Major Crimes and GIS" – General Investigative Services, a five-man unit in Peace River. Bilodeau assumed their involvement would be "a no-brainer." So did Shel Kelly.

Just before Christmas, at 10 p.m., a blast occurred outside Dymphny Dronyk's house. The explosion shook the house and terrified her three children. Like every other AEC employee, she suspected saboteurs and called the RCMP. It turned out that a seismic crew had shot a line of holes too close to her house without notification. "While we were relieved that the noises had not been a Ludwig attempting to blow up the sour gas well east of our house," she later wrote, "our relief quickly turned to outrage at the crass and careless working practices of the seismic crew." The blast cracked the foundation of her home and ruined a $3,000 water filtration system – exactly the sort of damage Ludwig feared AEC's seismic crew would do to his farm and aquifer.

After Christmas saboteurs decorated more AEC well sites with damaged solar panels, cut cables, and busted-up heaters. On New Year's Eve a grader operator with the County of Grande Prairie found a barricade of snow three feet high and six feet deep on the Norcen road, north of the Ludwig property. Water had been poured on the snow, turning it into a giant ice bump.

Finally, on New Year's Day, Bilodeau got his first break. He'd been inspecting vandalized well sites until early in the morning. He'd arrived home cold and tired. Then the phone rang. It was Sergeant Charlie Brown in Grande Prairie. An hour later two constables showed up at the house. They met downstairs, and Donna remembers hearing excited phrases like "No kidding" and "Holy mackerel!" Before Bilodeau left again, Donna asked, "What the hell's going on?" Bilodeau said, "We have something on film. We know what we're facing."

On New Year's Eve an AEC surveillance camera had caught a bearded figure entering the former Ranchmen's well site, now owned by AEC. The saboteur broke the light bulb illuminating the hut, then removed the batteries powering the light. He loosened the fitting to the gas heater, which caused a fire, which tripped a safety alarm at the Hythe Brainard plant an hour later. Police found tracks in the snow leading back towards the Ludwig property.

After viewing the video, no one at the Beaverlodge detachment could identify the bearded saboteur. Everyone complained that "the Ludwig boys all look alike." But Bob Bilodeau recognized him: Ludwig's oldest son, Ben. The one who sat to Ludwig's right.

Chapter 5

War

On January 2, 1997, Shel Kelly was in his second-floor office at AEC in Grande Prairie, completing vandalism reports, when Wiebo and Mamie Ludwig sauntered in, arm in arm. Kelly greeted them coolly and noticed that they smelled pungent. Ludwig said he was looking for Ken Woldum.

Kelly said Woldum wasn't around. Ludwig asked to use the washroom. Once he'd taken a leak he withdrew a bottle from his pocket and dumped sour crude in a corner of the room. He proceeded down the hall, merrily spilling crude in two other offices. Kelly finally spied the wandering visitor and rushed down to tell him to leave.

Later, in court, Ludwig asked Kelly a pointed question: "You stated there was something very pungent and strong. Is that a sore spot that bothers you significantly about our visit there?" Kelly, a taciturn man, replied, "It was a very, very uncomfortable odour that existed in that hallway for many days, yes. It didn't bother me any more than anyone else."

"I see," said Ludwig. "It bothers and it doesn't bother. But it seems to me something very strong and pungent and it would bother you, it would be unpleasant. It did significantly bother you, then?"

"Of course," relented Kelly.

After giving AEC a sample of what his family had been smelling for years, Ludwig, this time accompanied by his son Josh, repeated his performance of "nasal persuasion" at the strip-mall offices of the EUB in Grande Prairie. Before they entered the building, a saboteur had cut the phone cables and shut off the gas line. The sabotage had prompted a police call.

Inside, Ludwig fumbled with the crude and spilled some behind the stairs. He left briefly to clean his coat, only to return and berate Darrold Banta for not taking the family's concerns about sour gas leaks and flares seriously. At that point two RCMP constables arrived to investigate the sabotage and were overwhelmed by the smell. Ludwig said it was about time the RCMP got involved and stopped Big Oil from killing people.

The Mounties asked if Ludwig had spilled the hellish crude on the floor. Ludwig replied that it smelled "like somebody had spilled something." The officers arrested Ludwig and charged him with interfering with the "lawful enjoyment of property." When Josh protested, one of the Mounties held his fingers an inch apart. "Do you want to go to jail, too? Well, you're about this close."

The other Mountie frisked Ludwig: "I've been in the force for 20 years and I know your kind. You're nothing but a 14-year-old teenager."

Ludwig was processed, complete with mug shot, strip search, and fingerprints. In the confines of his cell, the fumes from the crude on his clothes and hands knocked him out. He fell unconscious on the cement floor. After a while the RCMP called for an ambulance. A half-hour later Ludwig awoke, dizzy and numb, to find an attendant hovering over him, urging him to let himself be taken to hospital. Ludwig said he'd stay put. That afternoon a justice of the peace charged him with mischief, collected $2,000 in bail, and told him not to loiter around the EUB any more. "We've done a lot of strange things," Ludwig said, "but all above board."

Two days later, Bob Bilodeau called up Trickle Creek to inform Ludwig about Ben's vandalism spree on New Year's Eve. Bilodeau offered Ludwig two choices: he'd come and arrest Ben, or Ben could voluntarily come into the detachment. Ludwig offered to drive his eldest son. The family's diary records that "Ben was very surprised and wondered what the police were into." He denied involvement in the episode. After being charged, he was ordered to stay away from the property of AEC and other oil companies. The judge set bail at $5,000.

After these legal formalities, Ludwig sat down with Bilodeau in his office. He explained that Ben's wife had miscarried in April 1995 after being exposed to flare emissions for three months. He wondered why the RCMP didn't investigate such "murders." Ludwig sensed Bilodeau's growing unease over the scale of the vandalism. He joked about Bilodeau being "on our side," but the Mountie didn't laugh.

"Well, Reverend. What are you going to do? Go over the line?"

Ludwig liked Bilodeau but sensed he was weak ("trying to appease all the elements"). He assured him things would not get that wild. "Whatever we do, we'll never kill anybody. So relax."

"I just don't think this is worth losing lives over," Bilodeau said.

On January 9 Bilodeau again alerted Peace River that things were getting out of hand. He detailed the improvised explosive device at the well shack and the arrests of Ben and Wiebo Ludwig. "He and his people are not afraid of man's law and are in a self-defensive, self-declared war against the oil and gas industry in the area. He is not afraid to sacrifice his own family members to the cause and appears to have little regard for anyone that stands in the way of his objective. Contrary to what others may mistakenly hope, he will not capitulate until he is taken out of the picture or is successful in his attempt to extort AEC." Bilodeau warned of greater violence and stated that his detachment needed a "proactive operational plan in place with the appropriate human and other resources."

AEC's ever-expanding security crew could also have used a plan. Shel Kelly had now deployed some 15 people, many of them former RCMP officers, to follow Ludwig and his family members within a five- to ten-kilometre radius of Trickle Creek. Armed with CB radios, working around the clock in eight-hour shifts, AEC's security army never caught a Ludwig doing anything more sinister than driving to Dawson Creek for a drywall job or a McDonald's hamburger. Kelly despaired of their inexperience while the security guards fumed at his clipped military manner and nitpicking orders.

Patrolling in rented Jeep Cherokees and Dodge trucks, the guards were a gung-ho bunch. "We felt Ludwig was pretty far out there and had to be stopped, but it was just one big cluster fuck," recalls Kevin Wharton, one of the few licensed private investigators on the job. "There was no clear objective and it was never set up for arrests or convictions." Still, at least three of the security men expressed sympathy with the Ludwigs' struggle. Both the supportive and the scornful guards were impressed by the Ludwigs' organizational abilities and dismayed by their own confusion. Locals dubbed the guards "the Keystone Cops."

Ludwig called them a damned nuisance. One night he narrowly missed smashing into a parked security vehicle whose driver had turned out the lights. His sons almost rear-ended another vehicle. He and Mamie couldn't take a walk down the county road without a security vehicle shadowing them. "Instead of securing the well-sites," he complained to the RCMP, "they continually chase us up and down the roadway as we come and go in our vehicles."

When Bilodeau's superiors in Peace River finally got caught up on their after-Christmas mail, they fumed at Bilodeau's description of the mayhem. They even objected to his use of words like "compound" and "detonate." Guerrilla activity of this sort just didn't happen in Peace River. More important, they were pissed off that he had sent a copy of one memo to K Division in Edmonton, which had asked Peace River what was going on. Bilodeau got the message that hell would freeze over before someone freed up dollars in a chronically underfunded agency to pursue a bunch of mischief complaints.

People in Hythe and Beaverlodge approached Bilodeau or his wife to ask what the RCMP was doing about the vandalism. "Why are you sitting on your hands?" Bilodeau didn't know what to say.

Meanwhile, the protests moved from one dramatic stage to another. In the second week of January, Bilodeau arrived at Trickle Creek with tension in his face and the Edmonton bomb squad in tow. A fish and wildlife officer had found an eight-foot-high blockade of snow on the Norcen road just behind the Boonstras' cabin. The blockade came with a homemade sign: "Danger! Buried Explosives." AEC's chief security man, Kelly, showed up to take notes.

Bilodeau asked the Ludwigs to stay away from the blockade. Josh, the family's video expert, filmed the whole scene, and the highly charged footage appeared in *Home Sour Home,* a video that the Ludwigs produced and began distributing that spring. The video is one of the most strident anti-oil documentaries ever made. In it Ludwig allows that "someone sympathetic to the Ludwig plight" had erected the blockade.

As the bomb squad prepared to blow up the snowbank, Bilodeau and a bomb technician barged into the empty Boonstra cabin for shelter. Ludwig followed the men, haranguing them.

Ludwig accused the sergeant of trespassing. Bilodeau said that Josh had invited him in, which Josh said wasn't true. Bilodeau told Ludwig to take all the pictures he wanted because the camera didn't intimidate him.

Ludwig asked about the windows that would break when the barricade exploded. "If we damage the windows, we will pay for them," said Bilodeau. "Baloney," Ludwig barked. "I get charged when I break people's windows."

Bilodeau said they were blowing up the blockade in the public interest. In the cold morning air the two yelling men in the shack looked like dragons breathing fire on each other.

"The public interest are my children. They are dead out there buried in the woods," shouted Ludwig.

"You may not be in a safe position here," the bomb technician said, trying to usher Ludwig out.

"There's a resistance building against this stuff, and I'm glad," said Ludwig.

When the squad finally blew the barricade, it settled back to the ground in a large cloud of wispy snow. The RCMP found no hidden explosives. As Shel Kelly later thanked one of the RCMP bomb technicians for his help, Josh looked up from his camera and asked, "What was that?" Kelly shot the young man a contemptuous look. "I'm not talking to you, asshole."

The blockade didn't deter Norcen – not much deters the oil patch – but the company took to using a large RCMP escort to get to its well site. Bilodeau even camped out in his Suburban as a Cat operator cleared ground for the drilling rig. Soon a fleet of semis and flatbeds carrying pipes, generators, ATCO trailers, and other paraphernalia rumbled up the Trickle Creek road and turned east at the Boonstra cabin. On Crown land, by a marsh that harboured beavers, ducks, and swans, Norcen selected a spot for its sump pit and cleared it. The Ludwigs had picked berries there for 11 years.

Oil companies traditionally dump oil-field and drilling waste in self-dug pits. Until recently the province kept no record of where sump pits were located or even what toxic waste might be buried in them. Over time, the contents of these pits often leach out and contaminate well water. The Ludwigs were concerned about their aquifer. As the drilling began, family members several times walked out to the sump pit. Each time Bilodeau, steely and weary, told them they were trespassing. Security guards took pictures of the Ludwigs, and the Ludwigs took pictures of the security guards. The family watched in disbelief as a truck sucked water out of a beaver pond for drilling purposes.

From his cubbyhole office in Beaverlodge, Bilodeau again pleaded for help. He wanted detectives from General Investigation Services and a unit from "Special I" to do a proper investigation before a hydrogen sulphide leak from a vandalized well killed one of the Ludwigs or an oil worker. No one from GIS, however, would even meet with him. Shel Kelly, the former Mountie, got on the phone and used his clout to force a gathering in Beaverlodge.

At two meetings in January, Bilodeau virtually begged GIS for help on behalf of his detachment and the local community. He told them, "This thing has legs." If anyone from GIS met with Ludwig, they'd understand he was a "man of conviction." The men from GIS said only that they would review the file.

The GIS men knew what their superiors thought about the whole thing – that it was a simple case of mischief – and ultimately they told Bilodeau that's how they saw it too. Shel Kelly, sympathetic to Bilodeau's awkward position, took notes and silently fumed. As for Bilodeau, he realized that he had placed his career in jeopardy. He was on his own with Ludwig. The RCMP rank and file have a saying about management: "White shirts look after white shirts." Bilodeau was a grey shirt.

At the end of January the despondent grey shirt received a personal letter addressed to "Sarg Bilodeau" in heavy blue lettering. Postmarked Dawson Creek, the letter contained a table napkin that read: "DON'T FUCK WITH OUR PREACHER FRIEND IN HYTHE SGT. SHIT HAPPENS. LOVE YOUR FAMILY 'FROG' – WHILE THEY ARE STILL ALIVE MAN." It was signed "HDB." AEC executives later got similar mail, signed with the same initials. Bilodeau suspected the threat was part of Ludwig's psychological war, a calculated attempt to rattle his cage, but no one could figure out who had sent it.

Bilodeau faxed copies of the letter to Peace River and put in a request to carry his service weapon off duty. "I do not take this lightly and will ensure that my family will be protected." He also asked for a threat assessment, a routine practice when a member of the force gets unfriendly mail. It was never done.

Bilodeau's last job as an active police officer consisted of a short visit to Trickle Creek in early February. On a cold, sunny day he and a court sheriff drove up to the property with registered mail, the kind Ludwig always refused. Mamie Jr., the goat herder and tanner, came out to the porch. Bilodeau asked to see her father. Mamie Jr. said her dad wasn't in. He asked to see her mother. Not in either. He asked to see Ben. Mamie Jr. said he, too, was out. Bilodeau smiled at the young woman and said, "Well, you're here."

Mamie Jr. said she was surely here, but that he should talk to one of her brothers. Josh came running over in the deep snow, camcorder in hand, and told the men they were trespassing. Bilodeau said he had some papers to deliver. When Josh refused them, Bilodeau put the envelope on a snowbank in front of the porch. Josh picked it up like a piece of garbage and threw it on the hood of the

Suburban. As Bilodeau got back into the truck, he told the sheriff to drop the papers in the snow. Then the two men drove away.

Bilodeau had just delivered the opening salvo of one of Canada's most remarkable lawsuits. Overwhelmed by the sabotage, AEC management had decided to strike back with a comprehensive statement of claim. It had pressed Highridge Exploration, a minor player with some shared wells in the area, to join in. The suit named Wiebo and Mamie, their married children and the children's spouses, and all their unmarried children, right down to nine-year-old Levi and seven-year-old Ishshah, the youngest. AEC claimed that "the Ludwig defendants operate and act as a single enterprise with common interests, objectives and actions" and were "vicariously liable" for the harassment, intimidation, and assault of AEC employees. It listed the recent vandalism, threats of war, and hostile encounters, and asked for $300,000 in damages as well as a permanent injunction restricting the Ludwigs from coming anywhere near AEC property. It even accused the family of stealing "No Trespassing" signs.

The idea that AEC would sue a seven-year-old horrified Ludwig and generated much righteous prose. "Now having smelled the blood from the many wounds they have inflicted and boundlessly excited by the thrashings of their victims, these two particular corporate wolves (AEC and HE Ltd) unleashed by the EUB are rushing in for the kill in a feeding frenzy as these reckless charges betray." Ludwig accused AEC of trying to revive the concept of *Sippenhaft*, "a legal construction used by the Nazis to send not only the accused offender, but also his entire family to the concentration camps." His reply also made clear that AEC had misinterpreted his war declaration: "The word war according to contemporary dictionaries means also hostility, enmity, contest, conflict or struggle. I meant to say that I would increase the intensity of the struggle by legal means and/or publicity and public action (even as we are doing) to protect the health, welfare and very existence of my family and flocks/herds." He called for another, impartial public hearing.

After delivering the lawsuit, Bob Bilodeau got an unexpected call from Staff Sergeant Paul Hurl in Peace River. Hurl ordered him to "attend" the office of a K Division psychologist in Edmonton the next morning.

"What's that got to do with the situation here?"

Hurl didn't elaborate. Bilodeau said something about being a good soldier and hung up. "I knew I was being taken out of the picture and that it was all over for me."

Superintendent Al Bunn later sent a briefing note to K Division accusing Bilodeau of sending "bizarre messages" about Ludwig and hinting that Bilodeau's post-traumatic stress disorder might have something to do with it. Bilodeau, Bunn concluded, was unable to "operate his detachment when dealing with a complaint of mischief." The only peace officer who had talked meaningfully with Ludwig, empathized with the family, and sought to mediate between Ludwig and the oil industry was being transferred to Edmonton.

Chapter 6

Dance Floor

No one in the Peace knew where Allan Johnstone was coming from and most had given up trying to puzzle it out. That suited the self-proclaimed "comprehensivist environmentalist" just fine. Though the good citizens of Beaverlodge accused him of being everything from a conceited intellectual to a blabbering idiot, no one called him predictable. In Beaverlodge, he was the town eccentric, complete with black-rimmed glasses, a luminous shock of white hair, and a mouth like a torn pocket. He kept a sign in his two-storey house that read, "Trespassers Welcome, Beware of Flying Arrows."

In his mid-60s, the father of two girls, and a former oil-patch geophysicist, Johnstone had no routine. Some days he got up at four in the morning to think and read. He read as many as 3,000 books a year. Most were on the history of Peace River country, the chemistry of benzene, other grim petrochemical chronicles. He didn't think people reflected enough on life and often told them so. He liked to say things like "Computers reduce incoherent sound data to coherent true sound wave forms by a process called deconvolution. I use my brains but the process is not finite."

When not pondering life or his wife's strained beneficence (Esther, a schoolteacher, had supported his "partial retirement" for a decade), Johnstone put on a camouflage hunting outfit, started up his AMC Eagle wagon, and drove for hours to survey the Peace from the Saddle Hills in the east to Bear Mountain in the west. The steering wheel became a dowsing rod in his hands, his truck a weathervane in the wind. He stopped on impulse and talked to anyone who would listen. He called the Peace his "patrol area."

For nearly 20 years Johnstone had been on the lookout for environmental hazards. He had chronicled "oil/condensate poison gas flaring" throughout the county, indiscriminate pesticide spraying along roads, extensive clear-cuts, and other foul deeds. He also watched over the affairs of the Horse Lakes Indians, some of whom spent more time in jail than out. (He once challenged a local chief to a duel with bow and arrows after police charged the Indian with selling cigarettes to children.) He believed industrial pollution in the region was altering minds and leading to "memory loss, depression, dread and personality change." He didn't consider himself exempt.

Most of his findings, sooner or later, found their way into one of his "Whistleblower" faxes. These faxes rambled on for two or three pages and occasionally crackled with wicked statements and gross insults. Whether attacking the Canadian military, Calgary oil companies, or the leadership qualities of the Horse Lakes Indians, Johnstone ended his Whistleblower reports with postscripts such as: "The naive majority of Canadian liberal weak-kneed spineless wimps reading this letter will label me as a WASP – a White Anglo Saxon Protestant red-necked bigot! I say, if the shoe fits – wear it! Someone has to tell people what is going on in this country. Newspaper reporters refuse to do it."

Johnstone's letters and faxes gave him great notoriety. His comments and opinions got him kicked out of the Christian Reformed Church in nearby La Glace more than once. One angry recipient of a Whistleblower knocked the man unconscious in the post office. When Johnstone's big mouth and environmental activities resulted in his wife's being fired from the local school board, he wrote the authorities a warning: "Imagine yourself lying on a desert island beach – white sand below you. Blue sky above you. Blue waves lapping at your feet. Bare breasted maidens fanning you with palm fronds. All is right with your world! Beware! You may be in the eye of a hurricane." It was vintage Johnstone.

Johnstone's bane was the oil patch. His father had worked in the Turner Valley in the 1940s, when flares burned so furiously they lit up Calgary's night sky. After working in Alberta's first sour gas field, known as "Hell's Half Acre," the father died of stomach cancer at the age of 32. "I have only two memories of my father," Johnstone wrote. "Once he backhanded me off the wall when I was insolent. I am proud of this memory. Also I can recall him being brought home on a stretcher to die." Johnstone was only 10 and still attributes his offhand and cynical behaviour to his father's horrible death. Then again, it could also have had something to do with his mother. "She dropped me down the cellar stairs when I was a baby. I would have forgiven her but she dropped me twice."

After working for two decades in the oil patch as a landman and geophysicist, Johnstone targeted benzenes as his dad's probable killer. He also believed that benzenes had killed thousands of other Albertans who lived downwind from oil and gas facilities. He called it the "60-year poison gas holocaust of Alberta." Using industry reports, he calculated that in the mid-1990s the industry dumped nearly 9,000 tonnes of benzenes into the atmosphere every year by flaring and venting. Leaky storage facilities, tank vents, and sump systems release loads of the toxic substance. So do glycol dehydrators, noisy rural facilities that remove water from natural gas.

Johnstone often came upon these unmanned and unattended dehydrators. The ones with the highest emissions are in the Peace River area. He noticed that the EUB didn't bother much about the dehydrators or monitor their emissions. Many are located just 750 metres from people's homes.

As Johnstone often wrote in his faxes, "Benzenes will penetrate human garments, damage all parts of the body, cause cancer and contribute to heart attacks and strokes." Wherever he found dehydrators and other benzene spreaders, he found cancer. He claimed industry covered up the subject and even boycotted the word. "We live in the world of truths, half-truths and absolute cover-ups." He dubbed the age of petrochemicals the age of missing information.

Wiebo Ludwig approached Johnstone in the fall of 1996 wanting information on hydrocarbon flaring and its health effects. Johnstone obliged and soon was dining with the Ludwigs at Trickle Creek. He took to them immediately, viewing them as "brushfire anarchists" and assuming they were responsible for all the vandalism going down. "I only associate with people with a reasonable IQ. I'm a snob. But Ludwig was smart." They talked about benzenes, hydrogen sulphide, and the hazards of flaring. Johnstone explained that venting raw gases is more serious than flaring, because none of the hazardous compounds are burned off. He also explained to the family how sour gas drops and lies at the bottom of dugouts and sunken fields. By the spring of 1997, Johnstone had become an unofficial spokesman for what he called "a shadowy group of people" and was signing his Whistleblower reports with "Long Live the Ludwigs."

One day Ludwig asked him why he called himself Moose Man. Johnstone explained that his mother and father met at the Moose Hall in Calgary in 1930. He also told Ludwig that one of his greatest disappointments in life was never being able to call in a bull moose. "I had a particularly embarrassing hunting trip in which two cow moose followed me down the trail, to the amusement of my hunting companions. When I got home, I tried the call out on my wife. She called out, 'Allan, will you please check the basement furnace fan – it's making a terrible noise.'

"Yes, I divorced her shortly after that. Otherwise, she was a good wife. I love her as much as my second wife – and vice versa. However, my present wife is better at carrying moose quarters out of the bush. I help her to load."

Ludwig came to refer to him as "Alien" Johnstone and tired of his constant banter and endless faxes. Despite his admiration for the family's struggle, Johnstone felt the family failed to appreciate his genius. After he threatened to "fry" Ludwig on a local radio station over some long-forgotten environmental issue, Ludwig barred him from Trickle Creek. The ban didn't last long; Johnstone was simply irrepressible. Over the next two years he appeared and reappeared at the farm like some prodigal son.

After Bob Bilodeau's abrupt departure, the war in the bush raged on. Björn Sommervold marched through it like a dog soldier. The 50-year-old security consultant worked 18-hour days, seven days a week, driving around Hythe trying to protect property the RCMP didn't want to defend and AEC didn't want to admit publicly was under assault. "It was crazy," he says. The Ludwigs saw so much of him they nicknamed him "Big Nose" and made more than 20 notations in their diaries about his "harassing" presence.

A former prison guard, Sommervold had come to Grande Prairie from Edmonton after his marriage went sour. He reported to Shel Kelly. With the Beaverlodge RCMP detachment essentially leaderless, Kelly and Sommervold grew more disillusioned by the day. Sommervold got more than 20 flat tires that winter while patrolling AEC well sites. He once found propane tanks near AEC property with their valves open, bleeding away like leaking wells. The growing scale of the vandalism astounded him. "I'd arrive at well sites and find hundreds of thousands of dollars' worth of damage." One morning he found three all-terrain vehicles and the instrument panel of a hydraulic excavator, all belonging to an AEC contractor, smashed to smithereens.

Some days the women at Trickle Creek would approach Sommervold and other guards and drop a dead lamb or a goat fetus on their vehicles, screaming, "Look at what you're doing." Other days the boys startled guards by setting off firecrackers near or underneath their vehicles. On several occasions Sommervold thought the explosions sounded more like stun grenades. "Those were the kind of nerve tactics being used." Ludwig later explained that "boys will be boys."

One winter morning Sommervold was sitting at the foot of the Trickle Creek road when he got a call from a fellow security guard that Ludwig was walking down the road with what he thought was a gun. "I need to know. Is it a gun?" said Sommervold. The guard said he couldn't see properly but it looked like a rifle.

"Are you sure?"

"No, I'm not sure."

As Ludwig came closer, Sommervold could see the outline of a weapon cradled in Ludwig's arm. He ordered his security guards out of the area and beat a retreat himself. (Ludwig says it was a pellet gun.) "The goddamn police never investigated that one either." Sommervold says he had countless encounters with Ludwig's "scary side." Ludwig and two of his sons held Sommervold "hostage" for several hours once, when his Jeep Cherokee was cornered and a tree was felled in front of it. "I couldn't get out and there was no way out." Ludwig accused the consultant of tearing down signs and then let him go. When Sommervold reported the incident, an RCMP constable made light of it.

Sommervold had orders to take pictures and get in Ludwig's face. He did just that. When he found Ludwig and Shane Hartnell, a British Columbia environmentalist, out for a walk in February, he drove up and pulled out his camera. He pointed his camera at the bush as the two men approached, then swung around within arm's length of the walkers, snapping away. Hartnell shouted, "Great. Now I'm a criminal too." Ludwig put his hand in front of the lens and said to Big Nose, "Don't bother, friend. Leave him alone."

Sommervold warned Ludwig to back off. "Don't touch me or I'll charge you!"

Ludwig says he then touched the security guard on the shoulder. Sommervold says Ludwig knocked the camera to the ground. "The shit I can tell you...," says Sommervold. "The public doesn't know half of it, and the police weren't interested. The man is a menace." The RCMP did lay charges that day but later dropped them.

Ludwig complained to the RCMP that if Prime Minister Jean Chrétien could choke a protesting citizen without any police hassles, "then it was hardly reasonable" to charge Ludwig "for such a harmless and normal human reaction to a security guard who after all was coming on to us, not vice versa."

RCMP Superintendent Al Bunn met with Ludwig over the matter, cautioning him: "What's happened up to now is one thing, but if it escalates there will be a major investigation. You and Allan

Johnstone are the only ones we've ever heard complain about oil and gas."

Ludwig, dumbfounded, told Bunn, "You are either very naive or you're putting me on." When Sommervold heard about the meeting, his respect for the force sank even lower. "The RCMP told him, 'Please don't be so bad.' I mean, give me a friggin' break."

Ludwig's war presented Sommervold and other security guards with odd temptations. One evening he found a bottle of wine, a wineglass, and a food platter in a snowbank about 200 metres from the farm, on the north side of the Norcen road where he often parked at night. A note said: "Big Nose. Enjoy." Sommervold took a picture of the platter and left it, wondering how it had got there. "It just bugged the shit out of me." His security guards watched the road with night goggles and never caught anyone crossing it. He later found a culvert that ran under the road, as well as a camouflaged observation post.

Sommervold deliberately invaded Ludwig's space as often as he could. Kelly even offered him an assignment that was illegal ("You know, Björn, I can't ask you to do this"). The RCMP needed pictures of the inside of one of Ludwig's outbuildings, suspecting it might contain explosives or weapons. Sommervold thought it over and agreed. At two o'clock in the morning he trespassed onto Trickle Creek, entered the building, and "took pictures from every angle." The photos identified nothing of interest. "But I'm sure they would have shot me had they caught me."

Sommervold says he never really knew what the war was about. He just assumed Ludwig was an evil publicity hound and thrill-seeker. Ludwig's skill amazed him. "The man was a master at hiding his tracks. If I could say anything good about him, that would be it." Many times Sommervold sat with AEC's private army of security personnel over coffee and talked about oil and gas pollution in the Peace. "You know what?" said one man. "Maybe he knows something we don't know."

"How true," replied Sommervold.

That year Sommervold built up a foot-thick file on all the sabotage, complete with hundreds of pictures. "The paperwork never stopped." He often started his day over breakfast with Shel Kelly, who ranted and raved, and ended it at two in the morning with Kelly despairing, "I can't believe the police force I used to serve has come to this."

"You know," Sommervold said to him one night, "somebody is going to die here."

Wiebo Ludwig decided to learn more about the politics of industrial pollution and enlisted Paul Belanger to help. A quiet French Canadian who had grown up in the Peace, Belanger had owned a million-dollar oil-field supply and safety company in Valleyview and knew the industry inside out. He'd given up the money, the hard drinking, and the hectic 60-hour weeks to become an environmental consultant. He now spent most of his time designing eco-friendly houses; he lived in his own self-designed, solar-powered home in Edson, three hours southeast of Grande Prairie. Alien Johnstone had told the Ludwigs and Belanger about each other.

Belanger made several trips to Trickle Creek in 1997. The more he saw, the more he liked the family. It was everything urban environmentalists tended not to be: organized, focused, resourceful, direct. The seventh of eight children, he recognized a certain recklessness and sarcasm in Ludwig that one finds only in later-borns. "Wiebo was the seventh of eight children, too," recalls Belanger. "We both had all these older siblings telling us what to do and – well, we got rebellious."

A lapsed Catholic ("I live by the golden rule"), Belanger regarded Ludwig as a classic anti-establishment rebel. Although he heard much about Ludwig's capacity for verbal nastiness, he never witnessed it. As time went by and the war progressed, the two men became friends. Belanger provided Ludwig with alarming information, particularly on flaring. They'd drive around the countryside and stop by a flaring well, where Belanger would explain exactly what was happening. One large test well often released more pollutants in a week than a large gas plant did in a month.

Belanger gave Ludwig a copy of a controversial 1994 study by the Alberta Research Council that the government had refused to release for two years. The study found that flares didn't burn efficiently and left anywhere from 16 to 38 percent of the gases intact. While the burning of waste gas destroyed some toxins, it created others – as many as 250 compounds, including known cancer causers and brain fuddlers such as benzene, styrene, carbon disulphide, hydrogen sulphide, and carbonyl sulphide. The industry said these emissions weren't much different from the stuff coming off a barbecue, but Belanger said that was nonsense. Besides, no one lived downwind of a barbecue and breathed its fumes day in and day out.

Belanger also told Ludwig the strange history behind the Alberta Cattle Commission report. In 1994 the government had hired Udo Weyer, a respected Calgary-based scientist who often worked for Germany's environmental protection agency, to examine what the world's scientific literature said about animal health and oil and gas emissions. Weyer also did original research on water contamination. His findings supported the anecdotal experiences of the province's cattlemen: that flaring released heavy metals and radioactive material that sickened cattle; that unlined garbage pits for waste drilling muds could contaminate groundwater; that H_2S catches a cow's breath at just 50 ppm; and that more studies on the long-term health effects of low-level exposures were needed. The study also pointed out strange inconsistencies. Oklahoma had 6 million cattle and 90,000 wells and nearly 500 cases of suspected oil-field waste poisoning a year; Alberta, with more wells and fewer cattle, officially had none. Weyer's findings alarmed the Canadian Association of Petroleum Producers and senior staff in Alberta Environment because no government agency had ever admitted the existence of a pollution problem.

The government took Weyer's 850-page report, rewrote it, and released a 250-page version. The sanitized report infuriated Weyer, who threatened legal action if the government didn't release the full version. It did, finally, but the victory cost Weyer's company, WDA Consultants, a great deal in legal bills and lost oil-industry business. Some clients openly told him he had attacked the industry and they wouldn't do business with him again. Others used his data to clean up gas plants and discovered they saved money by doing so. Ludwig told Belanger that the whole story sounded like another massive cover-up.

During one visit Belanger gave the Ludwigs a copy of *Our Stolen Future,* by Theo Colborn. The 1996 book contends that chemicals produced by the burning of fossil fuels contain dioxins and other compounds that mimic natural hormones. These hormone imposters can set off all kinds of problems, including skin disorders (which the family had seen much of), certain cancers, birth defects, and reproductive problems. The chemicals even feminized some animals and birds.

One candlelit evening Belanger had a long debate with the family about homosexuality. He postulated that if enough hormone imposters bombarded the fetus at a critical time, the toxins could alter sexual orientation. Hormone imposters could well explain part of the increase in homosexuality. Ludwig, of course, considered men who defiled themselves with men abominable sinners. But he listened intently to Belanger's arguments. "Homosexuality might be a measure of toxicity rather than something that's morally wrong," argued Belanger. Ludwig didn't want to agree, nor did he want to disagree. "It was a dramatic discussion," Belanger recalls. "They were enthralled. They realized that the environmental problems they were experiencing might be a small part of something big."

After the RCMP banished Bob Bilodeau to Edmonton, his wife lived in a state of escalating fear. For two weeks after his departure, Donna stayed at her girlfriend's bed and breakfast in Grande Prairie. Neither she nor Bob thought it would be safe to stay in Beaverlodge. The threatening letter ("LOVE YOUR FAMILY 'FROG' – WHILE THEY ARE STILL ALIVE") had achieved its purpose.

The threat took on more weight when Donna received one of Allan Johnstone's Whistleblower faxes at work. It warned the RCMP to leave the Ludwigs alone or else. Donna, who worked with political refugees from Iran and Yugoslavia, now feared for her own safety as well as that of her clients, who had all been victims of government-sponsored terrorism. After receiving the obnoxious fax, she phoned a constable in Grande Prairie and said, "This is really serious." The constable replied that Johnstone did that sort of thing all the time.

When Donna finally returned to her dream home in Beaverlodge, she was alone. Bob had been assigned to a training division in Edmonton and could get home only on weekends. During the week she phoned him all the time, saying, "Hi. I'm still here." That winter, menace stalked her everywhere she looked. When a van drove into her cul-de-sac, she froze. She closed the blinds during the day and kept the lights on at night. Every evening she slept in a different room. Even walking the dog became a fearful exercise. "How do you go for a walk when you're not sure who's watching you?" She staggered her work hours and watched her rear-view mirror during the half-hour drive to Grande Prairie. She phoned Bob before she left for work and again when she arrived.

Donna realized the depth of her fright when she visited the Beaverlodge detachment to pick up something from her husband's old office. There in a neighbouring office sat Ludwig, waiting to talk to Superintendent Al Bunn. When she spied the man, her heart pounded in her ears. She rushed to her car and drove home, where she cried and cried. "I was proud to be a policeman's wife, to stand by my husband, to go into a community and make it my home, but to have it all pulled out from under you…"

When the RCMP refused to offer protection, or even give her a cellphone, friends stepped in to keep watch over her. AEC had provided cellphones, panic alarms, and even 24-hour protection to one or two of its threatened employees, and her friends couldn't understand why the RCMP couldn't do the same for Bilodeau's wife. Nor could Donna, whose grandfather had been a member of the RCMP.

Shel Kelly often looked in on her, too, and he promised Bob that if things got worse with Ludwig, he'd make sure she was taken care of. As Bilodeau later documented in an angry complaint to the RCMP: "This was a very good example of community-based policing, but unfortunately the action did not involve the Force."

Donna felt she had lost her freedom, her power, and her home. When people on the streets of Beaverlodge asked her what Bob was doing about the Ludwigs, she searched for an answer. "It looks like we're being transferred to Edmonton," she'd reply stupidly. What was she supposed to say? That Bob was in Edmonton because the powers that be didn't believe him?

That summer the Bilodeaus sold the home they were going to retire to and left Beaverlodge, casualties of what the RCMP still insisted on calling "mischief complaints, nothing more."

In the spring of 1997, AEC dug up a newly laid pipeline just north of Trickle Creek. Saboteurs had drilled the line full of holes. Workers discovered the damage while pressure-testing the new line. Everyone remembered Ludwig visiting pipeline employees and asking them to call when they pressure-tested the line. At the time it seemed odd. Ludwig teasingly told a worker, "We bring in friends from other areas to cause problems here and we, in turn, travel to other areas to reciprocate."

The pipeline vandalism, like the previous sabotage, stumped the RCMP. Nevertheless, Constable Blake Pickell requested that Ludwig appear at the Beaverlodge detachment. He showed up with Mamie and several free copies of *Home Sour Home*. When the constable said he was investigating the drilling of two pipelines, Ludwig got belligerent. He said the police couldn't be trusted to protect the public from corporate polluters and asked Mamie to be a witness as Pickell turned on his tape recorder.

The interview didn't last long. The Ludwig diary summarized the scene. "Mom and Dad were, of course, disappointed about the typical RCMP position of working for the interests of the oil companies at the expense of local residents' safety despite our main and unresolved complaints and concerns that we have repeatedly laid out before these very policemen. It is truly astounding." When Ludwig later asked Pickell for a transcript, Pickell refused. Ludwig pressed the issue and Pickell retorted, "Well, as far as I know you've already got it taped. You've done it before."

It cost AEC West nearly half a million dollars to repair eight kilometres of pipeline. Ludwig has neither denied nor accepted responsibility. He does say he spotted a new bird in the area that summer. "You've heard of sandpipers and woodpeckers. Well, we spotted a pipepecker up here. It has a carbon pecker and moves along pipeline rights-of-way. It's an endangered species, and I hear they spotted a pair near Hythe."

In April 1997, Judge Donald Patterson convicted Ludwig of mischief for spilling sour crude in the EUB's offices. He granted a conditional discharge, stating that he felt Ludwig deserved "a more widespread forum to express the problems that culminated on 2nd of January." The judge also banned Ludwig from the offices of the EUB and four oil companies. Even the Crown prosecutor, Al Munro, expressed sympathy for the way Ludwig's life had been encroached upon. "A courtroom of this kind is, I think, an inappropriate and at best, an awkward forum for dealing with issues of political consequence." Ludwig said he didn't intend to do AEC or the EUB any harm but was trying "to persuade them to come to terms on doing us harm."

Meanwhile the monkeywrenching continued. At various well sites AEC field staff found wires cut, valves shut off, bullet holes in a gas generator unit, acid dumped on monitoring instruments, and construction equipment of every description bashed up.

The sabotage of the pipeline – under the noses of his own security guards – combined with the RCMP's lack of interest upset Shel Kelly no end. In a sharp letter to Peace River Superintendent Bunn, the same officer who had relieved Bilodeau of his job, Kelly accused the RCMP of "insufficient investigation" and becoming a simple-minded spectator of industrial property damage. The RCMP wasn't interviewing suspects, approaching witnesses, or even taking statements. Moreover, no one from the force had ever interviewed him. "Our clients have lost confidence in the police action and are perplexed by the inability or unwillingness of the RCMPolice to commit resources to this problem when they [AEC] have committed so many of their own."

Kelly's letter created a flurry of briefing notes, internal memorandums, and faxes within the RCMP. Assistant Commissioner Don McDermid, commander of K Division, was alarmed. "It seems apparent somebody dropped the ball (if they ever had it)." Al Bunn didn't care for Kelly's meddling and objected to his suggestion that the investigation was beyond the Beaverlodge detachment's capabilities. He promised that every incident would be investigated in a "thorough and professional manner."

That didn't satisfy Kelly. He flew down to Edmonton and had a screaming match at the airport with senior officers from K Division about the non investigation. An RCMP memo out of Peace River later called the situation "sensitive – the initial complaints of damage may not have been dealt with in a satisfactory manner but that's in the past and Mr. Kelly's intimidating/demanding demeanor may be out of place." Rod MacKay, the division's superintendent of criminal operations, observed, "Shel's performance with our field investigators is to say the least questionable!"

In June 1997, Colleen Galenzoski, the manager of Security Management Consulting Inc., sent pointed instructions to the Peace River subdivision. After accepting the force's explanation that "staffing and human resource problems in the Sub-Division were responsible for an apparent lack of continuity in the analysis of incidents," she demanded that the RCMP check out several Ludwig associates including Allan Johnstone, Paul Belanger, and Shane Hartnell. Galenzoski said she had information that Belanger might be a suspect in pipeline vandalism in the Edson area and warned that the Hythe Brainard plant could well be the next target.

Two GIS detectives in Peace River replied to the memo with the wariness of deft public servants. Yes, they had investigated most of these individuals. Hartnell was definitely "anti-industry" and even operated his own website. Inquiries about Belanger hadn't revealed much. Johnstone may or may not have had pertinent information, but he seemed to share most of it in his annoying Whistleblower reports.

The detectives also found fault with SMC reporting procedures. Whenever security guards (as opposed to company employees) investigated sabotage, they created an information delay and breakdown in the normal investigation. Peace River would always consider the big picture, but it remained the responsibility of the Beaverlodge detachment to chase evidence. The detectives finally encouraged SMC to educate the oil companies to report sabotage promptly. "Without physical evidence and reliable witness testimony, many future occurrences will unfortunately remain unsolved."

Burned out by 16-hour days and discouraged by the RCMP's inactivity, Shel Kelly closed his notebook and packed his bags. The man who had shadowed Ludwig for eight months left the field of battle. Like Bilodeau, Kelly didn't like to fight wars he knew he couldn't win.

When the Peace started to turn green that spring, Allan Johnstone popped into Robert Wraight's sporting goods store and pawnshop in a yellow building at the edge of Beaverlodge. Wraight, his wife, Marita, and their three children had moved to the south Peace from 100 Mile House, B.C. Johnstone, the consummate gossip, had befriended the 36-year-old with the handlebar moustache and asked if he wanted to buy a video he was selling on behalf of the Ludwigs.

"I want to watch it first," replied Wraight.

Wraight had come to the Peace in search of cheap land and new opportunities. A high school dropout and former soldier, he'd bought a quarter-section 20 kilometres west of Hythe and set up his trailer in the bush. In his living room one night he watched the *Home Sour Home* video with great unease. There had been no sour gas plants or flares at 100 Mile House, and he knew nothing about them.

The startling video begins with music from *Braveheart* and a shot of a graveyard sign that reads, "Here lie small beginnings, Created and wholly known by God." Then a genial, bearded fellow arm in arm with his wife appears on a snowy country road. "Hello. My name is Wiebo Ludwig." The man says his family came to the Peace 11 years earlier with no money and no skills. They prospered until the gas industry arrived. Now he fears that their hopes and dreams won't pan out because the oil and gas industry hasn't left them any room to live and grow.

Wraight watched the dramatic re-enactment of the Ranchmen's sour gas leak, complete with Harmony tearfully placing dead baby lambs in a wheelbarrow and throwing them onto a funeral pyre. "I, as a shepherdess, know that I have the right to go after a predator of my sheep," she declares angrily. Wraight grew more disturbed as he watched the family re-enact an evacuation from the farm.

Ben talks about the environmental benefits of wind power. Kara, a soap maker, explains that they have lost a child after flaring near their place. A woman named Dania talks about rabbits with toxic overload in their livers, and a man named Fritz demonstrates the Biblical bounty of bees and speaks of the need to teach industry a lesson. That is followed by scenes of bucolic winemaking and wood-working. A tall farmer named Carl Bryzgorni talks about being vented and flared on by industry. He demonstrates how drilling and seismic activity have affected his well water by setting it on fire. Ludwig narrates, "Even water can burn in this crazy world of industrial exploitation."

The battle over the Norcen road blockade fills the screen, and Wraight watched Bob Bilodeau and Ludwig go at each other like junkyard dogs. Ludwig charges that Big Oil's security guards have turned the area "into a regular ghetto." Allan Johnstone pops up in the video, warning about "continued brushfire anarchy in the north" if the federal government doesn't intervene. The video ends with Ludwig admonishing viewers to stand up and resist industry because the police and the government won't.

Wraight wanted to meet the charismatic narrator. He took his family out to Trickle Creek on Mother's Day. When Ludwig cautiously asked what he wanted, Wraight said he had watched the video and wanted to learn more. The Ludwigs invited the family in for coffee and talked about pollution, self-sufficiency, the villainy of government taxmen. "You know," said Wraight, "people in 100 Mile House talk and complain about things but never do anything." Ludwig assured Wraight that Trickle Creek was full of doers.

Ludwig gave Wraight a grand tour of the windmill, the animal barns, and his extensive woodlot. Wraight was impressed ("I had a strong interest in alternative lifestyles") and the two families began to socialize two or three times a week. Marita, a keen student of the Bible, felt comfortable at the farm and enjoyed talking about health issues with Harmony, the family's herbalist.

Not everyone at Trickle Creek welcomed the newcomer. Shane

Hartnell was a bearded activist who had once worked as a roughneck in eastern British Columbia. After a near-fatal car accident, he'd developed an extreme sensitivity to air pollution. Ever since, he had carried on a public battle with Louisiana Pacific to get the multinational to clean up its smelly pulp mill in Dawson Creek. In the spring of 1997 he took up residence at Trickle Creek after Allan Johnstone told him about the family's struggles. Hartnell, an outspoken fellow, wasn't afraid of offending Ludwig's fundamentalism and often did. One night he argued that the book of Genesis really describes how a group of aliens inserted 223 genes into Adam – the world's first case of genetic manipulation. When Hartnell later said he wanted to marry Mamie Jr., both Ludwig and Mamie Lou choked on their breakfasts.

Hartnell took an instant dislike to Wraight. The pawnshop owner never talked about much at the dinner table – to which he always wore a baseball cap – except guns, knives, and old snowmobiles. As Wraight got more upset about the flaring, he also talked about the need for retribution. "He was all for terrorism," says Hartnell. "He tried to urge Wiebo on and get his respect that way." Wraight told the Ludwig boys about well sites he had shot at, how to vandalize equipment, even how to make a silencer out of a potato. (The boys blew apart the barrel of a .22 following his advice.)

When Wraight's own children broke out in rashes and lumps after being exposed to flare emissions, his rhetoric got hotter. "He was mad. He constantly wanted to get back at the industry," says Hartnell. Before Ludwig kicked Hartnell off the farm for a while, for chasing after his red-lipped daughter Mamie Jr., Hartnell warned him that Wraight was giving him bad vibes. "Pawnshop people are pawnshop people," he told Ludwig. "They buy and they sell."

Wraight became such a convert to the family's cause that he sold copies of the video at his shop. He also sat in on Ben's trial for mischief in June in Grande Prairie, offering moral support.

Crown Prosecutor Al Munro, the Peace's best-read attorney, had deftly handled Ludwig's sour crude case two months earlier. He had less sympathy with Ben's act and coolly presented it as an open-

and-shut mischief case, complete with videotape of the criminal wrongdoing.

Near the end of the trial Ludwig defended his son by expressing his disillusionment with the court system. He felt that it didn't want to hear what had provoked his son "in good conscience" to defend himself against an industry that had committed plunder, rape, and murder. "Most of us are coughing up the evidence because it is affecting our lungs, and still they refuse to discuss the real issues. I call it straining at gnats and swallowing camels." He politely reminded Judge Patterson about section 34 of the Criminal Code, which states, "Everyone who is unlawfully assaulted without having provoked the assault is justified in repelling force by force." He drove home his point by quoting John Locke, the 17th-century English philosopher: "And that all men may be restrained from invading others' rights and from doing hurt to one another . . . Every man has a right to punish the transgressor of that law to such a degree as may hinder its violation."

The judge thanked Ludwig for his comments but reminded him that a court of law didn't entertain such sweeping defences. He again suggested that Ludwig find other forums "to deal with those problems that have beset your family." He pronounced Ben guilty and asked the Crown to comment on a suitable punishment.

Munro, who once prosecuted a company after a hydrogen sulphide leak had killed two of its workers, had no patience for the vandalism of sour gas wells. Any talk of punishment had to grapple with the potential havoc the sabotage could have caused. The whole incident raised an eloquent irony, he said. What Ben sought to destroy "was one of the very mechanisms that are there for his safety. What he sought to destroy is the warning system for the sour gas about which he so vividly complains and acts against." Calling him "an extraordinarily dangerous man" who had put "his family, his community, and the public at risk," Munro asked the judge to temper justice with mercy, given that Ben had no criminal record.

"This is an extremely dangerous situation," said the judge. "I have no idea what you had in mind when you loosened the gas fitting and started the fire. I am contemplating sending you to prison and the reason I'm doing that, and I haven't fully disabused myself of the notion, is that you are not contrite, sir. You seem to be very proud of the damage you did. You seem to be very proud of the fact that you have committed a criminal offence because you feel that you have a right to do so." Suggesting that Ben had been misled by his father, the judge placed him on three years' probation and ordered him to pay the oil company $890 in damages.

Patterson's comments unnerved Ben, who explained himself in a letter to the court and to AEC. Ben thought people in authority had the responsibility to protect the family and especially the headship of the father in the home. "So now after having sought support from the court in our efforts to protect our family, I have instead found myself with my name slandered and a criminal record to prove it." Ben confirmed that he was indeed proud of trashing the facility: "I actually feel privileged to have a criminal record because it declares officially that I stand opposed to such wholesale injustice and corruption." He warned the court to "turn from its cruel ways" or face the wrath of God.

His wife wrote an even more blistering addendum. She said Judge Patterson's reckless remarks so enraged her that her "vision was literally blurred momentarily... I myself was taken aback by the irreconcilable spirits operating in opposition to justice." The family, she said, had spent years trying to honour God's grace in a province with the nation's highest divorce rate, only to have a court stomp on her husband's good name. Did the court not recognize that a high official is watched by one higher? "King David's words seem so appropriate," she wrote: "'Do I not hate them that hate Thee, O Lord? And do I not loathe them that rise up against Thee? I hate them with perfect hatred; I count them my enemies.' (Psalm 139: 21/22)."

Recent injustices, she wrote, had helped her appreciate Jael, a daunting symbol of Israel's resistance against Canaanite repression. Kara regarded Jael as a "very meaningful example and heroine" because she calmly drove a tent peg deep into the temple of a Canaanite general "after soothing him to sleep with sweet words and satisfying milk."

Ludwig drew similar conclusions. He told local reporters after the trial that the system was simply too corrupt to deal with the problem. "The only thing that will bring about change is a groundswell of protest which would undoubtedly require force."

After the trial Richard and Lois Boonstra ended their long exile in the Okanagan and rejoined the Church of Our Shepherd King. Richard felt it was time, even though Lois still had emotional and spiritual reservations. Richard called first to test the waters. "There was fear," he remembers. "It felt just like the last minute before you get married."

"Do you feel you are eligible to return?" asked Ludwig.

"No, I don't feel eligible."

"Well, why don't you come home anyway."

Lois followed several days later. "I just didn't want to go back. I had doubts instead of trusting." When the Boonstras' daughters and grandchildren greeted them with tears of joy, and Wiebo and Mamie received them with open arms, Lois felt she had been shown the Lord's mercy and forgiveness.

To the surprise and relief of AEC's security guards, the saboteurs took the rest of the summer off. The Ludwigs, for their part, continued building their Christian community. While the boys drove into eastern British Columbia to drywall, the girls milked goats and gathered currants and cranberries. Ludwig himself had a new agenda: building a groundswell of resistance.

The first people he sought out were the Lubicon Indians. They live five hours' drive northeast of Trickle Creek near Little Buffalo. In the last two decades Big Oil has taken nearly $9 billion worth of oil and gas from Lubicon land. The invasion has changed their way of life. Chief Bernard Omniyak told Ludwig that before Big Oil arrived in the 1980s, the band harvested more than 200 moose a year. Now they were lucky to kill 20. Trapping income had dropped from $5,000 per trapper to less than $500. In 1985 and 1986, as wells flared around the band, the women miscarried 19 of 21 pregnancies. Omniyak gathered 40 of his troubled tribe together to watch *Home Sour Home*. The chief said his people had suffered from the same skin rashes and eye infections as those documented in the video. The chief's long tale of "deceitful treaties and authorities that were bent on taking their self-sufficient lifestyle away from them" deeply angered Ludwig.

Ludwig's next visit was to Henry and Tille Pirker. A big-handed man with a pleasant Austrian accent, Pirker runs a cattle and bee operation east of Grande Prairie near the Smoky River. Since 1991 he has amassed data indicating that emissions from gas plants and pulp mills have taken a heavy toll on trees and vegetation. Some locals regard Pirker as a complainer, but many top scientists praise his research.

In a tree survey of two quarter-sections near his farm, Pirker found that 37 percent of the aspens and poplars were dead and another 50 percent dying. Spruce trees were developing weird tops, what scientists call the "stork-nest syndrome," a telltale symptom of acid rain. Tourists from Germany, a nation acquainted with acid rain and forest die-off, routinely commented on the stunted trees in the Peace.

Alfalfa, said Pirker, the mainstay of cattle production and a crop highly sensitive to sulphur, was turning yellow and spindly. Downwind of intense oil and gas activity, alfalfa wasn't forming nitrogen nodules on its roots, which meant less hay and, ultimately, fewer farmers. Pirker travelled around the province inspecting alfalfa crops and found the same problem wherever the oil patch flared and vented profusely, including Lloydminster, Wainwright, and Provost.

Pirker attributed the tree and crop damage to ozone, a kind of smog formed by fossil-fuel emissions. At more than 25 parts per billion, ozone can open up plant pores and kill vegetation by forcing it to give up its moisture. It also robs legumes of the ability to make nitrogen. Ground-level ozone around Beaverlodge often exceeds the critical level for healthy vegetation for up to 80 days in the spring, when bright sunshine turns gas plant pollution into smog. But every time Pirker tried to raise the issue with Alberta Agriculture, he was told "pollution damage was not feasible in Alberta." Pirker told Ludwig, "I can talk to scientists all over the world and they understand this. But not in Alberta."

The Bocock brothers, Bill and John, related more horror stories. With their wives, the Bococks operate a prizewinning dairy farm west of Edmonton. Their troubles began when Norcen built a sour gas plant six kilometres east of their farm in 1991. They fought the development at an EUB hearing and even managed to get a neighbour, a professor of corporate law, to represent them. The professor told the EUB that its legislation was draconian and made a mockery of democratic process and that landowners had a snowball's chance in hell. In the end Norcen got its plant, but with a special scrubber that was supposed to reduce 2.3 tonnes of sulphur emissions a day to next to nothing. The scrubber, however, didn't always work.

That same year Norcen tested a sour gas well south of the Bocock farm and vented and flared enough gas to heat Edmonton for a week. The ghastly flare shook the house; the two families could hear and smell it even with their windows closed. Several months later the Bococks started seeing abnormal sexual behaviour in cows, bulls, heifers, tomcats, wild ducks, and crows. The bulls showed no interest in mounting and one tomcat behaved like a female. In the spring their herd's twinning rate jumped from 1 to 6 percent. High twinning is bad news for dairy farmers because the female twin is almost always sterile.

In the first two weeks of the plant's operation, the Bococks lost eight cows; several other animals produced no milk or became hyperactive or dumb. But reproductive problems remained the central curse. Their prizewinning milkers didn't come into heat properly, and in 1996 only 11 of 45 calves were healthy at birth. In the past six years, the brothers told Ludwig, they'd had to cull 100 animals from their herd. The land also took a beating. The Bococks had twice the recommended level of sulphur in their soil. In order to boost crop productivity, they had to lime their land to neutralize the acidity created by the plant's sulphurous fallout.

When they raised these issues with Norcen, a plant superintendent replied that a flare stack analysis showed "there was nothing there to indicate anything would pollute the atmosphere or create problems to growth in the area." The company, which met all government standards, suggested that big piles of manure at the farm were releasing H_2S and causing the problems. The Bococks had some of the cleanest barns in Alberta.

As the Bococks studied the matter, they realized that H_2S was just part of the problem. Recent studies had shown that flare emissions from wells and gas plants also contain harmful chemicals such as benzene, toluene, carbon disulphide, and dioxins. Some of these pollutants cause cancer, kill fetuses, and mimic hormones. The Bococks believe their cattle absorb these toxins in their fat and release them at calving time, when cows draw on their fat reserves. That's when they see the worst problems.

The Bococks are also convinced that pollution has taken a human toll. After the gas plant came onstream, two of their neighbours got cancer and another suffered a nervous breakdown. One farmer shot himself after finding cracked hooves on all his cattle. Asthma, allergies, and multiple sclerosis also seemed to be on the rise. And one of the Bocock women developed a low-grade lymphoma.

Government indifference and industry denials are the most damning part of the problem, the Bococks believe. The industry essentially regulates itself, and no one does proper air monitoring. In 1994 an Athabasca cattleman told Bill that most air monitoring was an out-and-out fraud. He knew because his son did monitoring for the province. Whenever provincial environmental staff got readings above guidelines, he said, they ignored them or tore them up. Several years later, Bocock told Ludwig, a petroleum engineer confirmed the practice.

After hearing the family's tribulations, Ludwig asked them, "What do you do when you are faced with Hitler? Do you fight?" The Bococks said it was important to fight in every legal way possible and to get the media's attention. Ludwig assured them he wasn't about to take further abuse from industry lying down. The Bococks suggested that he and Mamie should visit with the Johnstons down in Sundre.

Several months later they did. Wayne and Ila Johnston ranch by the James River in heavily wooded country in central Alberta. Their modest beef operation sits atop one of Alberta's richest gas fields. In 1996, with more than a dozen flaring gas wells and sour gas plants surrounding their bungalow, the couple could read the paper at five in the morning without turning on the lights.

Wayne, a gentle 50-ish man fond of suspenders, showed Ludwig a dozen binders documenting their struggles. The Johnstons had written more letters and accumulated more papers than even the Ludwigs. The industry went nuts in the 1980s, he said, and industrialized the countryside. "Every time you looked around there was a new flare or a pipeline break," said Wayne, who quit his job in the oil patch in 1991 to work on the farm. By 1994 the couple had a fine herd of 160 Angus. But because most of the land around their farm sits at a slightly higher altitude, the Johnstons started smelling and breathing flare emissions all over the farm. "It was just constant harassment."

In 1994 a sour gas pipeline owned by Shell sprang a leak under an ice-covered river as calving season started. The leak was three kilometres from their farm. The break released about 40,000 cubic metres of sour crude and gas into the air, including the usual suspects: hydrogen sulphide, methane, benzene, toluene, ethylbenzene, and xylene. Shell employees later burned the spilled hydrocarbons over a six-week period and in so doing created a nasty ice smog. The Johnstons' cattle breathed this chemical brew and started to go down. That spring the couple lost 26 calves to irritated lungs and hypothermia. Some of the calves had spongy hearts; others had lesions on their spines. The hooves on some calves simply dropped off. Other calves lost their hair and appetite. Adult cows became highly aggressive; some tried to mount other females. "It was an ungodly sight," said Wayne. A neighbour, he said, witnessed a similar holocaust in his herd.

A detailed toxicological study later commissioned by the Alberta Research Council found that the Johnstons' cattle had suffered damage to the lungs, brain, and immune system. The study concluded these impacts were "compatible with exposure to assorted hydrocarbons in other species... No consistent pattern of disease could explain the high death losses observed in calves on ranches." Shell blamed the deaths and calving problems on the cold winter, even though local ranchers had experienced colder winters without problems. Oil workers in the area spread the false allegation that Johnston beat and mistreated his cattle. He'd spent $54,000 on lawyers' fees, he told Ludwig, and still hadn't received any compensation.

Meanwhile the flaring continued. After one massive H_2S leak at Shell Caroline, the world's largest sour gas plant, a few kilometres to the west, the Johnstons' cattle all came down with pink eye and were reluctant to rise when disturbed. After other flaring incidents the Johnstons found dead cattle or dazed animals with phlegmy lungs and burned nostrils.

They also told the Ludwigs of their disappointing experiences with the EUB. In 1997 Shell Caroline, one of the Johnstons' most offensive neighbours, asked the EUB for permission to expand. The Johnstons opposed the move, demanded a public hearing, and got one. Many other ranchers signed up to testify. They all believed their ailments – including asthma, coughs, headaches, aching muscles, shortness of breath, and memory loss – were connected to pollution from the plant.

Dr. David Bates of Vancouver, a leading researcher on air pollution, testified on behalf of the ranchers. He told the EUB's professional engineers that symptoms of ill health in the area clearly matched what the scientific community knew about hydrocarbon exposure. He cited a study in the eastern United States, where foul air from a large chemical manufacturing centre had sickened the entire community. The EUB, however, dismissed Bates's testimony and approved the expansion: "While the Board does not doubt that the interveners are experiencing the symptoms described, it cannot conclude from any available evidence that these symptoms are necessarily related to emissions from the flares or the incinerator stack." Bates, who has testified all over the world, couldn't believe the board's unwillingness to consider basic health issues. "It convinced me that I would never want to testify in Alberta again." And he hasn't.

The Johnstons finished their tale with the results of monitoring done by Alberta Environment. The monitors picked up some of the province's highest levels of benzenes, toluenes, and xylenes near their home. Ila explained that Alberta didn't have regulations to govern these toxins. She said that benzene causes leukemia and can impair fetal development, while toluene undoes the nervous system. Xylene affects fetal body weight and poisons the brain. "There are days when it's almost too much – you drag yourself out and don't know what you'll face." She now had lung problems, she said, and thought flaring emissions were the cause.

The more Ludwig travelled, the more he heard. Martha Kostuch, a Rocky Mountain House veterinarian, said she got a call every week from gassed ranchers who didn't know where to turn. The problems extended as far away as Manitoba. Bill Campbell, a straight-arrow rancher, related how venting and flaring from a nearby sour gas battery had killed 60 of his cows and knocked down his 18-year-old grandson for 12 minutes. Campbell got such a dose one day that he couldn't stand for hours. The next day his toenails started to peel off. The government did nothing.

As more farmers learned of the war in the Peace, Ludwig spent more time on the phone. He was becoming a receptacle for all the rage landowners had kept to themselves, in some cases for decades. He wrote to anyone he could think of: Ted Turner, Jane Fonda, Robert Redford. He also informed the RCMP and the EUB of his findings. "I sense everywhere I go that if things continue this way – if the police, the courts, the government and its Agencies continue to suppress these many very legitimate and serious complaints from so many people so ill-affected by these industries – these people are poised to take matters in their own hands, as they indeed already are. People are getting sick, nervous and angry. It is not wise for government and industry to join hands in an all out attempt to silence them."

He got no reply.

Chapter 7
Numbers

Through 1997 one of Ludwig's neighbours, AEC's $200-million Hythe Brainard plant off Highway 43, wheezed and coughed like an angry dragon. Some days it flared as much as 6,000 cubic metres of gas. Dogged by mechanical trouble and chronic power shortages, the sour gas facility burned off more hydrocarbons that year than it had in the previous decade. Gary and Anne Smith, who lived southeast of the plant, watched and smelled the luminous fires and black smoke with fear and alarm.

When the two immigrants from Ontario bought a house and 10 acres in 1985, they knew nothing about the province's 600 gas plants or their propensity to expand. They had come to the Peace to take up nursing jobs and thought a place in the country would be a pleasant change. Save for the occasional odour, the Smiths hardly noticed their industrial neighbour until it started to grow from a three-building outfit into what Gary called "a monstrous facility" in 1997. At first the expansion seemed innocuous and the Smiths didn't mind the traffic and noise that accompanied new pipelines and power lines. But then the plant added a new gas inlet to collect all the sweet gas that AEC's aggressive approach to development in the Hythe area had discovered.

Bigger flares brightened the sky. More noxious fumes drifted by the house. The Smiths noticed the top half of their spruce trees dying off, and spots began dotting the poplar leaves in the front yard. Someone suggested it might be the first sign of acid rain. The plant had become so noisy both day and night that the two couldn't sleep properly. After seismic activity near their house, they found cracks in their basement foundation. Then their well water went bad and started to taste like sulphur and iron. If you drank too much, you farted all night long. They couldn't even get their white uniforms clean without using Iron Out, a caustic cleaner.

By fall clouds of black smoke and white steam issued irregularly from the plant. At times the Smiths felt as though they were living at the end of an airport runway. "We half expected to see a 747 come over the trees," says Gary. During one plant upset he phoned and inquired what all the flaring and sirens were about, only to be told to evacuate. When he called another time, he heard nothing but sirens, panic, and confusion in the control room. A plant operator finally shouted, "Sorry, we have an emergency right now!" before hanging up.

When Ludwig and Mamie heard about the Smiths' troubles, they paid a visit. "We believe you're having some problems," Ludwig began. "We've had the same problems on our property." The Smiths didn't know much about the Ludwigs except that they were a bit eccentric and held strong feelings about the oil and gas industry. Anne had once visited Trickle Creek to buy a turkey. Her co-workers had gossiped that the Ludwigs were "evil and awful" because of the way they treated their women. But none of that dissuaded the Smiths from being their garrulous, hospitable selves. While Anne chatted with Mamie, Gary told Ludwig his experiences with the plant and his concerns about his daughter, Freya, who was pregnant. He added that he was keeping a detailed record of all the flaring, odours, and noise.

The plant's increased production had also caught Ludwig's

attention. He and Mamie had seen 25-metre flares rise up into the sky. Every time the facility lit up the night, the people at Trickle Creek smelled H_2S and hydrocarbons around the farm the next morning. Many of the children developed blisters and sores after playing on the wooden rail fence in their yard. Ludwig suspected that sulphurous plant emissions had contaminated the fence. He congratulated Gary on his record-keeping and said it might be valuable in pressuring the industry. Gary promised to help out if he could and met with Ludwig three or four times that fall. The couples exchanged gifts.

The Smiths weren't the only people having problems with the gas plant. Peter von Tiesenhausen, a contemporary landscape artist, lives on the south side of the facility with his wife and son. Like the Smiths, he noticed an exponential increase in noise, lights, and fumes issuing from Hythe Brainard in 1997. For nearly seven years he had battled the industry as it drilled and altered the landscape around his land. "It takes away from the spirit of the land. It's like rape. You never get over it."

Von Tiesenhausen's immediate concern that fall was the approaching Alliance pipeline. He'd scrimped and saved to buy his land, and now a Calgary consortium wanted to put part of a $3-billion pipeline in his backyard so people in Chicago could buy more Canadian gas. "I made a decision at the age of nine to live here, and I won't leave. If someone is attacking you, don't you fight? I'm not one to run."

Von Tiesenhausen, who grew up in the Peace, isn't keen on the logging in the area either. He knows people who clear-cut their land just to buy a mobile home so they can escape all the ugliness they have created. He can't understand that kind of thinking. He once met a logger clear-cutting the forest scene he was trying to capture on canvas. "I'm not going to stop until I can see the ocean from my house," boasted the logger.

"What the hell are you doing this for?"

"My kid needs a four-wheel-drive."

Unlike most of his neighbours Tiesenhausen regards his well-treed land as a living sculpture and a gift. You can't walk his quarter-section without bumping into Viking-like ships made of long willows or ghostly wooden baskets hanging from trees. "I haven't a clue what they are about, but I sure like them." Medieval-looking towers of entwined branches surround lofty poplars. Five eight-foot-high "bog people" carved from solid wood guard one open field. Von Tiesenhausen made them with a chainsaw and then scorched them black. Some people call them the burning men. Von Tiesenhausen has shown them in Calgary and Toronto to much acclaim. "I see the figures as martyrs," he says. "They are the blackened refugees of the industrialization of the Peace."

And then there is the 88-foot-long fence that symbolizes the passage of his life. One end is paintless and rotting while the other end looks white and beautiful. Every year von Tiesenhausen adds another eight-foot length. He never makes repairs. The fence reminds him how little time a man has to live in this world. "It's about a commitment to my land, my work, and my integrity."

To protect the fence, the burning men, and the trees from the Alliance pipeline, von Tiesenhausen came up with a novel weapon: he put a copyright on his land. When the oilmen came to negotiate a price for ripping up his place for the pipeline, he said nothing was for sale. "I have a copyright. I make films and videos about my land. A pipeline would be a copyright infringement." The oilmen didn't know what to say. They offered him an obscene amount of cash; he still said no. Several months later they rerouted the pipeline around the place, spending nearly half a million dollars to do so.

Ludwig tried to enlist von Tiesenhausen in his cause that fall but the artist politely declined. "We are fighting a similar battle," he said, "but we are doing it differently."

As Ludwig sought to woo allies, the war in the Peace escalated. On October 27, 1997, at about 5:30 in the evening, a bullet smashed through Mike Weeks's office at the Hythe Brainard plant. The large-calibre bullet sent glass fragments flying through the air and put a hole above the plant manager's desk the size of a basketball before lodging in a pipe. Weeks, who had just gone over to the Sexsmith plant, missed being killed by an hour. The power engineer, the son of a military man, once described himself to one of Ludwig's sons as "a good church-going Christian and not an evil oilman." He had tried to convince Ludwig that he was "an environmentalist working in a gas plant," but to no avail.

The shooting scared the hell out of Hythe Brainard's 25 employees, mostly family men, and deeply unsettled Weeks. When he showed up that evening to calm down his co-workers, he took one look at the mess and wondered, "What am I doing here? This is crazy."

The seven-member Beaverlodge RCMP detachment, overworked as ever, sent out a constable to investigate the incident. The Mountie suggested that maybe a hunter or some Indians had taken a potshot at the plant. Such things often happened in Alberta. The constable calculated that the shooter had probably knelt or crouched about 160 metres from the facility. When Weeks asked why no one was being interviewed, the officer replied, "Oh, well, in that case I'll interview you."

The next day Weeks phoned many people, including Allan Johnstone. He woke the sleeping comprehensivist from a dream in which trees served as space satellite dishes for his extrasensory galactic perceptions – the subject of many recent faxes. Weeks believed that Johnstone was a cranky gossip and knew he was a friend of the Ludwigs. When he told him about the shooting and how unhappy he was about it, Johnstone laughed. "Finally, we'll get some publicity."

Menacing letters followed the shooting. Weeks's secretary at the Sexsmith plant opened one the next day. The dark black lettering made her hysterical: "LOOK AT YOUR OFFICE WINDOW ASSHOLE IF YOU DON'T STOP PISSIN ALL YOUR SHIT OVER THER NEXT ONCES REEL BAD." Several weeks later the plant supervisor got another threat, with better grammar. "YOU A-HOLE. NEXT TIME IT WILL BE RIGHT THROUGH YOUR HEAD."

In Calgary the shooting got the attention of AEC's senior management in a way that drilled pipelines hadn't. After spending literally millions on security and repairs to vandalized wells and pipelines, the company finally realized that its strategy of hiring guards and not talking to Ludwig wasn't working. Weeks flew down to Calgary and told one of the chairman's senior managers that the company needed to try something different. "If windows in Calgary were being targeted," he told the executive, "your employees would be just as stressed as ours."

In response to the shooting the company authorized a $50,000 reward. AEC West's vice-president, Ken Woldum, condemned the shooting as terrorism of the worst sort: "What we have is neighbours shooting at neighbours," he told the *Daily Herald-Tribune* in Grande Prairie.

That statement struck Ludwig as presumptuous. "How do they know it was someone in the neighbourhood of the plant who did the shooting? Slanderous conjecture like that is characteristic of oil thugs in Nigeria." He then promised to give up the identity of the responsible party if AEC West changed its reward to a "zero-tolerance policy on flaring and emissions emitting from their putrid and deadly oil and gas exploitation." The company ignored the verbal dare, as it had tried to avoid Ludwig himself for nearly a year.

In Edmonton, Ludwig's audacious statements caught the attention of Richard Secord, a British-educated lawyer with Ackroyd, Piasta, Roth and Day. Secord, who represented aboriginal communities and landowners battling government or corporate polluters, gave Ludwig a call. Despite Ludwig's abiding dislike of lawyers, the two hit it off. If there was unhappiness with oil-field activities in the area, Secord said, people should ask for a public inquiry before the Energy and Utilities Board to examine air pollution from oil and gas installations and its effects on human and animal health. Ludwig said he had a flock of people ready to testify. After visiting Hythe (and smelling the hellish fumes by the Smiths' residence), Secord proposed to bring AEC, Norcen, and Rigel before the EUB. To do so he needed the families to detail their concerns in writing.

Each letter told a graphic story. With Ludwig's assistance, Bob Wraight wrote that he had moved to Alberta to find clear air and opportunities. Instead his wife, Marita, got sick and lost weight when a sour gas well flared east of his property. Now his children had lumps on their necks. "Everywhere you go the industry blocks roads, destroys crown land around us. Worst of all is finding skin rashes and lumps on your family members. A doctor won't tell you what it is. All they say is call me next month. I've failed my family by not finding out about this before I brought them into the area."

Carl Bryzgorni, an organic grain farmer near Sexsmith, wrote about a sour gas well owned by Rigel that had vented and flared by his house for seven days in 1990. The highly acidic fumes made him and his wife sick, destroyed crops, and rusted out farm machinery. "Normally, vandalism of this magnitude, reported to the RCMP, would result in charges and prosecution in a court of law. Unfortunately the AEUB does not have the authority to press for damages."

The Smiths documented their woes with the Hythe Brainard plant, including their concerns about the way AEC's private security firm was investigating the plant shooting. With little or no evidence, the investigators had targeted Gary's son-in-law, Peter Smith, as a suspect. Smith had worked on and off at the plant but had quit before the shooting because of injuries. In the absence of a thorough RCMP investigation, the two consultants, both former RCMP officers, conducted their own. It largely consisted of threatening Peter with arrest if he didn't take a polygraph test.

In his letter Gary Smith accused AEC's security of "engaging in inappropriate, harassing behavior." Security personnel not only followed visitors to their home, he wrote, but shone lights in their yard and flashed high beams at visitors, supposedly to get licence plate numbers. "They were even caught once standing against our property fence, staring inside our property, watching our daughter take a walk with her newborn son. Another worry is the persistent rumour that the gas-plant workers are determined to shoot back if another shooting occurs."

All the families at Trickle Creek wrote letters. Ludwig's began, "It is certainly no public secret anymore that I and others in this area here are fed up." He called for a study of the health effects of flaring as well as an investigation of such industry practices as the dumping of sump fluids in swamps and farmland. One company had spent well over a million dollars on security rather than install much-needed pollution controls, he noted. The letter concluded by suggesting the recent shooting was, "in all likelihood," part of a larger protest against "the effects of thoughtless, reckless and life-threatening industrial practices."

Mike Weeks realized he needed help to deal with Ludwig. He had seen lots of bad practices in the Peace's sour gas fields, and now, with his hands on the buttons of two sour gas plants, he was finally in a position to do something about them. But Weeks, a Catholic by birth, didn't understand Ludwig's infuriating Protestant character or the complexity of the environmental issues. Working seven days a week, he also didn't have much time to plan a Ludwig strategy. To fill in the gaps he hired Ludwig's environmental adviser, Paul Belanger. "He wanted to get all the insights I had and what I was saying and what I believe," says Belanger. The first thing Belanger advised him was to stop "demonizing this guy. You've got to talk to him directly. Don't view him as a shithead."

Weeks, determined to resolve the conflict civilly, followed Belanger's advice. Shortly after the shooting, he parked his truck at an AEC well off Highway 59 and walked his dog, Bo, up "the Ludwig road," as locals called the county road, to Trickle Creek. When he knocked on the door, Ludwig tried to brush him off. Weeks, however, begged to be heard out, and the two men held a tentative conversation on the porch. Weeks said he could have been killed had he been in his office the evening of the shooting and wondered if Ludwig "couldn't cool things down a bit." Ludwig shot back, "Why talk to me? Why not find the guy that did the shooting?"

Ludwig told Weeks it was easy to understand why someone would want to shoot at the plant, considering how it spewed emissions. Weeks explained that workers had been upset by the shooting, that there had been talk of retaliation, and that he was concerned for the family's safety. But he didn't consider Ludwig a suspect and wanted Ludwig to know that. Weeks believed the shooting might have been part of a bizarre scheme to get AEC to hire more muscle to protect the company against oil-patch saboteurs. He said he was doing his best to control flaring at the plant and wanted to put forward a proposal for limiting flaring in the field. Ludwig agreed to read any proposal Weeks might produce, but said he would deal only with "higher-ups" in Calgary.

Weeks also approached all the letter writers. He told Gary Smith, "You knew the plant was here and would expand." Smith shot back: "If a kid grows up to be a raucous teenager, do you have to put up with him?" Weeks offered to install a water filter, check out the tree damage, and put up noise guards. In conversations with Carl Bryzgorni, Weeks promised not to flare near his property. The only one who refused to talk about his troubles was Bob Wraight, who referred to the plant manager as "Mike the Weasel." Ludwig later told Weeks that Wraight assumed all talk would be useless and that it had been a big step to get Wraight even to write a letter.

On November 30, Robert Wraight and his family visited Trickle Creek to chat and have coffee, as they often did. By now Wraight admired Ludwig as something of a father figure and looked upon Boonstra as a happy-go-lucky brother. He'd started to wear a cross, and he boasted to strangers that he lived on a self-sufficient farm with wind power, though his own property was nothing but bush.

The Smiths felt that Wraight's association with Ludwig had changed his attitude towards women. Whenever they asked Bob how Marita was doing, he'd just say "fat." Wraight also didn't permit Marita to question his decisions any more, treatment that Gary Smith described as "very Ludwigian." Wraight, however, felt comfortable at Trickle Creek. He enjoyed the long evening dinners and the fact that the Ludwig girls automatically babysat his children. He liked that feeling of being taken care of and the fact that everyone talked in the evening instead of watching TV.

Ludwig invited him to come along on a walk. "I have something to show you," he told Wraight. Marita and the children stayed behind while Wraight, Ben, Josh, Fritz, Bo, and Richard marched with Ludwig up the snow-covered Norcen road, the same contested track that had been spiked with nails and blocked with snow the previous winter. Wraight noticed that Ludwig had socks over his tennis shoes and was wearing camouflage gear Wraight had sold him at his shop. Ludwig said the socks were a little idea he picked out of *Ecodefense: A Field Guide to Monkeywrenching*. ("If the terrain requires boots, cover them with large socks to obscure their distinctive waffle print.") Ben and the others also wore socks over their shoes and had donned ski masks.

Trevor Schilthuis followed in an old red Sprint, then parked and stayed with the car, as a lookout might do. When the party turned north and got close to the controversial well, Wraight noticed that one felled tree after another lay across the road. "What's up?" he asked. Fritz started to fell another tree but got his chainsaw jammed. Wraight, who had done some logging in British Columbia, finished the job properly.

A few minutes' walk farther, Wraight beheld what seemed a queer apparition. The entire 10-foot-high wellhead, or "Christmas tree," had been encased in nearly a tonne of cement. It looked like some misshapen tombstone. Two signs on the concrete sculpture read, in red lettering, "R.I.P.," and below that, "Norcen." Particleboard still encased part of the cement and bits of rebar stuck out here and there. The odd shotgun shell appeared to be embedded in the tomb. Ludwig explained that the shells might slow down any attempt to reclaim the well. "How did you get the cement here?" asked Wraight incredulously. Nobody answered.

Josh, the family photographer, videotaped the scene as Richard Boonstra cautioned everyone to be quiet. Someone started a fire with debris and straw around the wellhead to help cure the cement. The group stood back and watched the fire rage, like guests at an outlawed picnic. Before they left, Boonstra placed a piece of paper on an oil drum and weighted it with a piece of lumber. It was a $2-million invoice for labour and materials and compensation for "pain, grief, intrusion of privacy and death" owed to the Ludwig family.

On the way back to Trickle Creek the group erased their tracks by dragging tree branches behind them. They downed more trees across the service road. Wraight showed Fritz how to do a back cut properly so the poplar wouldn't fall on the cutter. He left Trickle Creek that day mightily impressed with the lesson the Ludwigs had just taught the oil and gas industry.

Ludwig maintains that Wraight's version of events is poppycock. When reporters asked about the incident a year later, Ludwig replied, "I didn't involve myself, but I don't have an alibi either."

On December 1, 1997, a television station in Dawson Creek aired a newscast with a short clip of a burning well. A note accompanying the mysterious tape said protesters on the eve of the Kyoto conference on greenhouse gas emissions had done the job. "Several of the Ludwig family members who stood by to watch the fire consume the debris around the wellhead were deeply stirred by this symbolic gesture against reckless oil and gas exploitation, which has also seriously affected their health and plans to develop a self-sufficient alternate lifestyle including organic farming and the development of clean home energy systems."

Both Norcen and the RCMP had trouble getting out to the site the next day because of all the fallen trees. Sergeant Dave MacKay, Beaverlodge's new detachment commander, had never seen vandalism like this. A white-collar crime specialist, he was more used to Internet or securities fraud than damaged wellheads. But the force had largely disbanded his Calgary-based Economic Crime Unit in 1997 because the RCMP couldn't afford laptop computers for its investigators. A KPMG Consulting study later revealed that members of the unit "were emotionally distraught not only over the ongoing cutbacks but by the overall poor state of the Economic Crime Program." White-collar crime, MacKay liked to joke, didn't exist in Canada any more.

MacKay and his family had arrived in Beaverlodge around Thanksgiving. A bear-shaped man with a deep voice, MacKay struck many people as a tropical fish in a boreal pond. Unlike many of his peers, he hadn't been a hockey player. He liked to read books on quantum physics. One of the highlights of his career had been serving as a VIP guard for Mikhail Gorbachev for a week. After all the political fiascos in Economic Crime, he'd looked forward to worrying about little more than drunk driving in the Peace. There were no briefing papers on Ludwig or "the war." He'd suspected that the Hythe Brainard shooting and other vandalism were the work of disgruntled employees, but the Norcen cement job gave him second thoughts.

To MacKay the live .410 shotgun shells embedded under the surface of the concrete indicated the saboteurs weren't kidding. "It was apparent that vandalism to this well site was not simply a prank but an action designed with the potential to injure, blind or kill a person," he wrote in the first of many incident reports. "That person would in all likelihood be a Norcen employee." MacKay also found the note on the oil drum highly unusual. Criminals don't normally leave sarcastic invoices behind.

The sergeant asked a few veteran constables what they knew about Ludwig. Cal Mosher, who'd retired after serving as Bilodeau's file-keeper, reported that Ludwig's behaviour "was unlike anything he had dealt with in his entire career." He said that Ludwig always brought a large audience with him and that Mamie often concealed a tape recorder in her dress. (Mamie never did; the Ludwigs just kept careful notes of their dealings with authorities.) Mosher advised that MacKay just build evidence for an arrest. Another Mountie told him that talking to Ludwig about vandalism was "absolutely useless."

MacKay started a Ludwig file and made inquiries about industrial sabotage. He learned that Grande Prairie was fast becoming an epicentre of eco-terrorism in North America. Not only Big Oil but Big Timber appeared to be under attack. In 1995 a saboteur had set fire to six of Weyerhaeuser's pulp freight cars in the town. In 1996 another five pulp cars were torched. And just before the Norcen incident another saboteur jumped aboard one of the firm's front-end loaders, dug up a rail line, and rammed the machine into a power unit. The vandalism cost the company $1.6 million. But nobody in business circles wanted to talk openly about the damage; they all told MacKay that they were afraid of inspiring copycats. When MacKay started running into small oil and logging companies that refused to report $300,000 worth of bashed machinery, he knew he had a big problem on his hands.

Mike Weeks, meanwhile, worked on AEC's management, pressing for more dialogue. In late December he dropped by Trickle Creek to warn Ludwig about a new sour gas well, owned by a small Calgary firm, that was going in just south of the property. He had even bigger news: AEC's president, Gwyn Morgan, had agreed to meet with Ludwig in Edmonton in mid-January. Morgan had but one condition: "Nothing happens between now and the meeting."

"What makes you think I can guarantee an end to the vandalism?"

Weeks said he reckoned that Ludwig had so much influence in the area that he could make it happen.

"And he did," Weeks reported later.

Paul Belanger figured that a productive meeting between Ludwig and Gwyn Morgan was a long shot, but worth trying. As advised by Weeks, he cautioned the Ludwigs and the Boonstras not to bring along tape recorders, briefcases, or pepper spray. "They must feel very guilty," said Ludwig. Belanger explained that company officials were nervous. Even the RCMP had advised Morgan not to go to the meeting.

A short, fit, bespectacled, 51-year-old fellow, Morgan arrived at the Mayfield Inn in Edmonton wearing black trousers and a black turtleneck. He was accompanied by two security guards. With his bald head and clean-shaven face, Morgan bore an uncanny resemblance to Gumby, the cartoon character he had adopted as AEC's official mascot.

To Morgan, the elastic Gumby symbolized several of AEC's key values, such as the ability to stretch in difficult economic times in order to meet tight financial targets. It also represented the ability to have fun while working to win. In 1997 Morgan's latest Gumby goal was to make AEC Canada's largest publicly traded gas producer, and he was nearly there.

Morgan epitomized Calgary's oil-patch elite. He typically rose at 5:30 in the morning for an hour-long cross-training workout and didn't retire until late in the day. He was a trustee of the Fraser Institute, a conservative think tank, and a founding governor of the Canadian Association of Petroleum Producers. His peers viewed him as erudite, innovative, and entrepreneurial. After joining AEC in 1975 as a petroleum engineer, he'd worked his way up the ranks to become CEO in 1994. His success afforded him a large house in the affluent Calgary neighbourhood of Mount Royal and a salary of nearly $2 million a year. He once listed Adam Smith's *The Wealth of Nations* as his favourite book because it "actually captured the style of society that would take the dominant position in the world."

Morgan rarely talked to landowners and had a minimal understanding of their concerns. He knew, though, that he couldn't ignore Ludwig any longer. This strange prophet in the bush had cost AEC millions, terrified employees, and threatened to tarnish the company's public image. The notion that an individual could upset the operations of Big Oil wasn't something Morgan wanted in the press. He decided to treat the man as he would an aggrieved and successful competitor, with wariness and respect.

Belanger, who was serving as mediator, made introductions. Ludwig refused to shake Morgan's hand. "I'm not shaking your hand because I have a serious grievance against what you are doing. But I hope we can go beyond and settle these grievances and even reconcile our relationship."

Morgan, unfazed, began by advising Ludwig and Boonstra that his senior staff and his wife, Pat, really didn't approve of this face-to-face encounter. But Mike Weeks had insisted on it and he trusted Weeks. Morgan said he had watched the *Home Sour Home* video (almost every Calgary oil executive had) and expressed admiration for the family's dedication to natural ways. He was something of an outdoors person himself: "I often take 10-day treks into the Rockies." He had been raised on a farm in Carstairs, north of Calgary, near a sour gas plant, and he knew the industry could cause some headaches.

Morgan described his job as his "calling," a place where he could make a difference. His company contributed positively to the economy and gave its employees a good way of life. Natural gas, he said, is a benign fuel and a natural substance. "The employees that work for me are my extended family and are my concern. I personally believe the oil industry enhances the environment, but I see that we believe differently."

Belanger, the only participant in jacket and tie, talked about his experiences in the oil patch. He recalled a flaring incident at a gas plant that had killed 2,000 birds, an event that alerted him to flaring's dangers. Oil executives, he said, often inhabited ivory towers.

Richard Boonstra agreed. He said people didn't know where to go with their problems any more. "People have a fundamental Creational right to live their lives; it's more than spending 10 days in the woods."

Yes, there were problems, Morgan admitted, particularly with the supervision of contractors drilling wells. "I have confidence in the people running my plants but not as much in the contractors." After discussion of property rights and of Texas's stringent rules on flaring emissions, Morgan agreed that the industry had an obligation to curtail pollution as far as possible. But he wanted Ludwig to examine other possible explanations for his family's health problems.

"I'm not trying to give you a hard time," said Ludwig. "When a friend strikes you, it is unto healing. I am interested in reconciliation between people as the ultimate goal. As a Christian who understands the complexity of a situation, I will do the best I can, but I will not back down. I am not a pacifist."

Morgan made it plain that he wasn't a pacifist either. When people resort to violence and become terrorists and fugitives, "the system comes down hard on them. I have a sense of empathy for what you are saying. For those people who do take action that results in vandalism, shooting – that's stepping outside the bounds of our society, and we will act in whatever way to defend ourselves and use all possible components to deal with that." He referred to a recent bomb attack on logging equipment in the foothills that had caused $3 million in damage. "We can find better ways, because hate begets hate. This meeting is the start of a course that could be emulated elsewhere and is a beginning. When you step outside the system with violence, you'll either win or lose."

Ludwig argued that no system can determine what is right. If a man entered his house and tried to rape his daughter, he would take whatever action was necessary to protect his family, including killing the intruder.

"You have to make your choice and I have to make my choice," said Morgan. "I've told you what I will do."

The conversation turned to global warming. Morgan explained that carbon dioxide was one of the world's safest and most positive gases. There wasn't enough science to support the contention that industry's emissions, responsible for 50 percent of Canada's greenhouse gases, were altering climate. If Canada reduced CO_2 emissions, he said, another country would just produce more. And any effort to regulate emissions would simply hurt the economy.

Ludwig didn't buy Morgan's arguments. "I've been in homes where you could hardly walk, the floors were strewn with boxes, loaves of bread, clothes. I don't then go home and say to my wife: 'Oh, honey, don't worry about cleaning our home. I was just over to the neighbours' and their place is such a mess – why should you bother to clean?'" The industry had been derelict, he said, and had to change.

Ludwig brought up the $300,000 lawsuit: "I think it's a terrible thing, what you did."

"You push me – I'll push you," Morgan replied. "We are making good progress today – there is no reason why we would pursue that any further." AEC did put the suit on hold, although the company did not formally abandon the action until years later.

Morgan added that he didn't think a public inquiry would be productive. He felt such things tended to be costly and not solve anything and put everyone on the defensive. He agreed to press for industry changes on flaring, to improve AEC's practices in the field, and to study the idea of a citizens' committee to monitor pollution. Belanger left the meeting happy, feeling that good progress had been made.

After all the jawboning Ludwig, Mamie, Belanger, and the Boonstras retired for a few beers. Ludwig thought Morgan was a stupid man thoroughly in the service of the beast – "not a man with blood in his veins." Boonstra, though, felt the executive had been amicable and held out hope for reconciliation. In short order, two of AEC's ever-present security consultants, Howard Cox and Walt Sedler, joined them. The former Mounties both wore leather jackets. Cox was still investigating the shooting at the Hythe Brainard plant and wanted some answers. At one point he passed Ludwig a note: "Is Peter Smith the shooter?" Ludwig said Smith was innocent. "But I know who is responsible," he added playfully.

For a moment all conversation stopped. Belanger saw the smile disappear from Mamie's lips. But Ludwig merely told Cox to get off Smith's case because every man was innocent until proven guilty.

Whatever Gwyn Morgan may have thought of Ludwig, he kept

his word. The following month he wrote a blunt letter on flaring to the Canadian Association of Petroleum Producers, the conservative mouthpiece of Alberta's oil patch. CAPP had just received a recommendation from the Clean Air Strategic Alliance that proposed that industry voluntarily reduce flaring by 25 percent by 2001. The oilmen, who had debated flaring initiatives for nearly six years, hadn't yet made a decision. Morgan encouraged his peers to endorse "a clear policy that proactively decreases the amount of gas flaring in Alberta. Protestations by our industry citing economics and lack of scientific proof on the dangers of flaring are falling on skeptical ears." It would be best if the industry could address "this serious problem... without direct regulatory action."

Meanwhile, Mike Weeks pressed for better pollution controls on the ground. He authorized the installation of a new flare stack at the Hythe Brainard plant because the old one burned off only 60 percent of its waste gases. He also introduced a new system to test the economic viability of a sour gas well without flaring. Using other equipment, Weeks hoped to eliminate five-day test flares at as many as 20 new sour gas wells. The company also hired an ombudsman, an industry first, to deal with landowner complaints (a move many locals saw as a strategic effort to keep Ludwig from widening his base of support). In his first year the ombudsman dealt with 170 complaints, proving Ludwig wasn't the only fellow in the Peace with problems.

Weeks also proposed to central office a novel plan for restoring peace to the region. Why not buy Ludwig's farm and turn it into a camp for AEC workers and contractors working in the area? "Ludwig's not a bad man. He just needs more room. And a trapped man often does desperate things," reasoned Weeks. But AEC's Calgary bosses lambasted the proposal, declared Ludwig a "wing nut," and made fun of Weeks for even suggesting such a thing.

In fact most of AEC's executives didn't appreciate Weeks's proactive approach to Ludwig at all. Many pointed out that no laws required such anti-pollution measures and openly questioned Weeks's cleanup. Much to their chagrin, Weeks was admitting to problems most of the industry refused to acknowledge. Some also challenged Weeks's ongoing association with Belanger and accused him of working with a terrorist. Weeks's bosses and the RCMP both suspected Belanger of training Ludwig in pipeline sabotage. The logic of their allegations was pretty shallow: Belanger was a friend of Ludwig and lived in Edson, scene of a $1-million attack on a Nova pipeline eight years earlier; therefore he was guilty. The fact that Belanger hadn't lived in Edson at the time or that the incident took place during a messy union dispute didn't alleviate the suspicions of some at AEC. Weeks says he himself never believed the rumours, but the allegations infuriated Belanger.

While AEC executives questioned Weeks's efforts, Allan Johnstone welcomed them. He even praised Weeks's ongoing struggles during a public hearing on the 3,000-kilometre-long Alliance pipeline. In Fort St. John in February 1998, Johnstone entertained federal regulators with his sharp gibes and warned that the pipeline would be travelling through hostile country.

"Now we are looking at a situation where the man in charge of two gas plants making millions of dollars a day and connected to 100 wells has been shot at or intimidated. Nevertheless he is trying to straighten things out, and he says it's a no-win situation fighting Calgary. He's fighting Calgary because there are no laws." Johnstone warned federal regulators that if the new Alliance pipeline resulted in more flaring in the Peace, its Calgary owners would be "walking on the wild side of a group of people who are pretty angry out there."

Ludwig, however, was as hard on Weeks as he was on the rest of AEC. On January 23, he sent Morgan and Weeks a fiery ultimatum. It demanded an end to flaring and "genuine conciliatory if not due comprehensive compensation for damages done." Ludwig gave Weeks 10 days to respond. Either "assume responsibility for what you have done to people by clear admission, apologies and due compensation" or the Ludwigs "will truly know, once again, that we are at war with both a heartless as well as a deadly enemy."

The day he received the combative letter, Weeks drove out to the farm, tired and frustrated. A chinook had blown in, sweeping the sky of clouds. The emerging stars twinkled with surreal intensity, as they often do in the north. Weeks parked halfway up the Ludwig road and walked in the falling dark towards the main building, as he had done perhaps half a dozen times before. His dog loped ahead of him. Ludwig greeted him at the porch as one greets an unwelcome relative or a Midianite, then opened the door.

Normally a quiet man, Weeks stood in front of the family and told Ludwig that the ultimatum pissed him off. "Look, when you give us 10 days, you might as well say 10 hours. We're trying to do something, and we don't have to. I have been working 100 hours a week on this problem, and I'm just about ready to quit, because there is no winning this. So the oil companies will keep on flaring, they'll hire more security, there'll be more pollution. I've about killed myself working on this, and I'm just about done. I fight Calgary, I fight you people, and I'm done! Don't give us ultimatums!"

"You guys are a bunch of intimidators," replied Ludwig. "You figure you got all the money and the clout and you can slap people with lawsuits." Within seconds he was standing an inch from Weeks and yelling into his face. "Including little kids, little kids this high, and you're trying to tell me we're rough? Get your butt outta here, Mike! If you can't see that, you can't see much. After dumping this shit on us, forcing us to evacuate, you think you can come in here and tell us we're making it tough on you? Get out!"

As Weeks walked to the door and put on his boots, Ludwig shouted, "Wake up!"

In a restrained voice, Weeks said, "You, too, Reverend."

That night Weeks phoned Belanger, practically vibrating on the phone. Belanger told him not to take the tirade personally. "Wiebo is Wiebo."

Norcen took a different approach to Ludwig. After the cement job, Norcen's local gas plant manager, John Lieverse, vowed to connect the well northeast of Trickle Creek to the Knopcik plant via a new pipeline, come hell or high water. Lieverse even got into a shouting match with Allan Johnstone, swearing, "You and Reverend Ludwig are not going to stop us from working on that well."

For the testing of the well, the company assembled a small army of security. In addition to patrolling the access road with trucks day and night, the company hired four full-time security personnel to live in trailers by the well. The mayor of Beaverlodge, Leroy Durand, worked part-time as a Norcen guard to make extra money. The company also suspended video cameras and halogen lights from poles at the site.

All this activity alarmed the families at Trickle Creek as much as the exploration drilling had. Both Renée, Bo's long-boned wife, and Kara, Ben's wife, were now several weeks pregnant. Kara had already miscarried, of course, and now worried about losing another child. Renée had similar fears. "It makes us sad and angry that the gift of new life, which is such a joy and blessing, should be dampened (and maybe stilled) by the greed and exploitation of the oil industry," wrote Richard Boonstra's daughters in the community's diary. "The unborn child cries out with us – Is there no justice to be found?"

As more industrial vehicles roared past Trickle Creek, a new sign appeared on the Norcen road: "BEWARE NORCEN. Any flaring may result in deadly consequences." The production crew ignored the sign and went about its business. To improve gas flow, the crew sent a combination of sand, hydrochloric acid, and condensate at high pressure into the ground to crack open a collection of gas in the Montney formation. A successful fracking could increase a well's production tenfold, but when hydrocarbons mix with hydrochloric acid they create a host of deadly chemicals, including dioxins, that can affect the nervous system and the development of unborn children. Venting a fracked well almost always "blows back" these chemicals into the air.

On January 5, 1998, Norcen vented the well for five hours until sufficient gases rose to the top to be ignited. The well later flared for 41 hours, sounding like a jet airplane that had fired up its engines but couldn't take off. Belanger told the family that flaring after a frac job created a toxic brew. It was illegal in Texas and other states. "It's probably one of the most dangerous practices in the industry," he warned.

Whenever the Ludwigs or the Boonstras walked out to the site, security guards warned them not to proceed beyond the "No Trespassing" sign. Boonstra replied that the dirty stuff Norcen was spilling into the air was trespassing on his daughters and their unborn children. "Why not keep that on your own property?" The family wrote letters and sent faxes: "Urge that you cease development of said well" until a public inquiry had been held. They were ignored.

All spring Norcen felt the full brunt of the monkeywrenchers. In early March saboteurs tried to set on fire a Caterpillar D-8 tractor being used to build a summer road into the site. The tracks of four individuals wearing socks over their boots seemed to lead back to Trickle Creek but then vanished. One day Ludwig stopped a dump-truck driver and mounted his running board. He told the young man that anger was building in the area.

"Who's angry?" asked the driver.

"I am," replied Ludwig.

Saboteurs slashed tires on Norcen trucks and smashed windows on a well shack south of Trickle Creek. On March 2 someone fired a bullet into the Knopcik plant, five kilometres southeast of the Ludwig farm. The bullet travelled through two panes of glass and two walls, then lodged in a bookcase panel. The shooting caught Norcen's employees off guard: they thought that sort of thing happened only to AEC property.

The next day, the Boonstras paid the Knopcik plant a visit. Now grandparents of 13 children, they drove up to the office decorated with a bullet hole and grilled a lone employee. They wanted to know why Norcen hadn't responded to the family's numerous written requests for information on what the company had vented and flared back in January. The young man said he didn't know anything about it. Boonstra moved closer to him and accused him of killing unborn children and putting toxins, carcinogens, and benzenes in the air. The employee pleaded that he never got out in the field, didn't know much about flaring, and had himself been through leukemia treatments as a youth.

Another altercation resulted in a shoving match with the plant manager, John Lieverse. The company ordered the Boonstras to "cease and desist from entering onto" any company property again.

The Norcen shooting was foremost on Mike Weeks's mind when he met Ludwig and Mamie a week later at the Hythe Motor Inn to announce his departure from AEC. A German firm, Wintershell, had offered him a job in Libya for twice the money and vacation time that AEC gave him. Before he left, he wanted to introduce the new plant manager, Ron Bettin, whom he brought along. He also planned to tie up some loose ends about compensation and about the so-called Land Stewardship Council that Ludwig was proposing: an alliance of affected landowners who would monitor industry, establish fines for operational violations, and have the right to approve wells. But first he sounded out Ludwig about the shooting.

"I haven't heard anything about it nor read it in the papers," said Ludwig.

"I don't know why it's not in the news. If it was my plant, I'd want people to know," Weeks replied.

"What Norcen plant was shot at?" asked Ludwig.

"The Knopcik plant, at the office building. I've explained to you before how dangerous it is to shoot at a gas plant."

"There is a lot of restlessness out there; answers are overdue. I brought your letter along where you said you would make haste to deal with matters. It's been seven years of letters, tears, expenses, worries."

Weeks said he didn't want the lines of communication broken and that AEC would keep its promises. Then he brought up the subject of compensation. "We asked you to buy us out for $300,000 a few years ago and you turned it down," said Ludwig. "So you spend a million dollars on security because you think we are the problem. You would sooner spend another $3 or $4 million [than] cope with the anger that seethes."

Weeks said AEC wanted Ludwig to put his compensation needs in writing. He reiterated that the company was determined to improve its operations and had saved enough gas to heat 80 homes for a year by not flaring at one sour gas well.

Weeks asked about the Land Stewardship Council. How would other companies view Ludwig's proposal for a citizens' committee, now that Norcen was under attack? How would they know that the Land Stewardship Council wouldn't act as the political arm of a guerrilla army? "The perception is that the people who want to start

123

this council are the same people involved in direct action."

And so the conversation proceeded, the two sounding like 16th-century adversaries in some Reformation dispute between papists and Protestants. Before leaving, Weeks promised to introduce Ludwig to AEC's director of health, environment, and safety, Ed McGillivray, adding that McGillivray would handle the compensation issue. Ever conciliatory, he admitted that mistakes had been made. "We are trying to see to it that those things don't happen again."

"What we went through with the lawsuit you should not be proud of," Ludwig chided.

"I'm not proud of it. I explained it to you, whether right or wrong."

"There was no need for the lawsuit if you had talked with us and dealt with the problem."

"You are not easily approachable," said Weeks.

"*You* are not easily approachable," replied Ludwig.

Weeks said that gas workers feared for their lives driving anywhere near Trickle Creek.

"Don't you know what went on before? From the beginning the industry ignored our civil concerns and ran roughshod over our land. You're begging for a lawsuit. The industry needs to be disciplined, a stick across its ass."

Weeks said he wanted Ludwig to sit down with Ed McGillivray. "Will you be available?"

"Yes," said Ludwig. "Unless one of your men pushes me off the road."

Chapter 8

The General

When Ed McGillivray met Wiebo Ludwig, the former brigadier general had worked in the oil patch for only two years. Born and raised in Peace River country, McGillivray had spent 33 years flying CF-16s for the Canadian military. AEC hired him in 1996 to help out with the development of its rich oil and gas leases on federal military ranges such as Cold Lake. Generals like to talk to generals, reasoned the company. Like most of the industry's health, environment, and safety directors, McGillivray was largely a figurehead. He had no background in environmental matters beyond arranging garbage pickup at an air base. He knew even less about health matters. Even after a year of meetings with Ludwig, McGillivray still couldn't tell reporters the difference between a Level One and a Level Four sour gas well. (Level Four is the most dangerous well a company is permitted to drill.) But with Weeks's departure, Gwyn Morgan wanted McGillivray to be AEC's official Ludwig handler.

McGillivray's first meeting with Ludwig and Boonstra – an often testy three-hour encounter at the Grande Prairie Inn on March 13, 1998 – launched a long and tortuous negotiation process for a buyout. They discussed "conciliatory compensation" and Ludwig's novel proposal for a Land Stewardship Council.

McGillivray had never heard of "conciliatory compensation" before. Ludwig's four-page document put the bill at $450,000 and explained it was a "small investment to ensure the security of industry" after a history of all manner of suffering: "suffering the disenfranchisement of natural rights... suffering leaks and releases... suffering the abusive intimidation of a $300,000 lawsuit."

McGillivray generally liked Ludwig's idea of a Land Stewardship Council but expressed reservations about landowners having a greater say than the EUB in well approvals. He didn't think the industry needed another regulatory or approval agency. Ludwig explained that the council would merely give local landowners an "authoritative" say in where wells could be located before the EUB granted licences. McGillivray admitted that the EUB was stressed and understaffed. "I don't agree with how the process has been changed, from policing to self-policing."

Ludwig outlined his 18-point basis for compensation, for health problems, land damages, and "public slander and threats from industry personnel because we were pressed to defend ourselves." ("Well," said the general, "you can't stop people from talking.") McGillivray said some kind of payout was one thing, but it shouldn't "relieve our responsibility to make things better."

"That's our burning concern, too," replied Ludwig.

"You said you had property in Costa Rica. And I hear Costa Rica is a slice of heaven. Do you still feel like leaving?"

"No, we are going to fight you guys all the way. There's no place to fly to."

They talked about flaring and emission controls ("I'm explaining to you that we haven't done a good job and that we intend to do a better job," said McGillivray) before they turned back to conciliatory damages. The company didn't mind paying quantifiable things such as evacuation expenses, said McGillivray, but he doubted that "conciliatory compensation" fell into that category. Short of detailed

scientific studies, how could Ludwig prove that the oil and gas industry was responsible?

"I can't prove that you killed any of my children, but I do know
myself that we have very serious reasons to believe that you have."

"I believe that you believe that," McGillivray said warily. "If we've
done that damage, particularly AEC, I would be the first one to haul
out a chequebook. Let us solve that problem."

Richard Boonstra weighed in, saying the scientific proof the
industry demanded of landowners was an idolatry and an illusion.
Ludwig agreed: "You do not have to make the connection that a
certain particle went through the air into this or that person or animal
or plant before science does say, 'Stop, we may have some real problem
on our hands.' When I spilled a little crude in the EUB office, authorities considered me a criminal. But you can spew your crap over us
year after year and you don't get charged. It's a bizarre phenomenon."

The general called that "an interesting comparison."

"We can show that it was on purpose and without due diligence,"
added Ludwig, speaking of the 1996 AEC leak and Norcen's recent
venting and flaring.

In the end McGillivray agreed to forward the compensation
request to senior management, as well as the proposal for the LSC.
He also vowed to continue improving AEC's flaring practices.
Ludwig ended the talk, as he often concluded conversations on oil
and gas, with a little preaching on the meaning of violence or vindictive defiance.

After the meeting McGillivray wrote a lengthy memo to Morgan.
He believed the primary agenda for the Ludwig family had finally
surfaced: money. "In spite of all the arguments and the honest effort
of the industry and AEC, I firmly believe that Rev. Ludwig will not be
satisfied until he receives a substantial sum of money from AEC." He
noted that Ludwig seemed intent on staying in the area, which made
a buyout unlikely. All in all the general didn't like what he heard.
"Simply put, I feel that the Ludwigs are engaging in subtle blackmail
to achieve their ends and the company should not succumb to this
blatant tactic by providing compensation for perceived damages."

McGillivray set up a meeting with Peace River RCMP Superintendent John Spice to re-emphasize AEC's displeasure with the investigation into industrial sabotage in the area. Senior managers from Norcen and Rigel also attended and offered equipment or funding to help arrest Ludwig. Howard Cox, the security consultant for AEC West, later offered free access to SMC's equipment, including alarm systems, sweep equipment, and night-vision goggles. "Industry representatives are prepared to review and potentially subsidize any proposed enhanced positions or dedicated RCMP resources," added the former Mountie. Spice appreciated the offer but reminded the anxious companies that the law prohibited him from directly accepting corporate handouts.

Later that month Cox bumped into Ludwig and his son Josh (whom he mistook for Ben) near Trickle Creek on a routine anti-sabotage patrol. The men talked about the Norcen well that had flared and vented over child-bearing women. Cox said he just wanted to say hello; Ludwig said that he'd invite him in but "it was better to keep security dumb." As watcher and watched humoured each other, a group of Ludwig children surrounded the truck. Before the security consultant drove away he distinctly heard Ludwig admonish his grandchildren: "See this man? He's the enemy. If he ever asks you a question, do not talk to him."

That spring, Ludwig and the Smiths had a disagreement that ended their alliance. Ludwig and Mamie had dropped by the nurses' place to share news on the Land Stewardship Council, which Gary had agreed to join. Anne had misgivings about the group because membership was limited to heads of households ("I'm not a rabid feminist, but I found it rude and offensive to be relegated to a backroom"). She was also growing wary of Ludwig's incessant talk about civil disobedience. While Gary prepared for work that night, Anne and her daughter, Freya, chatted with the Ludwigs in the kitchen.

Anne, a forthright person, wondered how the young people courted at Trickle Creek. A relative of hers had met Mamie Jr. and was smitten. Anne also made comments about her previous husband, who had died several years earlier. Ludwig thought her comments slighted her present husband.

"Why do you treat Gary this way?" he asked.

Soon Freya and Anne were arguing with Ludwig, who calmly spoke of a woman's need to learn in quietness and full submission to her man. No family could function without headship. "Don't look down on the man in your life."

When Gary came downstairs, Ludwig advised him to exercise some control over his wife's sharp tongue. Mamie quietly nodded agreement. Gary was in a hurry to get to work. "This conversation is over." The Ludwigs departed. Anne still remembers Ludwig's presence as irate and caustic.

The next day Richard and Lois Boonstra turned up on the Smiths' doorstep, apparently as envoys of reconciliation. The Smiths offered them coffee and wondered what they had to say. Richard explained that he was a marriage counsellor and implied that Gary and Anne might need assistance. Any household that allowed a woman to run amok couldn't be happy for long. Lois, in her quiet, cheerful way, explained that she, too, had once objected to headship. When she finally submitted to her husband's will and covered her head – well, she felt much happier. Anne listened to the scarved woman and thought, "My God, if ever a woman looked more unhappy, I've not seen it."

Gary had read Paul's sermon to the Corinthians and disagreed with the Ludwigs and the Boonstras' interpretation. The sermon was about genuine equality and love, he said, not submission. He asked the Boonstras to leave. When Bob Wraight came by the next day, Anne kicked him out too. "I was tired of people telling me how to behave in my own house."

After the breakoff, the Smiths' concerns about flaring remained. Fearing for their health – they still couldn't drink the water – and besieged by foul odours, they put their house up for sale. An appraiser from Hythe valued the structure at $91,000 but cautioned the Smiths that no buyer could get a mortgage because of the cracks in the basement caused by nearby seismic activity.

Nevertheless, the Smiths listed the house at $110,000. As Gary recalls, "A number of bizarre things happened." For starters, the family immediately got three mysterious offers. One buyer said he wanted to start a buffalo farm in the middle of their swampy property; another put in an offer without even looking at the place. When the Smiths insisted that he take a look, he spent no more than 10 minutes. No one commented about the cracked basement.

Gary eventually sold the house for $140,000. He still doesn't know who bought his place but he suspects it was AEC through a third party, as indeed it was. Dozens of Alberta farmers and ranchers downwind of the province's 600 gas-processing plants have had similar offers. Most sign confidentiality agreements so that all evidence of the deal neatly disappears. The Smiths' old home still stands empty with its doors wide open. No buffalo have ever grazed the acreage. The Smiths purchased a quarter-section 12 kilometres south of the plant and made plans to build a new home.

Unlike the Smiths' hasty real estate deal, Ludwig's negotiations with AEC sputtered along for months. When the conciliatory compensation idea petered out, Ludwig tested McGillivray's interest in a simple land sale. McGillivray hemmed and hawed but then agreed that a buyout might be an option, suggesting half a million as a fair price. If an independent environmental study proved that the local oil and gas industry had damaged the family's health and land, then AEC would pay those damages too.

Ludwig, however, now wanted $1.25 million, or nearly $750,000 for damages and loss of his drywall business. Given what AEC had spent on security, Ludwig reasoned that this was one hell of a deal for the company. The $1.25 million roughly equalled the income generated by the Hythe Brainard gas plant in a single day.

The general told Ludwig the number was out of the ballpark. Ludwig irritably accused AEC of playing with other people's lives. He sent McGillivray a fax that raised the price to $1.5 million, what he had initially intended but withheld "out of due consideration for your many terrible corporate weaknesses and sins." McGillivray alerted Gwyn Morgan that his dealings with Ludwig were getting rocky. He also advised Peace personnel that "relations with Rev. Ludwig had broken down" and that they should be on the lookout for "renewed violence and vandalism."

Soon afterwards, Ludwig received a letter announcing AEC's plans to convert a sweet gas pipeline just north of his property to a sour gas one. The alarming news sent Ludwig to his typewriter. "Our collective advice to you all is: PERISH THE THOUGHT! at least until the grave cumulative industrial abuse suffered here is addressed and both a peaceful and proper settlement is made... Your timing is EXTREMELY BAD."

When Morgan heard about the ill-timed conversion plan, he told McGillivray sharply that he didn't want an AEC screw-up to scuttle talks or renew a war. He ordered McGillivray to make sure all AEC business with Ludwig went through senior management, and he insisted that the company promptly address Ludwig's concerns about the pipeline. Three days later AEC cancelled the pipeline conversion.

With assistance from Paul Belanger, whom the family called their "environmental adviser and corporate facilitator," Ludwig sent off a more political proposal on April 12. This one emphasized reconciliation as opposed to retribution. Ludwig called the revised deal "more beneficial to AEC than it is to us" because it would finally allow AEC to drill for gas under Trickle Creek. It included two pages that detailed why the family felt it had to move, such as forest decline, disappearing wildlife, and "teratogenic effects upon livestock and people born as well as miscarried." Ludwig noted that his community had grown from two to six families, "with a seventh family about to join while industry has literally surrounded us so completely that already all adjoining land has been inundated with pipes and wells leaving no room for expansion."

Ludwig's final "minimal financial deal in order to escape the horrors" included $750,000 for the six families; $500,000 to be put in trust for the South Peace Land Stewardship Council as compensation for the loss of his drywall business; and another $75,000 for moving expenses. Though Ludwig regarded a court action "as neither very conciliatory nor desirable given the adversarial character and corrupt nature of many of today's court rooms," he didn't rule it out. He gave AEC until May 11 to reply.

For the next month AEC senior management debated the

financial package. McGillivray called the proposal extortion and opposed it from day one. He also worried about setting a precedent and finding an army of disgruntled farmers on AEC's doorstep. Everyone agreed that giving the LSC money was insane; it would be like funding an executioner. Other AEC bosses wondered if Norcen and Rigel shouldn't share the pain. If Ludwig's removal from the Peace would benefit the entire industry, why should AEC foot the bill alone? But Gwyn Morgan had the last word. Fearing the vandalism might escalate and result in someone's death, he wanted a deal and he wanted Ludwig gone. Enough was enough.

Ludwig, meanwhile, was having his own doubts about the buyout. For months he had received daily phone calls from farmers and ranchers who had seen *Home Sour Home* and who supported his cause. "I am betwixt and between," he wrote to the dairy farmer Bill Bocock. On the one hand, "I am increasingly interested in more dramatic action – a revolution... We need to get our act together soon to form a new leadership that will take the bull by the horns instead of wasting more time jaw-boning with the present system." Only a Biblically inspired revolution could resist "if not overthrow" a power system "that has sold us out lock stock and barrel to corporate will."

On the other hand, he was torn by questions of his family's health. "It seems to me the part of wisdom to retreat, though I prefer to fight and alter the present state of affairs." Ludwig lived this debate in his heart every day that year.

Bob Wraight took a growing interest in Ludwig's travails as his own life fell apart. Since his appearance at Ben's trial a year earlier, fewer people frequented his store. Oil-patch workers tagged him as a Ludwig associate and refused to buy from him. In addition the RCMP now suspected he was selling stolen goods such as solar panels ripped off from remote oil and gas sites. (The industry remains the world's biggest user of solar panels.) Other townspeople believed Wraight was selling hand grenades and automatic weapons on the side. At Sergeant MacKay's urging, the town of Beaverlodge passed a bylaw requiring Wraight to keep records of all pawned items sold. Rather than comply, Wraight closed his shop.

Trickle Creek (above, in 1999) was a virgin 160 acres when Wiebo Ludwig bought the property in 1985. When he moved out from Goderich, Ontario, he was unaware that land title in the Peace did not include mineral rights, which the Alberta government leased to an oil company.

The community's goats, cared for by Salome Ludwig, experienced a dramatic increase in stillbirths after exposure to sour gas. Mamie Ludwig, Wiebo's wife (left), was only one of the women at the farm who suffered a miscarriage, which the family suspected was caused by the pollution.

NOTICE

THIS DRILLING OPERATION HAS PROCEEDED DESPITE AND WITHOUT DUE CONSIDERATION OF THE SERIOUS OBJECTIONS OF THE NEIGHBORING RESIDENTS WHO PROTEST:

1. THE RUTHLESS INTERRUPTION AND CESSATION OF THE PRIVACY & SERENITY ONCE ENJOYED AND HIGHLY PRIZED BY THEM FOR THE DEVELOPMENT OF CHRISTIAN FAMILY AND COMMUNITY LIFE HERE.
2. THE RELENTLESS GREEDY GRABBING OF CREATIONAL RESOURCES NO MATTER WHAT THE ULTIMATE COST TO HUMAN LIFE AND ENVIRONMENT.
3. THE CALOUSED DISREGARD FOR THE SANCTITY OF THE LORD'S DAY AND ITS SPIRITUAL SIGNIFICANCE FOR THE LOCAL RESIDENTS AND CHILDREN
4. THE LEGISLATION OF A LAND & MINERAL OWNERSHIP POLICY THAT DOES VIOLENCE TO THE GOD-GIVEN "RIGHT TO PROPERTY".
5. AND, THE ESTABLISHMENT OF ARBITRATION BOARDS THAT ARE FUNDED BY AND FAVOR OIL INTERESTS.

R.I.P.

Ludwig spent years lobbying in a conventional manner, firing off letters to politicians and bureaucrats and erecting signs to demonstrate his displeasure. When that produced no results, the vandalism began: left, a Norcen wellhead encased in almost a tonne of cement.

RCMP Sergeant Bob Bilodeau (below, left) imagined the Peace would be an aptly named posting after a stint in wartorn Bosnia; it didn't turn out that way. Allan Johnstone (below, right) took pride in his nickname: "Alien."

To establish the credibility of Robert Wraight (inset), a Ludwig acolyte turned informer, the RCMP bombed an AEC well shack – and Wraight took credit for it. Richard Boonstra (with his wife, Lois), like Ludwig, was imprisoned largely because of Wraight's work.

As tensions escalated, Ludwig found himself in many confrontations. Some local businesses wouldn't serve community members, and the family received numerous death threats. Edmonton lawyer Richard Secord, who acted for Ludwig, wore a bulletproof vest to court each day.

Gwyn Morgan, the president and CEO of Alberta Energy Company, met with Ludwig, but the men were unable to resolve their differences. While Ludwig was out on bail, his van was blown up. Responsibility for the crime was never established.

Karman Anne Willis
1983 – 1999

Sixteen-year-old Karman Willis was the only girl among late-night joyriders at Trickle Creek. Shots were fired at the pickup trucks, and she was fatally injured. The RCMP, fearing a Waco-type shootout, sent a SWAT team to Trickle Creek; the community video-taped the invasion.

Thus unemployed, Wraight spent more time at Trickle Creek. Ludwig gave him $2,500 because he didn't think it was right for a wife to work outside the home, let alone support a husband. Wraight was grateful and put away the envelope as a keepsake. He tried to help out on drywall jobs but couldn't keep up with the fit, hard-working Ludwig boys. After several attempts he quit, believing he was more hindrance than help. Ludwig still paid him by the hour for the work he had done.

In conversation with Boonstra one day, Wraight expressed interest in the unfinished cabin at the corner of the Trickle Creek road and the Norcen road. It came with a dugout and 10 acres of trees and wild berries. Boonstra joked that Wraight could have it "for a cigar," but Wraight offered $5,000 for it. No money changed hands but Wraight thought the cabin was as good as his. He and Marita often stayed overnight in the cabin and soon filled it with unsold inventory from his failed business. The Wraights were seriously considering joining Trickle Creek; Wraight even joined the Land Stewardship Council and got weekly reports on the buyout negotiations with AEC. When Ludwig wondered aloud if he had asked AEC for enough money, Wraight replied, "Ask for more."

In early April 1998 the saboteurs came to life again. When McGillivray received a report of slashed tires on a backhoe at an AEC well site near the Hythe Brainard plant, he asked Paul Belanger what was going on. "I thought we were in a truce period." The Ludwig diaries record: "We can only say other angry people out there who feel oppressed by the industry must be acting out."

Later that month Ludwig noticed activity near a Norcen well south of the farm and came by to check it out. A hostile supervisor warned that he'd call 911 if Ludwig didn't leave the site. When Ludwig asked McGillivray in one of their talks if a pipeline had corroded at that site, McGillivray replied, "No. They found two drilled holes in the pipe. Neither had gone through completely so there was no leakage, and one still had the drill bit stuck in the pipe. They are replacing that section."

Norcen wasn't the only company being visited by long-beaked

"pipepeckers." Near Valhalla a grain farmer got his pant leg caught on a metal rod sticking out of the ground over a Rigel pipeline. When he pulled up the mysterious rod, he found a drill bit welded to the other end. The damaged pipeline lay right next to a large pond and conservation area used by swans and ducks.

The vandals targeted other facilities. On April 28 two bullets hit an AEC well site near Hythe, blowing holes through the well shack door and window. The production manager faxed McGillivray a report on the incident that began, "Life goes on."

The war against Big Oil flared into a war against the county in late spring. That's when a backhoe working for Norcen narrowly missed hitting Elias, Ludwig's two-year-old grandson, as it drove past the homestead. Enraged by the reckless driving, Ludwig decided to keep the company off the county road by erecting a metal gate complete with ominous signs at the southern boundary of the farm.

Ron Pfau, administrator for the County of Grande Prairie, soon got complaints about a public road being blocked. He drove out to the farm hoping to remove the illegal obstacle, only to find Mamie and Lois sitting by the gate in lawn chairs with a video camera. Upon closer inspection it looked as if the women had chained themselves to the gate.

Realizing he had arrived at a Mexican standoff, Pfau told Ludwig that he didn't have the authority to gate a public road and that the county could be sued if someone ran into it. After much debate, Pfau agreed to consider a formal request to approve the gate if Ludwig agreed to keep it open. Ludwig made an application, which began by berating the county over a number of tax issues dating back years. It then brought up the gate. "Do the very people, for whose convenience the road was put there in the first place, have nothing to say anymore about whether or not it serves them well? Do they also not even get the courtesy to explain emergency decisions they need to make for the safety and security of their children even with respect to their very own habitat? Have we all become unwitting wards of the state so that differentiation and recognition of various kinds of authority, including parental, is no longer respected?" Bob Wraight, who now lived at the farm most of the time, signed the letter as a concerned resident.

Pfau and Ludwig lobbed faxes and phone calls at each other like hand grenades. County employees had instructions never to accept calls from Ludwig but to transfer them to voice mail. That way they could filter out the abuse before replying. In one month Pfau played back four death threats on his voice mail. A young or raspy voice, clearly not Ludwig's, instructed Pfau to leave "people's gates and personal property alone" because it was not healthy for Pfau to be involved; he had children, after all. No one knows who made the threats.

Meanwhile, Grande Prairie's council members debated Ludwig's unusual request. "We even had Wiebo and half his crew at the council, all shined up," recalls a long-time councillor, Richard Harpe. Ludwig told the largely agricultural assembly that his family was negotiating a settlement because a "developing sour gas field is just too dangerous to live in. Under these circumstances it might prove wise for the Council to exercise a little restraint rather than to agitate with more heavy-handedness a situation that is already grievous enough for the families involved."

Harpe strenuously argued, as he had for years, that Ludwig should obey the laws of the county like everyone else. Since 1996 Harpe had urged his fellow councillors to take a stand against the property damage associated with Ludwig's "paramilitary" crusade, to no avail. He knew the industry had done terrible things but didn't think vandalism was any way to address the issue. He called Ludwig a bully and warned council members that the more mayhem Ludwig got away with, the more he might commit. Most councillors didn't share his view. A few secretly enjoyed watching the industry squirm under Ludwig's verbal assaults. "Leave the man be," they replied. "It will pass. If we aggravate him, things will just get worse." But on the matter of the gate, the council eventually sided with Harpe and ordered its removal.

Pfau gave Ludwig a week to take it down before the county arrived with a sheriff and a backhoe. "Be prepared for a standoff," warned Ludwig, though not much happened when the county came to collect the gate. The backhoe lifted the sturdy structure out of the ground and dumped it on a trailer bed. "You'll pay for what you are doing somewhere down the line," Ludwig warned Pfau. Josh, who videotaped the incident, reminded the administrator that the gate had been built to combat reckless oil traffic.

The next letter to Pfau – a well-known drinker – admonished him to hear the word of God and to stop extorting people on tax matters: "Mr. Pfau, you as the County Administrator have indeed some reason to take to the bottle already in the early hours of the day. You would do well to repent." After the battle of the gate, someone added "The Ludwigs Are" atop the word "Dead" on the road's "Dead End" sign. About a year later Pfau's heavy drinking landed him in an early grave.

McGillivray presented AEC's counter-offer to Ludwig in late April 1998. There were two options: $575,000; or the best of three land appraisals plus 50 percent for "industrial advantage," plus $75,000 for moving expenses. Ludwig chose the latter package. AEC hoped to haggle the $500,000 for the LSC down to little or nothing.

As these negotiations proceeded, the EUB finally issued a ruling on Ludwig's request for a public inquiry. It found "no compelling argument to justify the need for a review or inquiry." The EUB based its denial on letters presented by the three oil and gas companies arguing that they "had complied with all applicable laws, regulations, government directives and industry standards."

Norcen told the board that all the complaints raised by Secord's clients were too general to be investigated and that its Knopcik plant, which processed sweet gas, couldn't "cause adverse irreparable harm to the public health." Rigel noted that it had "installed H_2S monitors on most of [its] well sites" and that it had no control over how AEC eventually processed gas from its wells at Hythe Brainard.

AEC's argument against an inquiry took up seven pages. It dismissed Wraight's complaint on the basis that his family had voluntarily "located in an area of intense exploration and development activity." Although it agreed that the Smiths had legitimate concerns, it assured the EUB that all "operational problems" were being resolved and were largely due to "a new sweetening solvent to improve... efficiency."

As for the Ludwigs, AEC felt that their concerns dealt with broad regional issues such as industrial density and air quality. If the EUB wanted to address these issues, it should involve all industry players in the Grande Prairie region. After detailing its own initiatives on flaring and emission control, AEC offered an "alternative mechanism" – a public information meeting. The EUB liked that idea. When it denied a public inquiry, it offered this AEC-inspired compromise instead.

The decision didn't please Ludwig. "First the bureaucrats say to us, 'You don't have proof of your allegations.' So we say, 'OK, let's have an inquiry so we can give you proof.' Then they say, 'No. We're not going to give you the opportunity to collect and show us the proof.' How absurd!" Ludwig wrote to the EUB, saying "the pollution of the bureaucratic process" now rivalled that of petrochemical toxins in the area. The board was now "establishing another process to establish yet another process by which to resolve concerns expressed." The EUB accepted his reply as a yes and set up a meeting for June 4 with an independent facilitator from Vancouver.

The so-called "communication" meeting didn't go well. The night before, Ludwig got into an argument with Howard Cox, the man Ludwig had warned his children about, while having a beer in Grande Prairie. When Ludwig tried to explain the seriousness of the industry's impact on his family, Cox replied, "I guess I don't know where you're coming from." Ludwig explained that he had spent nearly $60,000 of his own money battling industry. "Well, it's tax deductible, isn't it?" replied Cox. Ludwig left the bar wondering why he had agreed to the meeting. That night Boonstra convinced him not to attend and to protest the EUB's decision not to hold an inquiry.

The next day Richard Secord arrived at the meeting in Beaverlodge and patiently waited for Ludwig, along with 50 other people, including representatives from the EUB, Rigel, and Norcen. McGillivray had assembled a big delegation to do a show and tell on what good corporate citizens they were. When Ludwig didn't appear, Secord got nervous and called the farm.

Ludwig told Secord he wasn't coming because he had been rudely treated by a security guard. After some persuasion over coffee at the Teepee restaurant in Hythe, Ludwig briefly showed up before the hostile crowd. He demanded a full-blown inquiry and then left. Local citizens made catcalls, and one lady declared that Ludwig's problems were due to inbreeding.

After Ludwig's exit the talk turned to sabotage and shootings in the Peace. "They're radicals," declared Jake Janzen, the beekeeper, whose sons worked in the oil patch. "It's ridiculous what's going on. This isn't Iraq. We're supposed to be living in a peaceful land, but we're not when people pull stunts like that."

The peculiar meeting ended at noon. "In retrospect the whole thing was doomed," says Secord. "Why hold a meeting when the industry is trying to get him out of the area?" Ludwig wrote an apology to the EUB for his early departure, noting that, by not holding a proper public inquiry, the EUB had put the cart before the horse. He instructed Secord to start working on another request for an inquiry.

In early summer three real estate appraisals of Trickle Creek crossed McGillivray's desk. The general was surprised: they estimated Ludwig's property, with all its outbuildings, at a value as high as half a million dollars. After Ludwig did his own math, he came up with a final bill of $920,400, including $100,000 for the value of his trees. But Ludwig wanted to be reasonable. He'd settle for $825,000, forget the half-million for the LSC, and they'd vacate the premises by October 30. Instead of haggling, he wanted to spend his time looking at real estate in Nova Scotia, Montana, British Columbia, and Idaho. The family was looking for a remote idyll in preparation for the coming collapse of consumer society, as far as possible from the sour gas industry.

He eventually found what he was looking for in the Robson Valley on the Fraser River in British Columbia – a 300-acre parcel of stately cedars and firs. When Wraight visited the site, Ludwig offered to buy Wraight's family 15 acres nearby. After nearly eight years of constant struggle with the oil and gas industry, the family "seemed pretty pleased," as Belanger put it, "to get back to Project Shangri-La."

On June 12 Ludwig visited McGillivray in Calgary while en route to Montana to check out real estate. McGillivray told him AEC was prepared to offer $775,000 – less than what the company had promised by its own formula. But McGillivray said he would add on another $50,000 if Ludwig gave up the name of the saboteur who had shot at the Hythe Brainard plant. Ludwig, outraged, said a deal was a deal. If the company couldn't honour its commitments, there wasn't any point in talking any more. As he walked out, he told the general: "The truce is over. The war is back on."

Five days later, an area production supervisor for AEC reported what looked like a hole drilled in a sweet gas pipeline south of Grande Prairie. When the Mounties investigated, they found a crude device tied with rope. Constructed of angle iron and pipe, the mechanism worked a bit like a primitive gun. Once detonated, its explosive charge drove a half-inch stainless steel rod into the pipe, causing a small leak. An oil worker later found a similar pipe bomb tied to a Pembina pipeline in Drayton Valley, west of Edmonton. North of Grande Prairie, an employee with Rife Resources found another oddly shaped bomb, untied it, and put it under the seat of his truck, not knowing what it was. He drove around for a week before someone identified it as a bomb.

The device on the AEC pipeline prompted Ken Woldum to issue a press release expanding the $50,000 reward for information on the Hythe Brainard shooting to include "life threatening criminal acts." The release noted that 160 acts of vandalism had taken place against utility companies, forestry firms, and the oil and gas industry in the Peace. "If the people responsible for these random criminal acts are doing it for a cause they believe in," said Woldum, "then they are hypocrites, because they have no regard for public safety, community health or the environment."

Two days later, McGillivray got a long-distance call at home. Ludwig said he was looking at some property in Idaho and wondered if AEC couldn't come up with more money for "moral purposes." The general thought a moment and said there might be room for movement. The two sides eventually settled on $800,000, and the general said he would get final approval from AEC senior management.

AEC lawyers contacted Ludwig's lawyer, Secord, for details and clarifications. They wanted the Ludwigs to relocate "out of the area" and sign a confidentiality clause. The lawyers also said they didn't want the family to return once the property was sold. Nor was the company prepared to offer any cash up front. AEC would drop the lawsuit when the deal closed.

Ludwig thought the clause about not coming back was "far-reaching and precluded reconciliation." He also wanted a comprehensive written apology to all the children named in the lawsuit. In addition, the family needed $600,000 of the total up front to purchase land and construct new buildings. "Fourteen years ago we solemnly repented of being indebted to anyone save, of course, the perpetual debt of love which we owe every man. We wish to keep that commitment now too in the momentous purchase of an alternate place to live."

While the two sides finalized the details, Sergeant Dave MacKay sent a private e-mail to Gwyn Morgan. It quoted Rudyard Kipling: "Once you have paid the Danegeld, you never get rid of the Dane."

On July 31, the eve of the buyout, AEC's lawyers faxed Ludwig a 31-page covenant. Section 3.2 stipulated that the Ludwigs and their children couldn't reside or buy land within 800 kilometres of Grande Prairie (ruling out much of British Columbia) – ever. Another section bound the Ludwigs to eternal secrecy about the covenant and forbade them to ever talk about environmental problems on their land.

Even AEC knew these conditions were unorthodox. Curtis Bunz, a lawyer with Burnet, Duckworth, and Palmer in Calgary, warned McGillivray that the relocation restriction could, in fact, be unconstitutional: "There is an inherent risk a court could consider the geographic and temporal scope of the relocation restrictions to be too broad and thus either unreasonable as between the parties or contrary to public policy." McGillivray didn't bother reading the note and didn't think twice about the restrictive relocation clause. "We wanted them to move out and this was the only way to do it legally." He faxed it off and then went away for the weekend.

At Trickle Creek, Ludwig patiently pored over this long fax. He then called Secord, who advised him to cross out the offensive sections and sign it. Ludwig wearily sat down at the communal kitchen table and asked Harmony, who was on supper duty that evening, what she thought. He often asked his eldest daughter for advice. Harmony, now 29 and a woman as straight-talking as her mother, said she felt "icky" about signing such a servile example of "lordship" over people.

The family talked and debated, and a consensus emerged. Ludwig phoned AEC's lawyers and told them to "stick it where the sun doesn't shine." He left messages with Secord and McGillivray, as well, saying the deal was off: "We're staying."

Bob Wraight, eager to move back to British Columbia, couldn't believe Ludwig's change of heart. He argued that the restrictions were just corporate bullshit and that Ludwig should think of his family. "Wiebo, take the money," he pleaded. "If you have to say you're the fucking Easter Bunny, do it."

But Wiebo Ludwig had no intention of saying he was the Easter Bunny.

Chapter 9

Anger

The first bomb went off during a thunderstorm near the sleepy town of Goodfare, 12 kilometres southwest of Hythe, on July 31. The blast severed a pipeline leading from an inactive AEC sweet gas well and blew chunks of equipment into the bush. Although marked as a sour well, the facility had been converted to sweet gas three months earlier. An old couple living nearby heard a bang and saw a garish orange flash in the sky. They thought it was thunder and lightning, or a neighbour blowing up a beaver dam.

An AEC technician discovered the mess the next morning and called the RCMP. The police found few tracks in or out of the site because of the storm's heavy rains. One investigator took 287 photographs of the scene. Members of K Division's Explosives Disposal Unit eventually recovered an electrical switch, some tape, and a nine-volt battery. The EDU estimated that the saboteurs had used five pounds of dynamite.

Two days later a second bomb ruptured a high-pressure sour gas pipeline at a well 200 metres off Highway 43 near the Hythe Brainard plant. Dan Stevens, a local farmer driving west to Dawson Creek, had stopped his truck around 11 o'clock near the clapboard town of Demmitt to shake off a mouse crawling up his pant leg. "And then I heard a big boom. It was really loud. And then this Dodge Caravan went across the road. And I thought not too much of it and left." As Stevens drove on he heard a loud hissing noise in the bush. He had no idea what it was.

The hydrogen sulphide leak set off alarms at the Hythe Brainard plant and sent nearly a dozen AEC employees as well as members of Interline Security to the scene. They closed Highway 43, which leads to Alaska. The last thing AEC needed was a group of summer tourists dying in a suffocating cloud of H_2S. It took about two hours to isolate the small leak and get it under control. Meanwhile the RCMP evacuated homes southwards along the highway. At some residences H_2S monitors recorded readings as high as 1 ppm, enough gas to abort a fetus or cause an asthmatic reaction in a child.

The bomb squad calculated that saboteurs had cut the locked chain securing the well site and taped a bomb to the sour gas line. An extension cord ran from the explosive device to a light switch equipped with a spring and attached to a battery. Fishing line tied to a nail or stick on the ground kept the switch in the off position. A burning cigarette lying on top of the fishing line probably served as the fuse that set the whole device off. The electrical switch was identical to the one at Goodfare. The same bomber had done both jobs.

Reaction among residents to the Friday and Sunday detonations was one of disbelief and terror. They could have died in a haze of sour gas had the second well's emergency shutoff valve not worked properly. After inspecting the scene, Sergeant Dave MacKay told reporters, "In my whole career I've never heard of anyone blowing up sour gas wells." Nor had anyone else.

Len Racher, a heavy equipment operator and jazz musician, lived four kilometres from the Ludwigs and couldn't stomach the mayhem. "His actions aren't hurting the bad guys. His actions are affecting the poor little guys." Racher had no idea where the violence would end. "In this country we still have the old ways where you deal with a problem yourself. I hope it never comes to that." In Peace River country, the old ways included shooting a troublesome neighbour.

At the Teepee in Hythe, a restaurant once owned by the Horse Lakes Indians, the local gossips known as "Knights of the Round Table" held long debates. "They have a lot of queer ducks in this country but never any terrorists," argued Aubrey Greben, a retired liquor store manager. The queer ducks included Roundhouse Jones, who built a round house, and Baldy Red, an inventive bootlegger who used nuns to smuggle rum through police blockades during Prohibition. But the knights agreed Ludwig was a special case. "He's a complete little dictator in his own empire," noted Frank Webb, Hythe's mayor. Webb owned a business that tanked potable water for the oil patch. "Mr. Ludwig is a very clever man and excellent with his vocabulary, but he wants to take the law in his own hands. If an operator went to open a door at a well site and was blown up, I don't think we could control the people here. I really don't." When Ludwig and Mamie walked into the Teepee after the bombings, smiling and joking, the knights all scowled at them. "I say one thing," noted one. "He's got balls on him bigger than Superman's."

Distressed, Gwyn Morgan sent a memo to his employees at the Hythe Brainard plant ("Re: Violent Destruction of AEC Property"). It congratulated them on their resolve and good work "in the face of despicable acts." He denounced the "further escalation of the vandalism" and vowed to put together an "escalated effort to apprehend the perpetrators" by working with the RCMP. The talks with Ludwig were over.

The Ludwigs, 10 kilometres east of the second bomb site, heard the blast and felt the ground shake, but their diary makes no mention of it except for all the media coverage. Ludwig discovered that reporters are attracted to bombs like flies to honey. Both the *Edmonton Journal* and the Grande Prairie *Daily Herald-Tribune* ran front-page stories in which details of AEC's aborted land deal were also revealed. "It's blatant bribery that they wanted me to sign it in a last-minute rush," explained Ludwig. "They must think we're totally stupid – that they can wave the money in front of us and think that we'll go berserk or something."

Ludwig hinted that he knew something about the bombings and admitted that such attacks might not be terribly wise. But in the absence of government help, people had a right to strike out. "I don't know what planning went into it. I know that a woman who lost a child is involved. I don't know what role she played. I have some real sympathy for it." He expressed no discomfort about the blasts. "I think it's time the newspapers say who the real eco-terrorists are – industry. When are you going to wake up and realize that the companies are the dangerous ones?"

Carl Bryzgorni, the lanky Polish farmer who could light his tap water on fire, openly supported the sabotage. "Talking doesn't work. What other methods can you use? Maybe these bombings will wake industry up."

After the bombings and the revelations about the buyout, McGillivray and Ken Woldum held a safety meeting at the Hythe Brainard plant. Field hands, consultants, and landmen all attended. After enduring shootings, threats, and now bombs, local staff couldn't believe that their bosses had secretly negotiated a buyout, let alone a botched one. Senior managers had assured them the company would never do such a thing. Many had even ridiculed Mike Weeks's modest proposal.

"Is it true?" incredulous employees asked one after another, some with tears in their eyes.

"Yes, it's true," said McGillivray, red-faced.

The next day Ludwig rang McGillivray at home in the evening as though nothing had happened. McGillivray made no attempt to hide his embarrassment over the contract fiasco, which he blamed on AEC lawyers. "I feel like the worm at the bottom of the barrel." Since the bombings and the failed buyout, his popularity at AEC had sunk lower than a sour gas well. Even Morgan had become exasperated and reamed him out for fumbling the deal. McGillivray had violated one of the unwritten rules of the oil patch: when you buy out a disgruntled landowner, make sure no one hears about it.

Sensing the general's unease, Ludwig assured McGillivray that all was not lost. He proposed another meeting with Morgan to discuss a new proposal that would be of "great advantage to AEC's public name." The general said he would try to set up a meeting, which never occurred.

To AEC the only thing worse than a terrified workforce and bombed-out well sites was an implacable propagandist determined to dirty the industry's name with outrageous sour gas stories and Old Testament rage. To lessen the damage after the Goodfare and Demmitt blasts, the company issued an unsigned press release that played fast and loose with the truth. It claimed AEC had done its best to resolve the dispute but that "short of shutting down the oil and gas industry in northwest Alberta," nothing could be resolved. Ludwig, of course, had never asked for the industry to be shut down; he just didn't want sour gas wells around his farm. The release concluded that Ludwig had withdrawn from the discussions "for his own personal reasons."

Ludwig couldn't understand why AEC didn't want to immediately reopen talks. He called McGillivray repeatedly and said he was concerned about the standoff. McGillivray replied that Gwyn Morgan didn't want a meeting. Ludwig asked if AEC was a Canadian company, because he didn't want to hurt Canadian companies. He warned the general that people at Trickle Creek weren't about to lie down and get shoved around. McGillivray didn't say much. "I guess we're forced to sit tight, be patient, and behave ourselves," concluded Ludwig. McGillivray, who'd been told to string Ludwig along, faxed a memo on the conversation to his new ally, RCMP Sergeant Keith Hills.

The bombings had finally got the attention of RCMP senior brass in Edmonton. Two years after Bob Bilodeau's plea for help but mere days after the explosions, reinforcements arrived at last. On orders from Don McDermid, the commander of K Division, the force sent in a surveillance aircraft and an 11-member ground crew to watch Trickle Creek day and night. Sergeant Hills, head of General Investigative Services for Peace River, got the unlucky job of leading the investigation. Over the years the soft-spoken detective had reviewed the files detailing one incident of sabotage after another but had been told the force "didn't have the resources to spend time on vandalism complaints." Now on the verge of retirement, Hills had been handed the file from hell and the kind of resources only bomb investigators can muster, including wiretaps. Some days Hills commanded as many as 30 or 40 constables in the field. An RCMP functionary dubbed the Ludwig investigation "Kabriole" – the name of every operation in K Division began with a K.

Hills reviewed the files MacKay had assembled since the incident of the burning Norcen well. He defined his key targets as Wiebo, Ben, and Fritz Ludwig and Richard Boonstra. He later expanded that list to include all adult males at the farm and associates as varied as Allan Johnstone, Paul Belanger, and Shane Hartnell. Understanding that the suspects knew the forest well and had probably picked out oil and gas sites long in advance, he instructed the surveillance teams to be on the lookout for possible cache sites, industrial targets, and suppliers of dynamite.

Hills suspected that the Ludwigs knew something about police tactics. He guessed that the family monitored police and cellular frequencies and perhaps even engaged in counter-surveillance with their own aircraft. When the local chiropractor, a friend of the Ludwigs, innocently tried to land his ultralight plane at Trickle Creek after the bombings, he inadvertently flew over a two-man RCMP observation post. From this incident, Hills concluded that the man was a co-conspirator. He had Transport Canada issue the chiropractor a warning for flying too low.

While Hills marshalled his resources, AEC tried again to boost resolve with more money. The RCMP, which increasingly steered corporations to private security firms to save money, said thanks but no thanks: only the people of Canada could fund the RCMP. In September Gwyn Morgan wrote to Premier Ralph Klein, appealing for immediate action against the eco-terrorism disrupting industry in Peace River. A month later the government created a $3-million fund to fight "eco-terrorists." Steve West, the province's hard-nosed energy minister, called the bombers "hooligan anarchists. We better find them and show them what we do with Albertans who fool around with this industry."

By mid-August Operation Kabriole hadn't made much progress. In the absence of arrests or even suspicious activities, Hills's superiors in Edmonton warned him to "scale back the costs" of the operation. Surveillance alone was costing taxpayers nearly $100,000 a week. Hills phoned McGillivray and asked him to postpone a trip to Toronto and keep talking with Ludwig while Operation Kabriole got its wiretaps together. The RCMP had limited time and money for surveillance – could AEC "heat up the situation by breaking off negotiations" and saying it wouldn't deal with extortionists? The idea was to provoke Ludwig.

On August 17, McGillivray informed Ludwig that AEC had changed its mind about negotiations. It now wanted "a two-week cooling-off period," largely because of Ludwig's embarrassing disclosures about the earlier discussions. AEC had taken a beating in the press and suffered a loss of trust, he explained. Ludwig grew agitated, and McGillivray jotted down his blistering responses as best as he could, since the RCMP hadn't yet received permission to wiretap his phone or Ludwig's.

"Things are not going to get cool," said Ludwig. "I've tried resolving things through peaceful terms, and I'm tired of being jacked around. The company needs to get it through its head that they can't puke on people and walk all over them. Lessons will have to be learned. I will fight industry tooth and nail." He accused AEC of hiding behind a "thin skin of bravado" and hung up.

On August 21, death visited Trickle Creek. At one in the morning Renée Ludwig, the 23-year-old wife of Wiebo Jr., delivered a deformed baby boy whose grey, lifeless skin peeled at the touch. The baby's head contained no bones and felt like a sack of water. The deformities grimly reminded the women of all the stillborn goats and lambs. Renée had sensed something wrong a week earlier when she ceased feeling movement in her womb.

Josh videotaped the delivery of the ghostly fetus as well as the family's outpouring of grief. With tears running down his face,

Ludwig christened the dead child Abel Ryan and related how the Norcen well had spewed sour gas over the community in January. Abel, went his sermon, had been "killed by his brother's reckless greed." The family buried the child in a little wooden casket at the community graveyard under a canopy of poplar and spruce east of the main house. Abel now joined Kara's miscarried child, and Mamie's.

Renée wrote a poem about the death called "Abel Ryan Ludwig":

> We looked at you babe, through our tears of
>   great sorrow.
> For your eyes would never see the light of
>   the morrow.
> As you lay there we loved you, your broken body
>   we caressed,
> And we knew your open mouth would never suckle
>   a warm breast...
> Dear Abel Ryan, your blood now cries out from
>   the ground,
> For justice from the evil that all around us
>   abounds.

Later that day Ludwig and Mamie drove all the way to Rocky Mountain House in central Alberta, an eight-hour trip, to deliver a copy of *Home Sour Home* to Alberta environment minister Ty Lund. Lund, a bachelor who regarded acid rain as a quaint fertilizer and whose love of clear-cutting had earned him the moniker "Forrest Stump," wasn't home. Ludwig dropped off the video at a local coffee shop, where they met Joan McDonald, a councillor who said she knew Lund. Along with the video, they left a note to Lund: "Please review this video and let us know your reaction. We ask for your help with these formidable problems."

When the RCMP later interviewed McDonald, she described the Ludwigs as gentle but "sort of fanatic." She added that she and her daughter had watched the video before passing it on to Lund. "It's definitely a good study in self-sufficiency."

When Lund got the tape, he informed the RCMP that he had grave concerns about his personal safety.

Two days after the death of Abel Ryan, Operation Kabriole got its first break. A surveillance crew watched Ludwig's blue Dodge Caravan leave Trickle Creek around 6:30 in the evening and head east, then south to Grande Prairie. The police followed in unmarked cars while the surveillance aircraft, which continually circled the farm, tracked the van's progress from the sky.

In Grande Prairie Ludwig stopped for gas before heading south again towards the coal-mining town of Grande Cache. Highway 40 snakes through a mix of well-treed and clear-cut foothills hugging the Rockies, rising and falling like a paved roller-coaster. About 25 kilometres south of Grande Prairie the van stopped by the highway so its passengers could pee. A half-hour later the van stopped again; this time four people headed into the bush near a Precision Drilling rig. After studying the site they returned to the van. To the RCMP it finally looked like the family was on a bombing expedition. The Dodge rolled on towards Grande Cache and its elk-grazed hills. One unmarked police car travelled several kilometres ahead of Ludwig while two more followed the van's tail lights. When the surveillance aircraft abandoned the chase because of an approaching thunderstorm, the ground-based teams were left on their own.

About 80 kilometres south of Grande Cache, the Mounties lost their man near the entrance to a Suncor oil battery, an industrial square neatly cut out of the forest. The facility included a sweet oil well, a pumpjack, and liquid storage tanks. Located just 300 metres from the highway, the new well advertised its presence with a promi-nent flare. That's where the two unmarked surveillance vehicles travel-ling south suddenly realized their sandwich had fallen apart. Ludwig wasn't between them.

In a panic, Constable Blake Pickell made a U-turn and headed back north in search of the Dodge. About 10 minutes later he got word that the vehicle had reappeared and was heading south towards him. To keep his cover, the Mountie turned back into the Suncor site and concealed his vehicle. While he did so, his headlights caught a glimpse of a man in camouflage gear running through the trees near the battery like a phantom.

For nearly half an hour Pickell and another surveillance team watched the Dodge drive back and forth in front of the Suncor site. To the Mounties it looked like the driver was waiting to pick someone up. During one drive-by a Mountie standing by the highway finally shone his flashlight into the vehicle and spied Mamie Ludwig at the wheel. She accelerated and drove north to Grande Cache at about 120 kilometres an hour.

Having now lost three suspected bombers in the bush around an oil battery, the RCMP called in Constable Doug Hawkes, a dog handler, and Rex, his tracking dog. A call also went out to Edmonton's Explosives Disposal Unit. The Mounties suspected something had been planted at the battery but couldn't find anything in the dark. They sealed off the site. When Hawkes arrived later that morning, Rex picked up a scent west of the battery but lost it on the pavement.

Around one o'clock Mamie Ludwig saw flashing lights in her rear-view mirror outside Grande Cache. She kept driving. When the lights caught up to her, she pulled over. Two police cars did the same and the Mounties performed a "high-risk takedown." A Mountie with a megaphone shielded herself behind her open car door and shouted at Mamie in a gruff military manner. "Put the car in park! Put on the interior lights! Slowly put your left hand through the window and indicate how many people are in the vehicle."

Mamie put up one finger.

"Take your keys out and throw them on the pavement. Indicate once again how many people are in the vehicle."

Mamie stuck one finger up again.

"Now slowly open the door and kick it with your right foot. Put your hands on your head and slowly step out. Now take three steps to your left. Spread your hands. Start walking backwards. Don't look back. Get down on your knees."

Mamie followed instructions. She was soon sitting handcuffed in the back of a cruiser. A female officer asked again if anyone else was in the minivan. Mamie said no, adding in her Iowa twang, "You can use me as a hostage to check it out if you don't believe me."

A constable with a gun and a police dog searched the van for an hour but didn't find any explosives other than a few firecrackers under the front seat. Another Mountie checked Mamie's driver's licence, registration, and insurance. When everything seemed in order, the constable undid the handcuffs and issued Mamie a $155 ticket for failing to stop for a peace officer.

"Yes, but I thought you had to go 'Woo, woo' with the sirens before I had to stop," explained Mamie. "Maybe that's because I'm from the States." She said something about being treated like a criminal, to which an officer replied, "Well, that's your opinion and quite a few other people think that too."

"It's not just a true opinion. The Lord God above knows it's true. Can I go home to my 11 children now?"

"You have 11 children?"

"Yes," she said proudly.

Mamie drove home to Trickle Creek with a story to tell. But she didn't have much time to tell it. Around 11 o'clock that morning Sergeant Dave MacKay arrested her at the farm for mischief endangering life.

At the Suncor battery, the bomb went off around five in the morning, startling the constable standing guard. The explosion sent sparks and debris some 30 metres in the air. To Constable Hawkes the explosion sounded like someone taking a hammer to a tin garbage-can lid. The blast blew apart a well shack housing a fuel gas scrubber and separator, which triggered an automatic equipment shutdown. Technicians later figured the damage at $50,000 plus.

Not knowing whether the facility might be leaking sour gas, the RCMP fled upwind and closed the highway. Within a half-hour the bomb unit arrived, and Suncor's emergency crews followed. As soon as Hills got word of the explosion, he ordered a roadblock outside Grande Prairie and another north of Hinton, 40 kilometres farther south. He also called in a helicopter with an infrared camera to hunt for the saboteurs.

Around 6:15 in the morning Patrick Huntley, a British Columbia trucker, noticed a man by the side of the road about halfway between Grande Cache and Grande Prairie, waving his arms. Having seen three or four bears that morning, Huntley stopped and picked up the hitchhiker. The man introduced himself as "Paul" and said he was trying to get to Grande Prairie.

When Paul climbed into the cab, Huntley noticed he was soaking wet up to his knees. "What happened?"

Paul said he had tried to get a drink out of a river and slipped on a rock. His adventure had begun with a fight with his wife. Paul said he had left his house after an argument angrier than hell and tried to hitch a ride to Edson to visit a friend. He ended up sleeping that night in the bush because no one gave him a ride. He said he used to be a social worker but now painted houses.

Huntley didn't know whether to believe the stranger or not. But by the time he saw the flashing lights of the police blockade outside Grande Prairie, he could tell that his passenger had more than wife troubles. That's where the police arrested "Paul" – Richard Boonstra. Another hitchhiker, Bo Ludwig, father of Abel Ryan, was arrested at the same roadblock at 7 p.m. The family was surprised that the RCMP never noticed the absence of a fifth person from Trickle Creek at the time of the Suncor incident. Josh Ludwig, whom the police always confused with Ben, reappeared two days after the explosion.

Wiebo Ludwig eluded the police all day on August 24 as he marched south through the wilderness towards the logging town of Hinton. Whenever the helicopter with infrared hovered above him, he covered himself in moss and hugged a tree like some cursed environmentalist. Around 8:30 in the evening he sat in a ditch at the north end of Switzer Provincial Park, some 30 kilometres from the bombing, praying for a ride. He was dressed in a khaki jacket and blue pants and an olive-coloured hat. Tree moss stuck out of his hat like fashionable camouflage and sores covered his sandalled feet.

With dusk approaching, he decided to let the Lord determine if he would be picked up by a passing motorist or by the RCMP.

The Lord chose the RCMP.

Later that evening Corporal Dale Clarke at the Grande Cache detachment seized Ludwig's clothing and swabbed his hands for explosive residue. He explained that Ludwig had the right to refuse such procedures, but Ludwig was weary and remained for once a model of cooperation and politeness. At the mention of the word "explosive," Ludwig smiled and said, "Oh, there has been an explosion?"

The two men got to talking. "A lot of people may understand your cause but they don't necessarily agree with the way you're going about it," said Clarke.

"Some issues are worth going to jail for," replied Ludwig softly. He talked about the effects of sour gas on animals and said he had lost another child just days before. At one point Clarke asked if Ludwig wanted to call a lawyer. "No," he replied. "Lawyers don't help. They only cost you money." But he did want to call his wife.

Clarke, who had watched the *Home Sour Home* video, asked if Ludwig was injured or hurt. Ludwig said no, "just tired and thirsty." So Clarke ordered him two glasses of orange juice.

A couple of hours after Ludwig's arrest – like Boonstra and Bo, he was charged with mischief endangering life – Sergeant MacKay descended upon Trickle Creek with a search warrant. More than 20 carloads of Mounties from Edmonton, Peace River, Spirit River, and Grande Prairie came to look for dynamite, explosives packing boxes, blasting caps, detonation wire, timing devices, drawings, notes, diaries, videotapes – anything that might aid a successful prosecution and end Operation Kabriole's drain on the public purse.

Ben Ludwig greeted Investigator Rod Franklin of Edmonton GIS at the door and asked what was going on. Franklin read the warrant and directed Ben – whom he called Josh – to gather the family in the central cabin so the police could keep an eye on them. But the Mounties ended up collecting everyone themselves.

A large moving van belonging to the Explosives Disposal Unit wheeled into the yard, hitting the sign above the gate. As a family member yelled in dismay, an officer shone a light on the sign. And there, as the family diary noted, the painted sign swayed, pertinent as ever: "The Lord: He is God." The moving van headed over to the windmill and cold storage house where the RCMP expected to find explosives.

The police fanned out rapidly to all the outbuildings to make sure no one disappeared into the night. One team of flashlight-waving constables noisily approached Fritz and Dania's cabin. Barking dogs and beams of light woke the mother, who'd been sleeping with her three children. Clad only in underwear and a T-shirt, she shouted, "What's going on? What right do you have to come in the middle of the night and scare people like this?"

The police kept their lights on her, as police are trained to do. "Aren't you going to let me get dressed?" she yelled.

Fritz, the quietest of the Ludwig boys, had never seen his wife so angry and called the officers "fucking assholes." He later apologized for his unchristian conduct.

Later, around three o'clock in the morning, Harmony harangued two officers as they searched her bedroom over the garage. She told the searchers that they were working for a bunch of oil company thugs and she hoped the Lord would open their eyes to this damning reality. One officer confided that he was a Christian and said, "I have my eyes open."

For all their trouble that night, the RCMP found only a few items of modest interest: fishing line, two electrical switches, and instructions on how to build a Tattler, an intrusion warning device. They also found in Renée and Bo's bedroom a copy of *Ecodefense: A Field Guide to Monkeywrenching*, loaned to the Ludwigs by Alien Johnstone.

The 350-page book gives basic tips on how to defend wild areas from industrial assault by spiking roads, disabling heavy equipment, pulling seismic stakes, and plugging culverts. A publisher's disclaimer notes that the book is "for entertainment purposes only." First printed in 1985, it describes monkeywrenching as a deliberate, timely, ethical, and non-violent pastime that is never directed against human beings. "Explosives, firearms and other dangerous tools are usually avoided; they invite greater scrutiny from law enforcement agencies, repression, and loss of public support." The third edition also contains field notes on how to evade tracking dogs by contaminating the trail with pepper spray and a lengthy section on how to expose undercover agents. Agents usually tipped their hand by talking about "incriminating things" and "initiating conversations about monkeywrenching." MacKay recognized the book because someone had faxed him the chapter on sabotaging power lines after saboteurs downed 24 power lines near Gordondale, 55 kilometres north of Hythe. He and several other officers at the Beaverlodge detachment ordered copies of the book from Amazon.com. They were put on a waiting list.

After the police raid, Ludwig got more distressing news. The Crown would probably push for imprisonment without bail, send the three men to Edmonton's remand centre, and direct Mamie to a correctional facility in Saskatchewan. Ludwig earnestly petitioned the Lord to spare his people "this sting of imprisonment so far away especially for my wife's sake, knowing the pain it would bring to her tender and vulnerable spirit." He pleaded for a deal with Crown Prosecutor Al Munro. Munro said he would consider releasing all members of the family if Ludwig put up his land and home as bail. Ludwig agreed with tears in his eyes and was released that evening in front of a media horde.

Over the next few days Ludwig made full use of his newsworthy arrest. He told the Grande Prairie *Daily Herald-Tribune* that the battle was "to the death at this point. We had the perfect motive and I want the court to hear why." He informed the *Edmonton Sun* that "it'll get worse before it gets better." And he proclaimed to the *Edmonton Journal* that "the oil industry is tough, but I believe everything has its Achilles heel."

Paul Belanger, Ludwig's environmental adviser, repeatedly tried to reopen talks with AEC, but McGillivray wasn't receptive. Belanger feared a bloody war might break out if the families didn't move. He felt it was in everyone's interest to get them out of the Peace. But neither Ludwig nor McGillivray listened to the go-between any more. When Belanger met with McGillivray in his Calgary office at the end of August, the environmentalist warned that what had started out as a story about the dangers of flaring could wind up as a Wild West vigilante tragedy. McGillivray said AEC wasn't interested in further talks. Belanger advised him that Ludwig was going to release the videotape of Abel Ryan to the media. The general listened impassively.

Although McGillivray encouraged the go-between to continue his work with Ludwig, Belanger knew his role had been played out. When he drove back to his solar-powered home in Edson that night, he decided to withdraw from the whole drama and get back to the business of designing eco-friendly homes. He didn't want to witness the collision of egos any more. "When you take the operations of the oil companies and then you take Wiebo and put the two together, you have something much larger: two stubborn, arrogant actors."

Bob Wraight heard about the Hinton bombing while returning from British Columbia, where he had picked up his family after their holiday. He and Marita sat on the edge of their bed at the Thrifty Inn in Kamloops and watched a news bulletin about Ludwig's arrest. "It was hard to believe it was them."

Wraight had quarrelled bitterly with Ludwig about the meaning of headship. Every year Marita and the kids went to a popular Bible camp for two weeks, and every year Bob objected. He didn't like crowds, nor did he approve of Marita disappearing for a dose of religion he didn't understand. Marita took advantage of the event to visit her folks, whom Bob didn't like.

Ludwig advised Bob that as head of the household he should simply put his foot down and keep his wife and children at home. Get to know them, he counselled. Spend time with them. All through July, Wraight and Ludwig and Boonstra had wrestled with the matter. Boonstra finally lost his temper, poked his finger at Marita, and explained that a woman should submit to her husband. The straight talk offended her. Wraight, however, just fell into an angry silence. The next day Marita left in a huff for the sanctuary of Bible camp without him.

Wraight carried other hurts that summer. He still couldn't believe Ludwig had said no to an $800,000 buyout just because of some corporate silliness. Wraight's own quarter-section hadn't sold yet and he had no means of making a living. Boonstra had also killed the land deal Wraight thought they'd made. The nice little cabin at the end of the road wasn't for sale any more, which rankled him.

On their return from Kamloops, the Wraights drove over to Trickle Creek. The Ludwigs sat Bob down in front of a television and made him watch the video of Abel Ryan's gruesome birth. The children of Trickle Creek silently watched as well, as they had several times with reporters that month. "This is what the industry has done to us," said Ludwig. "This is what is happening to us." The delivery of the deformed child with the strange puppet-like head nauseated Wraight. He'd never seen anything like it.

After viewing the tape Wraight went outside for some air and brazenly asked Ben and Boonstra, "Why are you still here? And what were you doing in Hinton, anyway?" According to Wraight, Ben – who wasn't at the battery bombing – stood in a doorway and replied, "Well, Bob, we hadn't planned on getting caught."

When Bob and Marita left that evening, they felt like outcasts from some Eden that had turned dark and bloody. Wraight now wanted more than ever to leave the gas fields of the Peace, where his fatherly saviour had apparently taken up bombing. "After seeing the video I kind of felt betrayed," he later said. "I didn't keep a lot of secrets from them. I thought we were part of the community and were trusted. They were in Hinton after the little baby died."

Wraight nursed his growing resentment as he drove aimlessly around Hythe and Beaverlodge. He couldn't stop thinking about the middle-aged man he had sat behind at the Hythe coffee shop a while earlier. Dressed in white shirt and grey trousers, the man had looked like a plump Dean Martin and had been talking to Ron Bettin, the new manager of the Hythe Brainard plant, about bombs and security. Wraight had overheard the whole damn talk and even recognized the man's face from TV. He knew the man had the authority to make big-money deals at AEC.

If the truth be known, Wraight had wanted to go over then and there to introduce himself.

Chapter 10

Judas

Ed McGillivray was so surprised by the call he got on September 2 that he forgot to record the first five or ten minutes of it. He knew he was talking to a disgruntled Ludwig associate named Bob. But Bob was hard to understand because he didn't finish his sentences.

Bob mentioned something about threats to murder policemen. He said Wiebo Ludwig was becoming impossible. He said he was having a hard time with the situation and didn't want anyone to get hurt. McGillivray suddenly recognized his good fortune and turned on the recorder specifically installed to tape conversations with Ludwig. For the next 45 minutes he became a sounding board for a strange, desperate man calling from a phone booth outside the Teepee restaurant in Hythe.

"I'm having a hard time with this," said Bob.

"Yeah, it's just not working," replied McGillivray, smooth as a landman. "And he doesn't want to rationalize the situation?"

"No, he won't deviate from the plan. He won't change it. He's stuck on this. Things have been said there that you'd think come right out of a movie, you know. Knowing him kinda like I do, you know when he's fooling around or not."

McGillivray asked if more things were going to happen. Bob said another daughter was about to give birth and if it didn't turn out, a stillbirth would "spark 'em right off." He told McGillivray that the reverend was "kinda flying off the handle." He said if he knew something was coming down, he'd make a phone call. Then he made his pitch.

"I'm not looking for a handout. Basically all I want is my place. Like I said, it's listed with a realtor right now. If it was gone, sold – wonderful. You have my support and cooperation."

McGillivray asked if Bob would be willing to testify in court.

Bob sighed. "It could be a long day." He added that he wouldn't want to do it for one isolated incident. "If it was … um, something as serious as conspiracy to commit murder or something. But…"

"Do you think that's a possibility? Is he that deranged now?"

Bob said there was nothing wrong with religion, except when you make it work only for yourself. "And an eye for an eye comes up, you know."

"He's willing to hurt people without any proof that the oil and gas companies or the industry is the cause?"

Bob was inclined to think so.

"He's just a dangerous man that… uh, his hatred has got the best of him, then," McGillivray coaxed.

"Yeah," said Bob. "He's got a lot of support. Not publicly, but family. Like I said, I hope they can get caught and maybe things will have to get split up like a regular deal and half the family will pull through. There's, you know, there are some decent people in there."

"They don't have a chance because he's got so much influence," suggested McGillivray.

"Every time you turn around there's another family member breathing down your neck. With me, I'm pretty free to go and choose which way I want. I'm not really regulated at all. Funny thing to say."

Bob formally introduced himself as Bob Wraight. McGillivray said he had figured as much. "If I don't tell somebody and something happens, I'm just as guilty," said Wraight. He emphasized that he couldn't really cooperate unless his family was protected, not that he had much faith in the RCMP or its witness protection program. A private land swap would be a better deal. In fact, said Wraight, "the appreciation would be unbelievable." He added that he owed the bank $15,000 and didn't want to walk out of this thing empty-handed. "By the time I pay off the bank, I'll send my wife and kids off in the direction I choose with the balance."

McGillivray knew better than to make promises. "You're really upset, I can tell."

Wraight explained that he and Ludwig had had a big fight several months earlier over his wife. "He basically told her the way it is and how it's going to be. To make this work I've kind of stood there and took it." He said Marita didn't support the group any more but that Ludwig still tolerated him.

McGillivray commended Wraight on his courage for calling. He added gently, "By rights I should be talking to the RCMP on this. How do you feel about that?"

Wraight said he didn't want the Mounties coming to him because it was a small community and people noticed things.

"I understand."

Wraight talked about the organizations and companies being targeted but gave no specifics. McGillivray wanted to know if he himself was on any list.

"Not on a personal level," replied Wraight.

Wraight ended the conversation by saying he couldn't prove anything he was saying, but that "if you were 10 feet away you would hear it. They are not afraid to talk." He said he wasn't interested in the reward – which AEC had bumped up to $100,000 – but wanted the property deal arranged and his family protected. "I'll sign whatever there has to be signed to make it work. I don't care. If I have to be called the Easter Bunny, fine, I'm the Easter Bunny. Make it work."

McGillivray agreed to ensure the protection of Wraight's family. He promised to have a plane ticket left in Wraight's name at the Grande Prairie airport so the prospective informer could come to Calgary and talk. McGillivray had to run, he said, because he had a meeting – "of all things, with the Ecotrust environmental group. A legitimate one."

Bob Wraight's phone call couldn't have come at a better time for Operation Kabriole. After reviewing the evidence gathered from the Hinton bombing, Crown Prosecutor Steve Koval had concluded there wasn't enough to proceed. Unless the RCMP caught Ludwig with bomb in hand, the chances of conviction were slim. In fact Koval wanted to throw out the mischief charges, but Grande Prairie prosecutor Al Munro insisted he merely withdraw them. That meant the Ludwigs and Boonstra could be charged again if more evidence came to light from laboratory tests.

With Operation Kabriole seemingly falling apart, Sergeant Hills received McGillivray's news about a possible informant with keen interest. From the beginning Hills had recognized that the closeness of the Trickle Creek group "would make an undercover operation an extremely lengthy process." The sudden appearance of a long-time Ludwig "associate" had answered the RCMP's prayers. He assigned Corporal Dale Cox, a hard-edged Peace River cowboy with a love of rodeo, to check Wraight out.

After his conversation with McGillivray, Wraight drove over to Trickle Creek and found Ludwig bicycling along the road. Wraight recalls that he started an argument by expressing his regret about the death of Abel Ryan but then adding that he didn't want to see anyone else killed. He says he told Ludwig that the older man's attitude towards the industry had become extreme and aggressive. Ludwig said that people die and that Wraight shouldn't be afraid of that. If you have to put a bullet through someone's head, so be it. Wraight replied that killing was wrong and that Ludwig couldn't expect the industry to bend over backwards just for him.

Richard Boonstra entered the argument, daring Wraight to take a side and be a man. Wraight said later in court testimony that Boonstra invited him to firebomb a facility, which Boonstra says is untrue. "Just where do you stand when industry poisons children and the land?" demanded Boonstra. Ludwig told Wraight that if he didn't like what was going on, he could go elsewhere. Wraight left that evening burdened by a mess of emotions. He says he felt he had to pick a side and couldn't pick Ludwig's.

On September 8, Wraight flew to Calgary courtesy of AEC and met with McGillivray and RCMP Corporal Cox. After coffee and donuts at Tim Hortons, the men headed off to the AEC offices in Bankers Hall, one of the city's most expensive business addresses. There Cox set up his tape recorder and asked Wraight about Ludwig, the family's acquaintances, the number of guns at the farm, and Wraight's own history and motives.

Despite his distrust of the police, Wraight answered Cox's questions like a Catholic in a confessional booth. During the two-hour interview he talked about his involvement in the cementing of the Norcen well and explained how his friendships with those at Trickle Creek went bad after Boonstra and Ludwig started working on his marriage. He gave thumbnail sketches of Ludwig's associates, describing Paul Belanger as "a bit harsh" and Allan Johnstone as "harmless – he just likes to talk a lot." He accused the Ludwigs' lawyer, Richard Secord, of acting weird and staying at Ludwig's house several times: "He's very sympathetic." He portrayed Shane Hartnell, the environmentalist who wooed Mamie Jr. for a time, as "a loner and an emotional mess."

Ludwig, he said, was a macho type and somewhat baffling: "He'll take credit for something he didn't do just to throw you off. You don't know what he's thinkin' one day or the next. One day he wants to move to a better life, and the next day, 'No, I think I'll stay and fight.'"

Richard Boonstra – "the good guy in the family," said Wraight – would "try to smooth things over and make them work. He has a couple of daughters there that are married to the Ludwigs' sons, and I think he's seeking revenge for little difficulties in their lives." Wraight also repeated the wild talk about shooting cops. "They didn't specify how they were going to do this, except that the RCMP constables were dead."

Cox asked Wraight what would be the best way to investigate Ludwig. Here Wraight more or less offered his services: "To have somebody in there." He added, "They are going to commit more crimes, there is no doubt about that."

Cox, who had handled informers in the past, asked about Wraight's own background. Wraight spurted out a short biography in clipped phrases as though his life wasn't worthy of much elaboration: "Grade 11, went into military, injured myself, refused training, was discharged. Got into a car accident, got banged up, I was married. A couple of small businesses failed. I left the Vancouver area. Ah, then from there, nothing, nothing of any great amount of success." He added that he'd been in trouble with the law once, for a hazing ritual, and had a friend who'd committed murder.

The next day Hills and Cox put together an operations plan to use Wraight as an undercover agent "to infiltrate the Ludwig organization and thereby obtain evidence required to prosecute these persons." The optimum result, the Mounties reasoned, "would be to have Wiebo Ludwig and his group make arrangements to meet the U/C at a predetermined site with the intent of having the U/C place an explosion. When all targets attended the site to complete the criminal act, they could be arrested."

After the Crown withdrew the Hinton bombing charges, confounding every resident of the Peace, AEC decided to go on the offensive against Ludwig by breaking its silence on industrial sabotage. An AEC press release advertised the media event as a talk on "Terrorism and a Fractured Community" – a title that prompted the Ludwig diaries to ask, "What bizarre trip are they going on now?"

In mid-September Gwyn Morgan presided over AEC's first and only press conference on the sabotage. It was held at Calgary's Metropolitan Centre. McGillivray and other AEC executives attended, along with scores of business reporters. Morgan, meticulously dressed, did not mention Ludwig by name as he talked about the "corrosive hands of those who advocate or support violence and intimidation. I mean no humorous pun when I say those recent bombings were shattering." He described Peace River as "a funny name these days."

Morgan detailed the escalation of violence over 18 months and said more than 150 AEC employees and contractors were living and working in a state of siege. "We are mystified and dismayed that people would resort to such violent acts. We don't know who is doing them, and we don't understand why." He assured reporters that AEC had as good an environmental record as any company. He said farmers who blamed sour gas plants for livestock problems should check their own livestock management practices before blaming industry. Peace, order, and good government were Canadian values worth treasuring, he added. "I call industrial terrorism a creeping sickness that must be eradicated." To that end he promised to lobby the federal justice minister and Alberta's attorney general about the need for tougher legislation and investigative powers.

"No one has the right to threaten people or intimidate their neighbours. At AEC that line is fully drawn. Until now, in the interest of avoiding provocation, some employees and members of their families have endured personal threats, intimidation, and harassment. Threats to and harassment of our employees will be pursued through criminal and/or civil jurisdictions of our justice system." At the end of his speech Morgan announced that AEC, along with the County of Grande Prairie, would host a series of town hall meetings to help local residents deal "with the prolonged campaign of violence in the region."

No executive in Canada had ever given a speech quite like it. Morgan's talk made the national news, though it was notable for what it omitted: mention of AEC's lawsuit against the Ludwig clan, and Morgan's own lengthy meeting with Ludwig.

Grande Prairie reeve Roy Borstad spoke. He said it was time for local people to take back their community from "people who believe in violence and intimidation." AEC then put Rob and Gisela Everton, Ludwig's closest neighbours, in front of the cameras. The company had flown the farming couple in for the event. Somewhat bewildered by the commotion, the Evertons quietly talked about 40 rural residents who lived near Ludwig and reported no problems with the industry. "We would really like to see this come to an end," said Gisela. "It has been very frustrating, having this constant worry and

concern." The company also showed a short video starring frightened employees.

During Morgan's speech Ludwig and Mamie had arrived downstairs, looking harried and combative. On McGillivray's orders a
burly security guard had barred their entry. Ludwig told the guard he
wanted to speak with Morgan and give him a videotape showing the
stillbirth of Abel Ryan. Morgan sent McGillivray down instead.
Ludwig handed him the disturbing tape with the words, "You are
now my arch-enemies." He noted that the two men hadn't talked
recently. "Not since you closed off discussions," said McGillivray.
"Good day."

Later that morning McGillivray and Morgan found identical
anonymous letters waiting on their desks. Both were postmarked
Grande Prairie and signed by the same mysterious terrorist who had
threatened Bob Bilodeau's family a year earlier.

> Warning to AEC Calgary brass
>
> I have heard and read enough!
> You will pay "blood for blood" and "life for life"
> unless you and your corporate criminal associates
> publicly compensate the Hythe and Beaverlodge area
> farmers for your criminal damages.
> You get 30 days to make that the news of the day for
> the Canadian public!
> Your children are not exempt.
> Don't mess with this warning!
> You will only shorten the time of your well-deserved
> executions.   HDB

Ludwig followed Morgan's hard-line announcement with his
own hectic scrum in the chilly Calgary wind. He said tougher environmental standards would eliminate the problems in the oil patch.
"It would cost them some money but save us a lot on health and
agony and, perhaps, on bombings." He explained the necessity of
defensive violence to the *Calgary Sun* columnist Sidney Sharpe.

"Sometimes to reflect verbal perseverance, some force has to be exercised. I'm supportive of it." When she pressed him on the need for bombings, Ludwig angrily accused her of having a problem and tapped her on the shoulder. "You don't like women," barked Sharpe. "You're pretty snotty," replied Ludwig. The columnist called that day's event "one of the strangest the industry has seen in a long while."

Alanna Mitchell, head of the *Globe and Mail*'s Calgary bureau, later described the day as a remarkable study in contrasts. Upstairs Morgan, "dapper in a sober tie and navy-blue pinstriped shirt, his shoes polished to a high gloss," lectured the press on terrorism. Downstairs Ludwig, "a nightmare for the petroleum industry," protested against sour gas in "black jeans and discount store loafers" and dirty grey raincoat. She portrayed Ludwig as "a former evangelical preacher whose wavy grey hair and beard suggests Charlton Heston as Moses."

In her article Mitchell quoted experts who described sour gas as a dangerous concern and flaring as an unnecessary environmental hazard. One expert noted that the industry routinely bought out farmers living near highly polluting oil and gas facilities, a fact AEC denies. Dick Wilson, AEC's media spokesman, later phoned Mitchell and berated her for writing such nonsense. He also complained that the story gave Ludwig a platform, a stupid thing to do because the man was insane. Wilson, who taped the conversation, concluded his intimidating scolding by saying AEC would never deal with her again, a threat AEC routinely made to reporters who didn't toe the corporate line. Both Mitchell and the *Globe*'s publisher, Roy Megarry, received personal correspondence from Gwyn Morgan that called her reporting "pulp fiction."

McGillivray and the RCMP turned their attention to negotiating a deal with Wraight. Because of his doubts about the RCMP's ability to pay him, Wraight faxed McGillivray a three-page contract that stipulated the cost "of saving lives." In addition to $109,000 for his land, Wraight now wanted $43,960 for industrial advantage ("same as others who have been affected by industrial activity"), $59,000 in lost wages, and $600 a week for consultation fees – what he later called "snitch wages." McGillivray replied that this was a lot more than Wraight had originally asked for and that AEC would have to go back to the drawing board.

Two criminal lawyers, Chris Evans and Earl Wilson, advised the company that it shouldn't pay Wraight anything without the RCMP's permission. Gwyn Morgan was particularly concerned about tainting the agent's future testimony. McGillivray phoned both Cox and Hills about the matter but found them unhelpful. Cox told him to go ahead with a land deal "as AEC sees fit" but to keep the RCMP out of it. The debate eventually went as high as Neil McCrank, Alberta's deputy justice minister, and Rod MacKay, the second most powerful Mountie in the province.

The financial seesaw ended with a compromise of sorts. A private buyer agreed to purchase Wraight's property, and the RCMP signed up its informant. The agreement gave Wraight a $10,000 signing bonus, moving expenses, and $475 a week. McGillivray told Wraight that AEC had been unable to buy his land for legal reasons but encouraged him to seek the $100,000 reward. The RCMP agreed to help Wraight apply for it. It then gave him a new name: Agent K4209. On a form that assessed K4209's worthiness as a police agent, Cox recorded Wraight's chief motive as "monetary."

At the end of September, Sergeant Keith Hills reluctantly recognized that Operation Kabriole couldn't go anywhere without a bombing. Having Agent K4209 merely befriend targets as suspicious as Ludwig and Boonstra wasn't likely to produce evidence to support a new charge of mischief endangering life. Indeed, Ludwig appeared to be hesitant to discuss much with Wraight and called him a liability. In his notes, Hills wrote that Ludwig felt Wraight should "either take an active role very quickly or not bother associating with them any further."

To turn Wraight into a viable asset, the Kabriole team decided to blow up an AEC vehicle in the Hythe-Beaverlodge area and let Wraight take the credit. Given that the RCMP had previously burned barns, set off bombs, and even staged deaths, a vehicle bombing didn't seem outlandish. The RCMP's Explosives Disposal Unit confirmed it could easily do the job. When briefed, McGillivray not only warmed to the ruse but offered to locate a suitable site and sell the RCMP a 1995 Ford truck "for a good price."

Hills directed that the scenario be played out "complete with a controlled, prepared, media response. It is anticipated that once this proof has been supplied K4209 will be accepted to the extent that it will be privy to discussions of both past and future criminal activities of the targets."

But when McGillivray shared the staged bombing proposal with four senior AEC executives, including Morgan, they didn't like it. Morgan in particular got upset. He thought blowing up a vehicle would scare the hell out of his employees and make them even more jittery about going to work. He suggested that blowing up a well site would be smarter and gave Al Johnston, the AEC West production manager, the task of convincing the RCMP of the wisdom of his plans.

Dale Cox, like every other member of Kabriole, was intrigued by Morgan's proposal. The RCMP had never been offered a well site to blow up. Al Johnston assured him it would be safe. The well was 15 kilometres northwest of Beaverlodge, near Goodfare, and had been depressurized. He said the well wasn't sour, which greatly relieved the RCMP. Outsiders couldn't tell if the well was producing or not, and its location was advantageous: it was in a secluded bit of bush three kilometres from the nearest home.

The Kabriole team agreed that Morgan's plan made more sense than their own, but one Mountie, reflecting the agency's new emphasis on business models, asked about the force's financial liability. Johnston assured them that AEC wouldn't bill the RCMP more than $5,000 for the damage to the well. The notion of sowing more terror in an already terrorized community prompted only minor discussion. As Cox later explained, "I didn't think the fear level could have gone any higher. It was as high as it could go, and one more explosion would not heighten it in any way."

The next day Johnston drove out to the site with two Mounties. In the rain and mud, he checked out the wellhead and the equipment, which were housed in an eight-by-ten-foot shack, while Sergeant J.V. Dunn, the officer in charge of the bombing, took Polaroids. Unless there was one horrific explosion, said Johnston, the wellhead wouldn't rupture. Dunn suggested blowing out the left side of the main door: it was farthest from the equipment, and it could be seen from the road entrance.

Corporal Cox, meanwhile, was training Wraight for his informing duties. He gave him a black notebook and instructed him on how to take notes, complete with the date and a description of the weather. Cox also explained how the Nagra, or body pack, would work. Wraight would be outfitted with a green vest that contained a microphone and a transmitter. A receiver in an airplane or nearby car would pick up the transmission and record any conversation. He warned that the Nagra had a limited transmission range and that its recording tape lasted only two hours. The RCMP also gave Wraight a grey 1982 Olds Cutlass Sierra with a CB radio. The trunk of the car contained a police PACS radio system set to Tactical Channel 7. The radio allowed ground surveillance crews with hand-held radios to monitor conversations and possibly intervene.

During training Cox encouraged Wraight to visit the community "but not to get involved in anything inappropriate." On September 26, Wraight and his little son, Bobby, went to Trickle Creek and found Trevor Schilthuis making a motion detector "to monitor vehicles as far away as three and four miles." Wraight later reported in his black notebook that Ludwig was considering "a large lawsuit" against the oil and gas industry and that Boonstra didn't like all the security following him everywhere. "We should do something about it, teach these guys we're not afraid of them... put a bullet through their window."

According to Wraight's notes, the men also talked about getting back clothes the RCMP had seized after the Suncor bombing. "Richard B then says 1 cop told me to wash my hands up to my elbows. Wiebo then says, well, that's good. You had the stuff right up to your armpits." Wraight ended the entry by writing: "2:20 pm I say goodbye and take my son home, and leave for the day."

In between Wraight's visits, Ludwig continued to entertain scores of reporters. "So you've come all this way to meet the saboteur?" he said welcomingly to one New York writer. Whenever journalists asked if he had set off any of the bombs, Ludwig hemmed and hawed. "I don't remember. The bomb was too loud." He said he knew the saboteurs and supported them in spirit. You know, he often reasoned, "the Lord is perverse with those who are perverse."

While the RCMP finalized plans for the bombing, one of Wiebo Ludwig's ominous prophecies came true. For two months he had warned that something was going to happen that would "make bombing look minor." On October 3, 1998, something did.

Chapter 11

A Killing

October 3 was a Saturday, and Patrick Kent, the vice-president of KB Resources, rose early in his Calgary bungalow, as oil patchers are wont to do. He had a job to complete near Bowden, an hour's drive north of the city. He downed a glass of orange juice and told his wife, Linda, that he'd call around four in the afternoon to let her know if he'd be home in time for dinner.

Kent, fourth son of an accountant and military officer, was a big man with big plans in the oil patch. His mother, Hope, says he was always a determined boy: "The happiest day of his life was when he outgrew all of his brothers and stood six-five." After attending Trinity College School, a private high school in Port Hope, Ontario, Kent started working in the oil patch to help support a car racing passion. When his towering frame no longer fit safely into a Formula One, he got an engineering degree and joined the American oil and gas outfit Amerada Hess, working in Rocky Mountain House and in the boreal forest near Fort St. John.

Men who worked with him up north generally liked him. "Right was right to him and there was no diplomacy," recalls Ron Fipke, a drilling operator who once had to pull Kent out of a meeting with rural folk over a land dispute and send him to his car. "He had a bit of an irritating nature to him."

In 1995 Kent teamed up with some colleagues and became the K in KB Resources, a Calgary firm with eight employees. After years of burning the midnight oil for big multinationals, Kent wanted to be his own man. KB, like a lot of small companies in the province, figured it could make good money by reviving suspended or abandoned wells deemed uneconomic by bigger companies.

Kent called his wife "Blondie." An open-faced woman a couple of feet shorter than her husband, Linda took care of their four children and the household. She says there were two things they never did together: dance, and talk about the oil and gas business. The first she ever heard about her husband's two-year-long dispute with Wayne Roberts was after she had become a widow.

Eifion Wayne Roberts – Wyn to his friends – grew up in Wales during World War II. As a youth, he delivered butter and coal for his mother, a shop owner. Roberts stood only five-six and had been a boxer and sailor in his youth. He compensated for his lack of height with a wry and stubborn outspokenness, as short men often do. "Wyn is a person who has his own very strong sense of morals," says his wife, Jean. After working as a welder in Nova Scotia in the 1970s, Roberts moved to Alberta and started his own company, repairing pipes and boilers for oil companies, including Amerada Hess. In 1989 he married Jean, a former nurse – his third marriage – and bought Eagle Ridge Ranch near Bowden. They dreamed of raising Welsh cattle and converting a money-making gravel pit into a fish farm.

The destinies of the little Welshman and the big oilman converged in December 1995, a year before Ludwig declared war on AEC. Kent's firm bought two suspended wells and an old gas plant that his former employer, Amerada, had sold to Petro-Canada. One of the wells lay in Roberts's front yard, just east of his house and barn. Buying and selling wells is routine business in Alberta. Every year more than 17,000 of them change corporate hands. For landowners it's the equivalent of getting an absentee neighbour or a nightmare tenant.

The transaction caught Roberts off guard. In 1993, Amerada had suspended the well when it became uneconomic after nearly 20 years of production. Company officials had assured him it would be abandoned. As a consequence Roberts didn't press for a rent review on the well (he was then receiving $1,353 a year). With the company's permission he dug up ground around the wellhead to establish the particulars for reclamation. In the process he found an illegal valve that made it impossible to test well pressure accurately. No one ever explained how it got there or how many other wells might contain illegal valves. Roberts also noticed gas bubbling up from around the well and suspected a leak. Amerada's people suggested the bubbling gas was probably due to "a bad cement job down the hole" that could be taken care of during reclamation. They figured it might cost $20,000 to restore the site to farmland.

But in 1995 Amerada, then the eighth-largest oil and gas company in the United States, sold all its holdings to Petro-Canada. Instead of abandoning the well, Petro-Canada sold it to KB Resources. Roberts wasn't happy and expressed his concerns about subsurface contamination to Patrick Kent. Kent came out and inspected the site and agreed the illegal valve shouldn't have been there, adding that Amerada hadn't mentioned anything about contamination.

Roberts also called up the Energy and Utilities Board office in Red Deer. Because of sour gas emissions and gas-casing leaks, the Red Deer office receives more complaints from landowners (nearly a third of the province's total of 851 complaints that year) than any other of the board's eight offices. Joe Gormley, a chain-smoking inspector, checked out the well and ordered some tests. That action delayed the well's transfer to KB for a few months, but the EUB ultimately concluded that the leak was "non-serious."

In some dozen visits with Roberts, Joe Gormley got the sense that the Welshman "didn't have a whole lot of trust in oil companies" and felt large outfits shouldn't be allowed to sell off uneconomic properties to small ones. "He was concerned that KB would not have the financial resources to look after reclamation." Roberts's concerns weren't unusual. Many Alberta landowners suspect that major producers often sell off their "dog" wells to smaller companies to avoid reclamation costs. One of the big firms sold 200 wells to a fly-by-night company in Saskatchewan that promptly went bankrupt. Roberts feared the same would happen on his land.

A 1999 report by Alberta Environment later confirmed how widespread these concerns were among landowners. Farmers told a special committee on well-site reclamations that oil and gas operators didn't do a good job of "keeping them informed about activities related to the abandonment of a well." Citizens also called the inquiry process "unpredictable" and the appeal process "expensive and intimidating." In addition most landowners didn't know that the liability for poisoned land lay with the well operator in perpetuity, or – in the case of a company's bankruptcy – with the government. Like Roberts, most had no idea that the industry was in the process of setting up the multimillion-dollar Orphan Wells Program to deal with bad operators and the issue of environmental liability. The report recommended what Roberts and Kent never achieved: "improved communication between all parties."

Roberts often told Gormley he was concerned about "a cover-up" and he threatened, repeatedly, to "shoot somebody" if the leak and the contamination weren't addressed properly. Gormley thought little of Roberts's bravado. Farmers talked like that every day in Alberta. Roberts had other concerns besides. He wanted KB Resources to install a new cattle gate; during a snowy winter two of his cattle had got stuck in an unplowed Texas gate. He also wanted a bigger rent cheque; he wasn't about to be taken again. Having worked in the oil patch, Roberts understood the industry and knew which buttons to push.

Faced with growing demands on a well site producing no revenue, Kent hired a landman to deal with Roberts: Jack Evans, the same tall, pleasant, sandy-haired man who had dealt with Wiebo Ludwig on behalf of Suncor in 1995. Evans had noticed a change in rural temperaments and attitudes to the industry. As more landowners became better informed about their surface rights, says Evans, "even the nice guys weren't as nice as they once were." His job was getting harder, but he enjoyed it. He operated, as always, by an old credo: "Never send an engineer to do a landman's job, and never send a landman to do an engineer's job."

One day in the fall of 1996 Evans spent five hours carefully listening to Roberts. He toured the farm and inspected the man's prized Welsh cattle. Evans pegged him as "volatile and determined," though "nothing close to a Wiebo Ludwig." It became clear that Roberts didn't want the well on his property under any conditions. Evans agreed with Roberts that a rent review was long overdue.

Roberts says he threw Evans off his property when the landman offered to buy him off with a lump sum of cash. Evans says the meeting ended amicably but with no resolution. To deal with the growing imbroglio, Roberts hired a local lawyer, Daniel Harder.

As time wore on and Roberts's demands grew, Patrick Kent's feelings towards the man grew increasingly uncharitable. He came to view the Welshman as a problem "that was costing his small company money," says Evans. In a 1997 fax to Evans, Kent referred to Roberts as a "shithead" and dismissed his concerns about cattle guards and rent as "dribble." Added Kent: "If Wayne wants $3,000 a year for access, then he can go fuck himself." Normal rent for a well lease usually went for $2,000 in the area; at $1,353, KB had itself a small bargain.

Kent learned that Roberts had built both his barn and his corral either within the well lease or damn close, violating the standard 100-metre minimum distance rule in the industry. Evans, however, advised Kent that it would be unethical or counterproductive to use that "encroachment card" in negotiations. Evans knew the industry and the EUB granted exceptions to the rule every day.

After a year of fruitless negotiations, Evans concluded that both sides were too entrenched to resolve anything. "Wyn was not ready to reduce his position and KB's was to give nothing. This made it nearly impossible to reach any agreement," he wrote in one memo. As Evans later said, things went from "worse to worse." When Kent wrote out cheques to Roberts for well rent, he purposely addressed them incorrectly. Inquiries from Roberts's lawyer to KB often went unanswered.

Meanwhile, Roberts's concerns about contamination grew. He noticed more bubbling from the inactive well and wondered about his groundwater and his fish pond. He feared that the contamination could be going off the lease area onto grazing land. Gormley inspected the site again, confirmed "gas migration to surface around the well bore," and ordered remedial work. Kent paid for more tests, which found definite hydrocarbon contamination around the wellhead, a common finding around old wells. Kent didn't believe "this well is leaking or poses any threat to public safety," but he reluctantly agreed to replace soil around the wellhead and do more tests to pinpoint the source of the trouble.

Nothing happened for nearly a year. In July 1998, in a fit of frustration, Roberts threatened to dig up the well himself. Gormley told him he couldn't do that. After a talk with Gormley, Kent agreed to do the work "in two weeks." Roberts, meanwhile, phoned up Alberta Environment and requested some testing. Gormley says Roberts again threatened to shoot someone if things weren't done properly. He says he reported this threat to KB Resources. Ken Wilde, the geologist who took the call, remembers no such warning, only that the landowner was angry and had threatened to sue the company. When Wilde passed the message to Kent, Kent replied, "If he wants to sue, let him go ahead."

KB's initial excavation of the site began three months later and got off to a bad start. Kent didn't bring soil analysts to determine the scope of the problem, normal practice for a cleanup. He also balked at the cost of disposing of contaminated soil at a local waste facility. So he sent the load back to the farm and dumped it by the wellhead. Roberts, of course, complained; contaminated soil left on top of gravel could leach into the water table. Roberts says Kent later phoned and told him he should have left the damn soil in the ground. He says Kent told him, "I'm going to teach you a lesson."

In the late afternoon on Friday, October 2, Kent informed Roberts that another excavation would take place the next morning. Roberts faxed the company and the EUB, saying he would oversee the project and warning that "any attempt at cover-up of contamination or spreading contaminated soil or water on farm land will be subject to an arrest and criminal prosecution." Spreading oil and drilling waste on farm fields happens routinely in Alberta and Roberts, knowing the oil patch inside out, wanted no part of it. He also phoned his lawyer, Harder, to ask him to be there. Harder said he'd try.

On Saturday morning a host of workers descended on Roberts's farm, including Kent, Terry Ringheim, a backhoe operator, Darren Tomecek, an environmental consultant, Joe Gormley of the EUB, Lloyd Ross, a tank truck operator, Wayne Brown, a ditch man, and a party of surveyors, George MacPhee and Karry Kerhoulas. Kent directed the surveyors to measure and stake out the lease boundaries for the wellhead, an area of 4.5 acres. Everyone else concentrated on the well site. Soon the sound of a backhoe filled the air. It was a cool, blue-sky Alberta day.

Kent instructed Tomecek to determine the extent of the contamination and make recommendations about remediation. Having witnessed ugly disputes between landowners and oil companies, including cases where landowners pulled out handguns, Tomecek was apprehensive. Other consultants had warned him that this dispute involved a big man not wanting to be pushed around by a little man, and vice versa. The consultant, however, was pleasantly surprised by how smoothly things went. Kent and Roberts appeared calm and cordial. Roberts even helped out, filling sampling bottles around the wellhead. When Roberts spied some obvious contamination, Kent replied, "That's what we're here for."

Roberts mentioned to Ringheim and Ross that the well had polluted his land with cancer-causing hydrocarbons such as toluenes and benzenes, and that if KB Resources dug up the swamp below the well they'd have to replace all the peat moss, even if they had to buy it from Wal-Mart. He also told Ross, "They are just a small oil company. I'll break them. It'll cost $300,000 to reclaim this land. They can buy me out for a million dollars."

Kent, meanwhile, worked with the surveyors, who established that about 80 percent of Roberts's barn and corral was on the well's lease site. (Kent didn't know that Amerada Hess had given Roberts permission to build there.) He asked the surveyors to stake out the lease three times and "mark it neon," as one surveyor said. When Ross remarked that the house and barn were pretty close to the well, Kent said he might fence the whole lease off. Such an act was within the company's legal rights and would have made it impossible for Roberts to use his barn or house. "If push comes to shove, I can threaten to fence off the lease; I don't want to do that and I won't, but it gives me a lot of satisfaction to see those stakes there even if it costs me a day's pay for the surveyors." He shot Ross a smile and walked away.

Patrick Kent spent the last few minutes of his life measuring the distance between the lease boundary and the house, some 11.4 metres. The house, started in 1996 without objections from KB Resources, also violated the 100-metre rule. From a distance Ross watched Kent, in his white hard hat, kneeling on the ground as he made the measurements and pencilled them in a notebook. Ross later testified that Kent vowed to put the whole matter to rest that day, "once and for all."

Roberts was drinking tea and smoking a cigarette in the kitchen of his unfinished two-storey house when he noticed Kent outside. He thought he heard the snapping of a tape measure against a wall and told Jean he'd go investigate. Roberts, who owned half a dozen guns, grabbed his 9-mm Ruger pistol off the tack chest. He used the automatic handgun, a favourite among policemen, for target practice in his gravel pit and to shoot coyotes at night. He later said he picked up the Ruger because of Kent's enormous size and because of the threats Kent had uttered about "teaching him a lesson."

As he walked out, he held the pistol behind his back. Roberts approached to within about five metres of the man before Kent rose, extending his arms. It appeared to Ross that the two men hollered at each other. Roberts later testified that he asked Kent what he was doing. "I thought you were here to excavate and clean up. Not to survey."

Kent replied (no other witness heard this exchange because of the noisy backhoe): "Your barn is on the lease. Your corral is on the lease. Your house is too close to the well. Your barn is gone. Your house is gone. Tell your fucking wife to pack her bags. She's gone."

Roberts told Kent to get off his land and then threatened to arrest him for trespassing, as he had a legal right to do. According to Roberts, Kent erupted and said, "Arrest me, you shithead, and I'll tear your fucking head off."

Roberts said he "had never seen a more angry look on a man's face" and that Kent charged him like a middle linebacker. "He lost it completely and I lost it completely. I never thought he would have reacted that way. Surely you don't attack a man with a gun in his hand." Ross said he saw Kent take only one step.

Roberts fired at Kent's hip and then at his forehead, but the big man kept charging. Roberts says he doesn't remember the other shots, which shattered Kent's skull so thoroughly that even the pathologist couldn't figure out which bullet went where. Roberts then leaned over the dying man and said, "My God, what did I do?" Jack Evans, who wishes he'd been there that day to mediate, guesses that Kent "would have put his two cents' worth in about the house or barn being too close to the wellhead." He says neither party understood the insignificance of that fact.

Each of the men working for Kent near the wellhead, perhaps 20 metres away, saw something different. Some heard shots. Others saw Roberts standing over Kent, firing. One surveyor says he saw Roberts "put two bullets in him as though he were putting down an animal to make sure it wasn't suffering."

After the shooting the Welshman walked back into his house. He heard people shouting "Man down," which is what sour gas operators yell when hydrogen sulphide overcomes a man. He thought all the yelling strange because his home wasn't a sour gas plant. Jean called 911.

A few minutes later he walked out again, without the gun. He passed the body of Patrick Kent and marched towards the wellhead. Excavators and surveyors were talking frantically on their cellphones in the safety of their trucks. Terry Ringheim, the backhoe operator, had medical training and thought he might be able to help the prostrate figure in blue jeans on the ground. He approached Roberts.

"What the fuck's going on?" he asked excitedly.

"He's dead," said Roberts.

"Who shot him?"

"I did."

As Ringheim later told a Calgary jury, "It finally dawned on my slow-moving brain that, yes, it was time to get out of there." The eight men on site gunned their trucks and sped out of the yard like a confused family fleeing a burning house.

Roberts's lawyer, Daniel Harder, finally showed up two hours after the killing. He explained that he'd got lost.

When Wiebo Ludwig heard about the killing on the news, he and Mamie got in the car and drove down to Sundre, where they spent the night with Wayne and Ila Johnston, about 30 kilometres from the shooting. His prophecy about things getting worse and "the culprits in Calgary" getting hurt had come true, and he felt compelled to tell people so.

On Monday Ludwig made an appearance at the Didsbury courthouse, where Roberts was charged with first-degree murder. Ludwig told reporters he appreciated the gravity of Roberts's action because he too had suffered grievous losses at the hands of industry. He knew how a man could lose it in the face of a persistent aggressor and called the killing a case of "aggravated assault." He later tried to visit Jean Roberts, but police had cordoned off the farm.

In rural Alberta the murder became a compulsory topic of conversation. Most farmers sided with Roberts. In Medicine Hat several hundred landowners gathered to discuss oil and gas leases, but the shooting occupied most tongues. Many ranchers wondered how "government would let things get this far." Nobody condoned violence, but many reckoned that oil company harassment could explain if not justify a bloody murder. At the weekly auction in Olds, Johnston even heard one farmer say, "Roberts shot the right son-of-a-bitch."

The murder stunned the oil patch. It was the industry's first killing. Dumbfounded administrators at the EUB had thought the dispute was an ordinary spat between farmer and oil company. Ron

Fipke, an old friend of Kent's, was so appalled by the murder and Ludwig's disguised support for the killing that he put a new licence plate on his truck. It read: "Piss On Wiebo."

The province's tightly knit oil community openly speculated that Ludwig was to blame. Many oil patchers continue to believe Ludwig secretly met with Roberts a week before the murder in a local coffee shop and used his powers of persuasion to convince him to kill Kent. The RCMP, which had Ludwig under 24-hour observation, recorded no such visit. Indeed, Jean Roberts says she and her husband had no idea who Wiebo Ludwig was until he showed up at court two days after the shooting.

In November, Ludwig sent Roberts, then in Calgary's remand centre, a letter of consolation with a strong congratulatory tone. He wrote that he was amazed "that more farmers and landowners haven't put their foot down on this very present plague of corporate leeching and murdering." He went on: "Whatever the more personal reasons for your actions may have been, Wayne, you have, in my opinion, be it inadvertently, effectively disciplined a bull-headed and foolhardy industrial mind set which, again in my opinion, has repeatedly demonstrated that it will listen to nothing less and is in fact clearly in need of more of the same painful kind of judgments ...

"Despite what most (the democratic majority) will say and what you, yourself, Wayne may from time to time even seriously doubt, and regardless of what may have motivated you personally, your action was a much needed blow to destructive and, yes, murderous corporate ambitions throughout the length and breadth of this province and was as such also a much needed wake-up call to a lot of sleepy and hood-winked people throughout the country and perhaps even throughout the world.

"I (all of us here actually) wish you a rich measure of God's wisdom and the indispensable consolations of His Spirit in all of this."

Ludwig enclosed a cheque for $500.

Chapter 12
Romans

Four days after the killing of Patrick Kent, Corporal Dale Cox sent Bob Wraight into Trickle Creek to test out the equipment. He told Wraight to move about the farm to see how well the Nagra transmitter functioned from different locations. He also instructed the agent to keep the conversations general and to mention the appearance of a large plywood sign by Hythe's campground on the highway. When Wraight had discovered it the day before, he had immediately torn it down and given it to the RCMP. In bright red letters the placard described Ludwig, Boonstra, and Wraight himself as "Scum of the Earth."

Wraight arrived in mid-afternoon to find Boonstra giving the children an English lesson. Ludwig and Mamie showed up 20 minutes later with a pile of newspapers. Ludwig briskly asked Wraight if he was a mole, just as he often asked visiting reporters if they had any bombs with them. The question stymied the informant. "I then looked on the floor and for once he laughed," recorded Wraight in his notebook. His printed notes also mentioned a long conversation about the shooting of Patrick Kent: "Wiebo said well there shooting C.E.O.s now. We'll have to start that too."

The Nagra didn't work well. Static made the entire conversation inaudible. Technical problems often dog big investigations, but Operation Kabriole was about to set a record. Short of the agent's car catching fire, everything that could go wrong did. One day the trunk of Wraight's car popped open; another time the informant left his vest in the car. Technical difficulties eliminated some key phone conversations. Even the surveillance aircraft had problems. On one flight a constable couldn't figure out how to work the record button.

In the first two weeks of October, AEC and the RCMP fine-tuned plans for their well-site bombing. Al Johnston had specific orders. After the explosion he was to visit the site with another AEC employee. When he'd viewed the damage, he was to file a complaint with the Beaverlodge detachment. Sergeant Dave MacKay would send out an investigating officer and issue a press release.

On October 14 at 5:30 in the morning, a team of seven RCMP members blew a hole in the shack. Because of pressing business concerns, Johnston didn't drive out until later in the morning. Once there he acted all chagrined and surprised and dutifully filed his complaint over his cellphone to Ron Bettin, the plant manager at Hythe Brainard. He also sent a memo to McGillivray and notified the police. The RCMP issued a short press release and waited for inquiries.

The morning of the RCMP bombing, Wraight phoned Ludwig around 7:30 and acted breathless and distraught, like a man caught in another man's bed. "Don't mind me, I'm just kinda shook up here," he said.

"What's that?"

"Just kinda a little bit shook up here."

"Why?

Wraight said Ludwig would be able to read about it in the paper.

"You're shook up about what, Bob?"

"Can't really tell you on the phone."

An hour later Richard and Lois Boonstra surprised Wraight by driving up to his trailer in their little red Sprint. The RCMP hadn't anticipated this and there were no recording devices around. Wraight invited them in and described the bombing and how he had nearly blown himself up. Boonstra warned Wraight not to talk on the phone about such things, adding that Richard Secord had warned them that the RCMP was using aircraft and a French satellite to gather information about them. Wraight let it be known that he could get more dynamite. Boonstra invited him over for a talk later that night.

That evening, Wraight pulled up at Trickle Creek in time to admire the new dairy cow that Ludwig had just brought home. At the dinner table Wraight called for a county map. After one of the Ludwig boys produced one, Wraight spent several nervous minutes trying to locate the site the RCMP had bombed. "It doesn't make any sense; should be over there somewhere. Well, here's Ray Lake, it must be close." After much fumbling he finally found the spot near Goodfare. Wraight said somebody must have heard the explosion. "It's so quiet up here you can hear a mouse fart a thousand yards." He said there were Canadian Hunter wells nearby, and so many oil and gas company signs he couldn't remember them all. He said he got about 70 yards from the site before the bomb went off. "I almost shit my pants."

Ludwig didn't seem terribly interested; he started speculating about whether a stick of dynamite could blow up a beaver dam. Wraight said sure, a man could blow a beaver dam 25 feet in the air – sticks, mud, beavers, and all. Ludwig asked if Wraight would have a problem getting over the bombing.

"I'm better now than I was in the morning," said Wraight.

"It takes about three weeks or so," Ludwig allowed, adding that he'd like to see the site sometime.

"You can't miss it," replied Wraight.

Ludwig warmed to the topic; he talked obliquely about fuses and fishing lines and cigarettes. He asked Wraight if his supplier had more dynamite.

"Well," replied Wraight, hardly believing his luck, "he's got more."

"You didn't tell him what you're using it for?"

"No. Oh, I did. Yeah. Beavers!"

"Well, we've got to watch it. They are very upset right now."

The rest of the conversation, much of which was inaudible to the RCMP handlers, centred on Wraight's unhappy married life, a subject the two men had spent so much time dissecting. Wraight said it was pathetic that a man would have to ask his wife for help to understand his own feelings. He said he felt all choked up because everything he touched turned to shit. "I barely get in the house and my coat off and shoes and... she throws it at me, whatever it is. You open the door and she's just like a mother hen."

"What you can do," joked Ludwig, "is tape duct tape right over her mouth."

"Well, I just told her to go to her mom's."

"Tie it around her neck a few times."

Ludwig urged Wraight to "lay this thing on the line and say that's it, either this or it's over. Somebody has to rule the roost and somebody has to say what is what." He talked about the strength to be found in the Scriptures and added, "I've done a few things here that if society would know about it I'd be in deep shit. I'd be in jail for the rest of my life." Ludwig looked Wraight in the eye and said he'd need bonds greater than duct tape to repair his marriage.

Before Wraight used up his two hours of recording time, he turned the subject back to dynamite. He said that one stick cost him $100, revealing his ignorance of the local market.

"That's expensive. He's gypping you. Twenty-five bucks is plenty."

After pulling out of the driveway at Trickle Creek that night, Wraight spoke into the malfunctioning Nagra, as he did at the end of every operation scenario, sounding like a stand-up comic in an empty theatre. "Man, these roads are slippery..."

Despite his ineptitude and the technical problems, however, Operation Kabriole was in full gear. Wraight had found a conspirator interested in dynamite.

The shed bombing didn't hit the news until October 16. Sergeant MacKay's press release claimed that "persons unknown used a powerful explosive to destroy an AEC well site building and equipment. Police are seeking the public's assistance." A Global Television crew chartered a plane and flew up to inspect the damage, while in media interviews MacKay suggested that the explosive was probably stolen dynamite. He described the bombing as "severe" and said the RCMP found tire tracks into the site but couldn't identify them.

Ed McGillivray played his part well too, acting as aggrieved as if the bombing had happened in his own backyard. "I classify it purely as terrorism," he told the *Globe and Mail*. "That's what it is. You're dealing with people's emotions here. Let's face it, our employees and the people that live up here, it's causing them a great deal of concern and angst and fear." He told the *Edmonton Journal*, "We can fix equipment but we can't repair anyone who gets hurt or killed." He told the *Calgary Herald* the only thing that might mollify the bombers would be the complete shutdown of the oil and gas industry. "I just scratch my head and question why our well sites are being blown up," he added. "To me that's a funny way of showing you care for the environment." McGillivray also used the event to advertise the two upcoming town hall meetings sponsored by AEC to warn the public about the dangers of political extremism and terrorism.

News of another bombing predictably heated up emotions in Grande Prairie. County councillor Brock Smith said he was disgusted. "I really think that those dirty criminals should be put in jail." Added a local store owner: "If the guys who are doing it would just blow themselves up, they'd get rid of the problem." Even Premier Ralph Klein got into the act: "It's against the law, and the people who do this kind of thing should be punished to the fullest extent of the law."

Like the RCMP, Ludwig made full use of the mysterious shed bombing. He told reporters it proved that an underground movement of resistance to industry had sprung up. He said the bombing might convince the industry to listen to people and not play hardball with their lives, "otherwise people will play hardball back." The oil industry, he added, could expect more grief if it didn't stop poisoning people. "No one cares to shoot people, but sometimes war has to be waged." A reporter asked if executives might be targeted next and Ludwig obliged him: "People are talking here that maybe someone should be shooting guys in pinstripe suits to get them to stop." He added that shooting executives made more sense than shooting employees at well sites. RCMP Sergeant MacKay nearly fell out of his chair when he heard about the targeting of executives. "I think that commentary is outrageous," he told a Canadian Press reporter. "I would go to the point of saying it's anti-Canadian."

The day after the news broke, Wraight visited Trickle Creek to take advantage of his new status as a terrorist. The RCMP wanted him to get Ludwig and Boonstra to talk about the Goodfare and Demmitt bombings, maybe even to coax them into a car and have them show him the sites. Cox also instructed Wraight to correct his dynamite economy to five sticks for $100.

When Wraight arrived at the farm, though, he learned that Ludwig was in Grande Prairie, talking to the CBC "or whatever poor soul's got to listen to him." Boonstra wasn't in a talkative mood and Wraight's leading comments about well sites and dynamite mostly elicited inaudible mumbles. Boonstra was mostly concerned about getting Wraight to move the junk in his cabin. As Wraight drove away that day, he confessed to the Nagra, "It was like pulling teeth today."

He got luckier three days later. As he chatted with Boonstra around the dining-room table, Ludwig popped in the door, hale and hearty. He'd been on a 12-kilometre walk in the bush, armed with a 30-30 rifle, a machete, and a knife. "I wasn't tired a bit. Even running for a while. That's pretty good for an old codger." He'd been sizing up a couple of well sites and had dodged a couple of RCMP spy planes by hiding under spruce trees. Boonstra asked if there were any sites "worth doing" and Ludwig said the wind had to be right. "We wouldn't want to fumigate ourselves." Ludwig also congratulated Wraight on his bombing.

"Beginner's luck," said Wraight modestly.

As Ludwig downed a bowl of soup, the conversation turned to two compressor stations. "We got to try to blow up..." Ludwig began, but the rest of the sentence was drowned out by the clinking of glasses and the noises of children. Ludwig said one compressor station was behind Dr. William Scott's place – midway between Beaverlodge and Hythe – while the other was near the junction of Highway 59 and Highway 43. He said he knew where to get "some stuff" free for Wraight and that he would drop off a package of cigarettes at the Bi-Lo gas station near Demmitt by the following night. "Behind a telephone booth."

Later that day Boonstra took Wraight for a car ride to scout another compressor station – one owned by AEC behind Wagon-masters, an old horse-trailer factory off Highway 43, a few kilometres northwest of Brainard. Blowing up one of the AEC compressors, enthused Wraight, "would really make them look like shit." When the two men returned, they talked to Ludwig about how best to get access to the site. "I might even take my rifle and walk through hunting," said Wraight. He told Ludwig to make sure his bomb maker used a simple model. "Yeah, you know, push A. I don't want to have to connect B, C, and the blue and green. No colours because I'm colour-blind. It has to be idiot-proof."

Ludwig said he'd have his contact set it up so all Wraight had to do was "pull the trigger or turn the knob." Wraight said if there was a connector and an egg timer on it, he'd be very happy.

"Egg timer?" asked Ludwig incredulously.

"Well, yeah, okay. I'm shaking already so I better go."

Before Wraight left, Ludwig made a quip about the town hall meeting on terrorism being held that night in Valhalla. "I thought maybe I should go in a pinstriped suit from Sally Ann with all kinds of holes in it and ketchup running out of it."

Ed McGillivray was the only AEC executive who knew that the company's anti-terrorism talks would end up focusing on the shed bombing. AEC's excitable media spokesman, Dick Wilson, believed that he was just organizing public relations events in Valhalla and near Beaverlodge to calm people down. He didn't realize his company had just helped the RCMP set off a bomb to stir everyone up. McGillivray, who went on holiday that week, later described the timing of events as "unfortunate."

The first gathering, in Valhalla, soothed nobody. The town's struggling grain and dairy farmers knew Big Oil intimately. Companies operated so many flaring wells in the community that local farmers, sons and daughters of Norwegian immigrants, swore you could drive around at night with your car lights off. Other farmers called the place a pincushion for oil and gas.

AEC security, headed by Howard Cox, guarded the doors as more than 100 local farmers and oil-patch workers solemnly marched into the hall. A row of television cameras and well-dressed urban reporters, many of whom had been jetted in from Calgary by AEC for the event, occupied one side of the room like a foreign army. Everyone drank coffee and ate cookies.

Each invited speaker brought a different community message. In his scarlet tunic Sergeant MacKay called for vigilance and the reporting of all suspicious activity. "We are only as good as the community we work with. Remember the five Ws: who, what, when, where, and why. If you can help us fill in the blanks, the information will help to protect your families and homes."

Sandy Jentze, a Calgary psychologist, talked about the nature of stress. Normally stress is just a short-term crisis, she said. "But in this case it has come and stayed." Unrelenting stress, she explained, can make people lose sleep or even hair. She said that individuals made anxious by "unprecedented events" in the area should probably see their family doctors.

John Thompson, the intellectual, beer-bellied director of the Toronto-based Mackenzie Institute and a long-time terrorism expert, explained that "ecotage" was really a form of terrorism. Terrorism generally seeks a wider audience than its victims and can strike anywhere. Terrorists "have little to protect and an endless list of targets." After defining the asymmetry of terrorism and talking about cells under the control of charismatic leaders, Thompson, a former military man, advised the crowd to be alert and to stay calm.

The farmers, who had survived drought, falling grain prices, and now bombs, generally held their tongues; nobody dared mention Ludwig by name. "How do we help you do your job?" ventured one oilman.

"Don't panic and worry unduly," replied MacKay.

A farmer in a baseball cap stood and complained bitterly about the lack of RCMP officers in the region. "We only see them after we have been bombed or robbed. Maybe if we had cops we wouldn't get terrorists." An angry mother added that people were scared and fed up with the bombing and the bombers. Every day her children walked by well sites on their way to school. "Did you call this meeting to deter terrorism or to deter anti-terrorist activity?" she asked.

MacKay said he'd heard much talk in the coffee shops and was definitely concerned about vigilantism. After months of investigations, "it would be unfortunate if we have to prosecute someone who thinks they can take the law into their own hands."

The mother didn't quit. "I think vigilantism is on the way. I don't think people here are expressing what's on their minds. They are intimidated by the number of media here."

At the end of the meeting the locals poured out of the hall like cold coffee. Gerald Loberg, a 60-year-old grain farmer, could barely suppress a laugh. "The police say to report everything unusual. But oil and gas has changed this country so dramatically that you'd be on the phone all the time." He personally didn't live in fear of being blown up but didn't approve of such things. Nor did his wife, Emily. But she thought the flaring should be stopped. "I hate it when they flare."

The Smiths also attended the meeting. They went to a restaurant with friends afterwards where they all shook their heads. "People were so disgusted that a person would come in and tell them what stress was," said Freya. "She assumed we were morons and hillbillies."

The next night the three speakers repeated their performances at the Albright Hall just west of Beaverlodge. There more than 300 residents, many them neighbours of Ludwig, bristled with anger. Rick Leismeister, a Beaverlodge oil worker sporting a black leather cap and many tattoos, couldn't believe what he was hearing from the professionals. "You're telling us we're not supposed to get mad at these people? All we're doing here is trying to make a living."

A farmer stunned MacKay with a popular question: "If he comes onto my property, can I shoot him?"

Most of the crowd agreed that night that if Ludwig had dared to show up, he'd have been hanged as high as Ken Saro-Wiwa. They believed there was nothing the four attending RCMP officers could have done to stop it.

Ludwig, of course, stayed home and fielded obscene and threatening phone calls, as he had for most of the month. Many callers took on cartoonish accents: "Looodvig, you're going to die." He told visiting reporters that AEC should hold information sessions on how to protect the environment instead of combatting terrorism. He later told Bob Wraight that the so-called terrorism expert was a jerk. "Should castrate a guy like that out in the back woods."

"I think he's already been castrated," said Wraight.

The Mounties were happy about the Trickle Creek plan to blow up a compressor station with a device Ludwig offered to supply and designed their next venture with the confidence of men about to finish a job. "We will have the Wescam in position to video record the laying down of these items." The bomb squad would be present to disarm and seize the bomb. The Mounties hoped finally to catch Ludwig in the act: "We are interested should Wiebo attempt to take any part in either the scenario or to pick up Boonstra after the bomb is supposed to have been planted."

True to his word, Ludwig left a message on the machine at Wraight's trailer on October 22. "Yes. Bob. Left something for you at the phone booth."

Sergeant Hills drove out to the Bi-Lo station and found a package of Player's on the south side of the phone booth. It was weighted down by several small stones. Inside was a note from a stranger. In red ink under the foil paper, it read: "SPARTICUS, TELL YOUR CONTACT THINGS ARE TOO HOT RIGHT NOW!"

Two hours after Hills's discovery, Wraight pulled up to Trickle Creek. The young man couldn't disguise his bewilderment. Ludwig was reading *Tactics of Christian Resistance*, a massive tome on how to defy authorities and gum up bureaucracies. Wraight was interested in only one topic: the "Sparticus" note. But Ludwig proved coy and playful.

"Spartacus, who's Spartacus?" said Ludwig absently.

"That's what I was going to ask."

"Everybody stands up and says I'm Spartacus," added Ludwig. Finally he focused his attention on the agitated young man in front of him. "What's up?"

"I don't know. Come over here for a minute." Wraight was still at the front door. "I – I got that note," he sputtered in a hushed voice.

"Yeah," said Ludwig.

"And I am confused. I don't know if they're talkin' about me bein' Spartacus or you. But anyway, somebody. I guess it's me. I don't know. Um, the cigarette package."

"What's it say?"

"It's in red lettering, big letters, says, 'Not tonight, it's too hot, tell your contact.'"

"Oh, I see. He must be nervous about it, I guess."

"I'm the one that's nervous."

"You're the one that was nervous?"

"All hyped up, ready to go. And all of a sudden it's like somebody took my new skates away or something."

"Oh. Did you have something planned for tonight?"

"You never know," replied Wraight.

"Well, the note was to me, you see." Ludwig explained that he was under surveillance. "They're pissed off. The last explosion got everybody pretty worked up." He mentioned the plane flying overhead, the anonymous calls, people phoning and saying nothing. Even local wildlife officers had been asked to join in the hunt for the oil-patch vandals. "Yeah, it's pretty hot right now and maybe it's too hot for him."

Wraight persisted, talking about the compressor site behind Wagonmasters, but Ludwig preferred to talk about the media. "One newscaster from CBC National told me it was now a national political issue." He also gave Wraight some philosophical instruction. "Your life is pretty fragmented in different directions right now. But you need to pull together because that is the bottom line, preserving ourselves from a lot of other things that are going to happen and are happening." He added that there was solidarity at Trickle Creek. "And in an underground movement you need a lot of solidarity," he added, looking Wraight in the eye, "because you can get moled by all kinds of people."

Whenever Wraight tried to direct the conversation back to bombing-related matters ("Kind of handy for lights and stuff," he said of .22 silencers), Ludwig steered him back to his family. "How's it going at home, Bob?"

"Yeah, it's kind of a stalemate. By the time you finish getting mad at the banks and oil companies. Everybody else seems to want to throw shit your way, and you throw it back."

"I can see where it's difficult for you to have motivation and a steady purpose while you have that heartache at home. If I were you, I would not get too preoccupied with this stuff at the expense of losing that."

"Well, she doesn't know about it, so..."

Ludwig explained a father's obligations in life: "To discipline the family in love. That doesn't mean to say beat the shit out of them because you're frustrated, but discipline will offset certain contours slowly, train them to focus in a healthier direction. It's just like an army. You don't get an army together without a certain amount of healthy discipline."

Wraight pressed the bombing issue, and at the end of the evening Ludwig agreed to ask Ben to make him an hour-long fuse. And if Wraight needed money for dynamite, Ludwig added, "I'll cover it."

The next day Wraight arranged to have coffee with Ludwig at the Teepee in Hythe. Thanks to the Spartacus note, the RCMP had abandoned its plans for catching Ludwig planting a bomb and would now settle for a simple dynamite sting. The Mounties told Wraight to offer Ludwig five sticks of phony dynamite and ask if he'd pay $100 for them. Wraight waited for Ludwig near the Wheat Pool building in Hythe. ("We'll drive over in my car so the whole world doesn't know. Everyone kinda knows your van.") Off and on he spoke into his vest. "Come on, you ungrateful old bastard, where are you? Come on, you old prick. Get here."

When Ludwig and Boonstra arrived, Ludwig surprised Wraight and his handlers, who were listening to the monitor, with more sardonic humour.

"Where are you taking us, Bob? Into custody?"

"Yeah," Wraight laughed nervously.

"Where are the cuffs?" said Ludwig.

"I forgot 'em."

Wraight said his supplier could get four sticks at a hundred bucks. He actually had five and wanted to get rid of them. "I can have them by tomorrow night." Wraight added that he couldn't pay for them himself, then started in about potential bomb sites. Ludwig said it was pretty hot and he didn't need any dynamite. "Go ahead and get four and hang on to them for future use."

The next day Wraight showed up at Trickle Creek to pick up money for the dynamite, saying he felt like a "pizza delivery guy." The voices of women and children and the singing of canaries greeted him at the door and nearly drowned out the entire recording. Ludwig went to his private bedroom, fumbled in a drawer, and came back with two US$50 bills. He said with a smile that the money came from Earth First, a radical American movement dedicated to monkeywrenching. "Earth First is funding us, you know." He was pulling Wraight's leg, and Wraight replied that he accepted only Canadian Tire money. Making sure his vest could hear him, he asked what the money was for.

"For the cause," said Ludwig.

Wraight asked for a pen so he could show Ludwig where the dynamite had been hidden, under a culvert near the Bi-Lo station. A cigarette package by the phone booth would spell out the exact location.

"I don't need it," said Ludwig.

"Well, I got mine. It's what –"

"I don't need any."

This news so unnerved Wraight that he asked Ludwig to step outside onto the porch. "A little communication gap here."

"No," said Ludwig calmly. "I thought you wanted them."

Wraight said he didn't know what to do with the dynamite.

"It's no problem stashing it, is it?" asked Ludwig.

"No, it doesn't matter."

On the porch Ludwig talked about the EUB inquiry Richard Secord was again pressing for, saying it would be "tougher on them than anything else right now." After more chat, Wraight asked whether Ben had made his timing device, or "hobby kit." Ben said, "I don't know. I can imagine it can be done." When a plane passed overhead, Ben pointed it out: "See that bloody plane."

"Yeah," said Ludwig. "It's checking Bob out."

After that visit, Cox and Hills decided to retire Wraight for a week. The evidence they had certainly wasn't enough to prove the offences they wanted to charge Ludwig with. The Nagra tapes were full of static and inaudibles. The Mounties also felt that Ludwig suspected too much. They decided future meetings with Ludwig should be held at more neutral locations, such as the Teepee. Rural surveillance was hard to do without being found out. Besides, they were running out of time.

On November 4, Wraight met Ludwig again at the Teepee. Mamie and other family members tagged along. Ludwig asked how Wraight had been keeping.

"Not bad. Relaxed now."

Ludwig looked at Mamie and said, "The heat's off him, but, boy, we've been tailed constantly 24 hours a day." He told a story about a man in a brown car who'd been following him all over the place, even to Grande Prairie and Dawson Creek. He tried to lose him a couple of times by going in and out of buildings. "I don't know how he got up to me again," admitted Ludwig. After five days of cat and mouse, Ludwig had pulled up beside the man, taking him by surprise. "I asked him to voluntarily turn down the window, and said, 'I don't appreciate you following me around. I don't think it will be good for your health if you continue.'" Ludwig said he'd even filed a complaint with the Beaverlodge detachment. "I mean, even God isn't watching me that close," he wisecracked, and the two men laughed heartily. Ludwig felt like Martin Luther, who once quipped of his enemies: "If I break wind in Wittenberg, they smell it in Rome."

Ludwig talked about the premier's announcement that the province would spend $3 million to fight biker gangs and eco-terrorists. He mentioned a funny bit in the paper about the "Hole in the Well Gang" terrorizing Peace River country. Wraight said he'd heard of the cowboy Hole in the Wall Gang, the one Butch Cassidy and the Sundance Kid belonged to. Ludwig repeated the name – Hole in the Well Gang – as though he liked the sound of it. Given all the money being devoted to battling eco-terrorism, he said, people should "thank the Hole in the Well Gang for job creation." The men talked idly about Wayne Roberts and the town hall meetings. The subject of dynamite never came up. When a couple came by to talk, Ludwig obliged, gesturing at Wraight: "You want to say hello to the bomber."

Two days later Wraight visited the farm again. Cox and Hills wanted him to ask Ludwig if he was "using him," and to complain about the amount of money he was getting for his land. "The Agent will suggest to LUDWIG that should the acts of terrorism they are involved in result in AEC buying out LUDWIG that the Agent would appreciate some consideration for the help he has given."

Wraight never got around to it. Ludwig greeted him caustically: "How many tape recorders you got in that vest?"

"Six," Wraight managed.

Ludwig was off to town, so Wraight did his best to interest Boonstra in another well bombing. There still wasn't any snow on the ground and you could get into a site without leaving prints, he explained. Boonstra didn't say much as he hammered away on renovations to his cabin. Wraight tried another tack, complaining, "I kind of got left holding the old bag here" – meaning with the dynamite – but Boonstra didn't appear interested. He repeated, as Ludwig had, that things were too hot. The oil and gas companies definitely needed disciplining, he said, but a man has to learn patience.

Hills and Cox had just about run out of scenarios to play. They also worried about Wraight's security. In one last attempt to put pressure on the targets, Hills advised Wraight to tell Ludwig he was moving. "This may put the initiative on the targets to inquire about the dynamite."

On November 11, while waiting for Ludwig to show up at the Teepee, Wraight sat in his car and chatted with his handlers. "Kind of cool today. Shit. I'm keeping the vest. You can't have it back. Too warm. Can you hear anything I'm saying at all?"

When Wraight walked into the restaurant, Ludwig and Mamie were already there. He gave them the news: "I'm moving to Kleena Kleene," near 100 Mile House in central British Columbia. He was going to look after a gun camp. During the winter he'd feed the horses, and in summer he'd guide hunters and fishermen. "I get a truck. I might even get paid. It's my new image."

"Are you going to take your, ah, your explosives with you?"

"I don't know if I really need them," said Wraight.

They talked about how Wraight's kids would like the place and what the family would take with them. Ludwig joked about Wraight leaving some machine guns, "because we'll be needing them."

"I don't have any spare ones," replied Wraight.

"Gatling guns?"

"I'll probably leave you one of those."

They talked about surveillance and security around AEC wells, and Ludwig mentioned that CBC's *the fifth estate* was looking for "terrorists" to interview. Wraight mused about posing as one.

"I'll do anything for $500," he said. "Well, almost."

On the morning of November 12, Sergeant Hills and Constable Curtis Zablocki drove out to the Bi-Lo gas station west of Demmitt. After checking out the area they decided to stash the fake dynamite in a culvert on a side road west of the station. The Mounties then returned to Beaverlodge, where they met Wraight. He drew a map on the back of a du Maurier cigarette package, then helped the police-men photograph the fake dynamite, the note, and two IGA bags for the explosives. After Hills drove back to the Bi-Lo to plant the bait, Wraight met with his handlers again. At one o'clock he phoned

Ludwig to say he had left a message, "from me to you," behind the telephone booth.

"Yeah, I can check it out," said Ludwig.

Shortly afterwards, Richard Boonstra's white Dodge van left the farm and headed west to the Bi-Lo station. Ludwig and his son Caleb got out. While Ludwig entered the phone booth, as if to make a call, Caleb scoured the ground. He picked something up and handed it to his father.

A surveillance aircraft followed the van for 50 kilometres to Dawson Creek, where Ludwig and Caleb went to Safeway and ate at McDonald's. On their way back, Ludwig abruptly turned right onto the side road. While Ludwig "struck a pose as if urinating," Caleb scrambled into the culvert. He lay low as several cars passed. Then he returned to the van with a doubled white bag in his hand.

From his vantage point in a hayfield, RCMP Sergeant Doug Dahl watched as an interior light came on. It momentarily lit up Ludwig's face just as he turned around in the driver's seat to inspect something in the back. In darkness the vehicle then headed east to Trickle Creek.

Wraight later phoned Ludwig to make sure he had found the dynamite. Ludwig said he had, and invited Wraight over. He said he'd have a "surprise" for him that night.

Sergeant Hills thought that the surprise might be an explosive device and that Ludwig possibly wanted Wraight to blow something up before he left town. He advised Wraight not to meet with Ludwig at the farm but to arrange another chat at the Hythe Motor Inn in the morning. He also wanted Wraight to give Ludwig a drop-off point for the device that surveillance teams could watch and photograph. Now that the Mounties had glossy photos of Ludwig and his son picking up fake dynamite, Hills wanted to catch Ludwig delivering a live bomb.

Wraight's last mission as an agent went about as smoothly as the rest of Operation Kabriole had gone. He greeted Ludwig and Mamie and Richard and Lois in the restaurant. When Mamie started to rub his shoulders, he thought she was checking his body pack. Before he could explain that he'd called them together to say goodbye and acquire a timing device, a talkative CBC camera crew joined the table. "I burst into flames with the media, you know that," Wraight told Boonstra.

The cameramen asked Wraight why he was moving.

"Don't want to be here."

"Why?"

"You drive around and you'll see."

"Sour gas," added Ludwig.

Boonstra and Ludwig chatted with the cameramen and talked about people's fear of sour gas. When the cameramen left, Ludwig talked about Frank Mink, the EUB man now handling the Ludwig case, suggesting that someone should put a bullet in his head. Ludwig also joked about Wraight being wired.

"He shouldn't joke about being wired and stuff. It's not funny," Wraight said to Boonstra. "I don't find the humour in it at all."

Wraight said he'd found a good site to blow up near Dawson Creek – "just for, in case, you have something for me." As Wraight tried to suggest a drop-off point, Ludwig interjected. "We'll let you know where we drop it." Wraight suggested he leave a note in the little inspection hole of the heater in "the guys' shitter" at the restaurant.

"Okay," said Ludwig.

Wraight asked that Ludwig put everything in big letters, instructions and so on. "You know me."

"Be sure you follow the instructions," said Ludwig, "or you'll blow yourself up."

"Follow the instructions," repeated Boonstra.

"Yeah, yeah, right."

Those were the last words Wraight said to Ludwig. After Ludwig departed, Wraight sat at the table alone with the Nagra as the enormity of his betrayal swept over him like a shiver. He had secretly taped 29 hours of private conversations with a man he once considered a father figure. He had informed on a family that had babysat his children, given him money, offered his family shelter. And now he was about to become another member of the RCMP's witness protection program.

Wraight walked up to the cash. A pretty waitress said, "Hi."

"Hi."

"How's it going?"

"Hey, I don't know where it's going. I'm just going."

"I said *how's* it going?"

"I know, that's what I mean. How? Where? Not a clue."

The waitress said something the Nagra didn't pick up.

"The shit you get yourself into," said Wraight. "Sometimes you wonder."

He ordered coffee and some "health food," a Coffee Crisp and a Snickers. The Nagra picked up the sound of the till. He walked to his car speaking to his vest like a lost drunk. "Just leaving. Stand by." Long pause. "Just making a note. I'm just leaving" – he cleared his throat – "pulling out onto the highway." A sigh. "Oh man." He cleared his throat several times and burped. His last words on behalf of Operation Kabriole were "Fuck me."

Later that day Sergeant Hills found the napkin note in the bathroom. With considerable anticipation he fished it out of its hiding place. He imagined it would detail the location of the explosive device and at long last tie up the case. But the instructions Ludwig had asked Wraight to follow carefully read: "Don't burden yourself. Enjoy your move."

During this chaotic time Ludwig heard a moving confession from one of his daughters. Two winters earlier she had crept out of bed and marched through the snow in the dead of night to a new AEC well site a kilometre east of the farm. There she found a 20-wheel trailer full of pipe parked on the lease. Filled with fury at how Big Oil had treated her family, she slashed every tire with a knife. She also beheaded all the metal signs on the site with a saw. She didn't tell her father or anybody at the farm for two years.

Her confession at the dinner table that fall filled Ludwig with a mixture of pride and wonder. "I'd call that an example of bona fide anti-terrorism," he explained to guests. The real terrorists, of course, were industry. That one of his own daughters had quietly struggled alone with this action "in her own soul" for two years struck Ludwig as remarkable. "So whenever the court or the media say I'm the one in control on this farm, they have another thing coming."

At the end of November Ludwig went for a walk on a trail north of the farm's residences, where the boreal forest is dark and deep. Mamie and Boonstra tagged along. Underneath towering white spruce and poplar Ludwig moved like some Hebrew king. Every now and then he stopped to inspect berries and plants used to feed and heal his children. Passing a spruce, he grabbed a tuft of tree lichen. The community had made baby powder from this "old man's beard."

The party pushed on until the trail opened onto the Norcen road, blanketed in snow. Here and there, strategically felled poplars lay across the road like white speed bumps. *Ecodefense: A Field Guide to Monkeywrenching* says that "the well-known methods of cutting a tree across or rolling a boulder onto a road are of limited value (but they are of value if enough people do them frequently)."

The party followed the road east and turned north where the road continued towards the Norcen well. Ludwig and Boonstra started talking in Frisian, a stark, fierce language that sounds like Old Norse. Then everyone stopped at a small hand-painted sign propped up against a stump in the middle of the road. Ludwig bent down and carefully wiped away the snow. It read, "Caution Site Rigged With Motion Sensor Explosives."

Ludwig playfully attributed the deed to "the Friends of the Ludwigs." When he later asked Bob Wraight if he did the bombing, the informer said he didn't know anything about it.

"There are people who say we don't have friends," said Boonstra. "But I don't believe it."

In early December, the RCMP Edmonton bomb squad found a gaping hole the size of a hot tub in the middle of the road. Road cratering is a rare military specialty. When Alien Johnstone heard about it, he exclaimed, "Now that the Ludwigs are mining roads, I'll have nothing to do with them," though he quickly changed his tune. When Constable Jackie Wheeler later phoned Ludwig and asked if he had heard an explosion, Ludwig said, "No. Why?"

To some residents in the Peace the last bombing of 1998 looked like the end of a campaign. It was as if a group of weary and chastened saboteurs had taken their last sticks of dynamite and safely exploded them far from anywhere in their own backyard.

Chapter 13

Revelations

On January 15, 1999, Wiebo Ludwig found himself in a small interrogation room in Grande Prairie facing a video camera and two members of Operation Kabriole: RCMP Corporal Dale Cox and RCMP Constable Curtis Zablocki. The detectives, in jeans, had looked forward to this moment. It had taken nearly three months to assemble all the evidence. After recruiting Robert Wraight, blowing up a well shack, conducting surveillance day and night, and spending $750,000, the Mounties figured they finally had their man. In another room, Richard Boonstra faced a similar audience.

Cox read out the nine charges on which each man had been uneventfully arrested. They dealt mostly with counselling or conspiring to commit mischief between September and November of 1998 by "interfering with the lawful use, enjoyment or operation of property" – something that, as Ludwig likes to point out, a lot of sour gas plants, batteries, and flaring gas wells do every day in Alberta. The Crown also accused Ludwig and Boonstra of attempting to possess, without lawful excuse, an explosive substance, contrary to Section 24 of the Criminal Code. In his dry reading the corporal omitted the object of all this conspiring and counselling: Bob Wraight.

Ludwig, who had been arrested outside the Tags convenience store while taking one of his daughters to the dentist that morning, calmly listened to the wordy allegations, then said he wouldn't mind hearing the officers' intentions. Cox advised him in police argot that a fairly lengthy investigation into numerous incidents of mischief victimizing oil companies had "surfaced yourself as a very prime suspect to the point I believe you are responsible for the charges laid today."

Cox wanted to hear Ludwig's side of the story, he said, but only if he wanted to tell it. When Ludwig said the charges were too fuzzy to respond to, Cox asked if he had ever thought about blowing up a well site.

"Oh, sure. I've thought about the possibility of doing all kinds of things. But I have not proceeded with it. Sure, I've talked lots. We joke about it in our house. We talk seriously about it when we get angry about things that have happened, but we've all done that in life."

Ludwig said he'd received a lot of publicity for threatening to kill an oil executive after Abel Ryan's death. Over a glass of wine he had told an American journalist, Mark Levine, "Sometimes I think we should take the president of the Alberta Energy Company hostage, tie him up, and make him watch the video of Abel Ryan, then slit his throat." It was one of those idle angry comments that had upset the RCMP, the press, and many oil executives.

Cox wondered if Ludwig ever dreamed about such violence in his sleep. It would take some aggravation to get a man to dream like that, replied Ludwig. "Think of Wayne Roberts. I have a lot of sympathy for that man. It's a tragedy, but I think the fault lies with the aggravator."

Cox said he wasn't a religious man but remembered something from the Bible about an eye for an eye. "Do you feel that way?" Revenge, replied Ludwig, wasn't a good idea and lay in the province of God.

Cox, who believed Ludwig suffered from a persecution complex, asked how he felt about the great industrial and police conspiracy against him. Ludwig said he had compiled up to 1,500 pages of records and letters in hopes of finally winning a public inquiry on the oil and gas industry's practices in rural Alberta. "And I'm hoping that the inquiry can cover all that with a retired judge and say, 'Look, there's a lot of bad stuff going on here.'"

"How sincere are you in what you are doing?"

Ludwig chuckled. He said what he'd been saying for nearly eight years to every government functionary with an address or phone number. "You know when you're squeezed in a corner – are you willing to be squished or are you going to fight? I mean, I think it's more honourable to fight than to just be squished. You know that I would do what is needed to defend my family from harm and that's the only reason I'm in it. I'm not an environmentalist who is trying to save the world from burning by the petrochemical industry."

Cox asked a question that had stumped his superior, Sergeant Hills, during Operation Kabriole: "Who's Spartacus?"

Ludwig gave a brief synopsis of the Stanley Kubrick film, starring Kirk Douglas. Cox had confused it with *Ben-Hur*, the Biblical epic starring Charlton Heston. Ludwig set him straight. Spartacus was a Christian slave who led a great revolt against imperial Rome. When the Roman legions finally quelled the uprising, they rounded up the survivors and asked (much as the RCMP was now doing), "Who's Spartacus?" One slave after another stepped forward, claiming to be Spartacus, until all stood in front of their persecutors. "So they just hung the whole pile of them," concluded Ludwig.

"And that's how you feel. You're just seeing yourself?"

"There are obviously people doing things. I will not help you find them by saying I'm Spartacus. I'll say I'm Spartacus with the rest of them. You can figure it out for yourself."

Ludwig said the absence of good government forced good people to protect themselves. The law protected industry when it assaulted citizens with baby-deforming and fetus-aborting pollutants, but it did not protect victims who tried to fight back. To make matters worse the RCMP just stood by. "And there are so many other things screwed up." All in all he felt the RCMP didn't want to know the whole story and was just playing "tiddlywinks" with his arrest.

There followed a philosophical discussion about the law. Ludwig argued that responsible representative government didn't exist in Alberta. Furthermore, the spirit of the law differed from the letter of the law. Ludwig had no doubt that he had violated the letter of the law, but never its spirit.

Cox asked Ludwig to define himself.

"Well, I'm just an ordinary man."

"What about this Wraight guy. What kind of person is he?"

"Mixed. I mean he's not a person that's easy to understand. He breathes threats. People who breathe threats generally don't do it. That's why they breathe them." He described Allan Johnstone as another multiple personality who was all bark and no bite.

Cox passed the torch to Curtis Zablocki, who'd been sitting quietly.

"Are you the good cop or the bad cop?" joked Ludwig.

Zablocki asked about the bombings. He noted that the Hinton bombing had come just after the death of Abel Ryan, and the Goodfare and Demmitt bombings after the botched AEC negotiations. "It seems very coincidental that you experience these significant events in your life and they're followed by acts of violence. I mean, anyone sitting from the outside trying to – and looking at this, would say, 'You know, this is related.'"

"They certainly would," agreed Ludwig.

"Exactly. They'll ask that question. Can you answer that question for us?"

"I already answered it. Code name Spartacus."

"Can you say they are not related?"

"I'm saying code name Spartacus. I happen to feel for people who do things of that sort."

Zablocki said he believed that Ludwig was an active participant in the Hinton bombing.

"Well, I'm glad you are not my judge," said Ludwig. "My judge is up above."

Cox asked how Ludwig would have felt if a bomb had killed an innocent oil company guy checking a well site.

"That wouldn't be justified," replied Ludwig. "None of the bombs have hurt anybody, you know."

"Don't you think they could have hurt somebody?" asked Cox.

"Well, we can say the same about industry. Do you not realize that when they develop sour gas wells, that the pipe could burst and kill people beside you? We don't therefore say you can't build a pipeline."

Ludwig grew weary of the narrow focus of his interrogators. As the loudest hollerer about gas emissions and corporate greed, he said, of course he was the prime suspect. "You know, you're looking for motive. Well, you got lots of motive in me. If that's the little catch you want to put onto your legalistic investigation, you don't have to prove that. I mean, just read all the statements I've made."

Richard Boonstra's questioning went very differently. Two RCMP constables did most of the talking, constantly interrupting Boonstra. When they asked if had ever attempted to obtain explosives to damage oil company property, Boonstra replied, "The burden of proof lies with you guys. I have told you before, I'm no criminal. I have nothing to hide."

Boonstra asked the policemen to spell out the meaning of the charges. "Did I conspire to kill Chrétien or something?" The cops encouraged him not to pass up an opportunity to tell his side of the story. They knew he had lived in Vernon until 1997. "I know for a fact that some of this stuff you couldn't have been involved in unless you were coming in by the darkness of night and leaving by the darkness of night in an invisible car," added one of the Mounties.

Boonstra let that pass. One constable then explained his theory about how people were driven to do things. "What happens if you fill a water balloon up too full? It explodes."

Boonstra didn't want to talk about balloons.

"When lives become endangered and when people die, the issue doesn't matter any more," one constable advised. "The issue goes out the window and people start looking at you and saying, 'We don't care what your reason was for killing somebody.'"

"Mm-hmm," Boonstra said many times. Finally he said, "I don't want to be disrespectful, but I'm not going to answer your questions. Okay?"

"Okay. Well, I'll keep you in here another 13, 14 hours, then bring in the guys in the bunny suits and – just joking around here, Richard."

The interview ended soon afterwards. Cox later paid Ludwig a short visit in his cell. "Well, Reverend Ludwig, you'll have lots of time now to contemplate the state of the real world."

After Ludwig's and Boonstra's arrests another small army of 30 constables descended upon Trickle Creek. Directed by Sergeant Hills, the Mounties tried to gather all the residents into the main house to begin an extensive search. Not everyone cooperated. Several mothers barricaded themselves in the room above the garage. Seeing a chartered bus outside, they feared their children might be taken from them. Trevor Schilthuis later convinced them to open the door and come out.

At her cabin door Renée greeted the officers with a can of pepper spray and demanded to be shown a search warrant. A constable eventually complied. The warrant said the police were looking for several sticks of imitation dynamite, two white IGA bags, photographs of the Norcen well, diary notes, and various papers. After finally coaxing everyone into the main building, the police separated the women and children and herded them onto the parked bus. One constable told the families the RCMP was going to do some things "that might be disturbing to you."

Several hours into the search, the family told Hills that 13-year-old Caleb was missing. When he saw the police cars pull up, the teenager had slipped downstairs to hide in the crawl space under the big house. During the lengthy search he got hungry, crawled out, and opened a can of saskatoon berries in the cold room. As he ate, he heard a constable stomp down the stairs, so he returned to his hiding place. The officer rummaged around but never noticed the open can of berries.

While under the floor Caleb heard the RCMP men talk among themselves as they searched the premises, a process that ended up taking almost 10 hours.

"Boy, those women are no pushovers."

"There were kids crawling all over me. It's quite something."

"I talked to Ben and asked him if he liked this life. He said, 'Yes, but I've had my times where I wanted to get out, but I know what it's like out there and I don't want to go out there.' It's not like some Christian people who are so definite about staying. You can tell [some of them] would have taken their families and gone if they had the chance."

"Well, you can talk to them for 15 minutes or an hour, but you can't change years and years of brainwashing."

"We know the oil companies are doing bad stuff, and I think the Ludwigs have a cause here."

"This is really weird – that one girl knew what my name was."

Outside, the mothers and 17 Trickle Creek children under the age of 12 spent seven and a half hours in the bus with little drinking water. Diesel fumes seeped into the vehicle and made two pregnant women sick. At one point the bus driver told Ben, "I wish I didn't have to be here for this."

Before the police left, Ben and a few constables looked for Caleb in the woods. When they couldn't find him, Hills warned Ben that the RCMP wouldn't be responsible for the boy. Then the Mounties left with a trunkload of seized items including a sour gas monitor, a 30-30 rifle, and Ludwig's taped sermons. The police never found the fake dynamite they'd given Bob Wraight to entrap Ludwig.

After the raid many family members slept poorly. In their dreams the RCMP chased their relatives, ransacked their homes, seized their children. A month later an ambulance rushed Trevor Schilthuis to the hospital with heart irregularities. The family's diaries say it had to do "with the stress of the false accusations that Bob Wraight and the police are perpetrating."

When Richard Secord got word of the arrests of Ludwig and Boonstra, he phoned Paul Moreau, a criminal lawyer in Edmonton with a commanding voice and serious crewcut. The former Crown prosecutor knew the Criminal Code the way Ludwig knew the Bible. He agreed to become part of Ludwig's defence team and started work right away on the 18 charges generated by Bob Wraight's undercover work for the RCMP.

Secord asked a lawyer in Grande Prairie to act as his agent and apply for bail. He thought it would come easily because Ludwig and Boonstra had been granted bail immediately on similar charges after the Hinton bombing. But the Crown argued that Ludwig was a public menace. Moreover he had a criminal record, didn't pay his taxes, and had a habit of exhibiting increasingly violent behaviour. Why, the man had even threatened to slit the throat of an oil executive. A Grande Prairie judge agreed with that bleak assessment and denied bail to both men, even though none of the arguments applied to Boonstra.

Stunned by the denial, Secord quickly applied for a Queen's Bench bail review in Edmonton. While scanning the police disclosures, Moreau came across the RCMP's operation plans for blowing up a vehicle and then a well. "This has to be wrong," he thought. "This can't be what it says." Secord was just as confounded. The disclosures read like the RCMP "dirty tricks" campaign in the 1970s, when operatives went around blowing up things as a ruse to infiltrate a national liberation movement in Quebec.

While arguing for bail before Justice Paul Belzil, Secord dropped the bombshell about Operation Kabriole and AEC's collusion with the RCMP. He also argued that jailing an individual for comments made to the media was "a travesty of justice." Although revelations on the shed bombing made national headlines, they had no effect on Belzil; he, too, denied bail on the grounds that Ludwig was a threat to the public.

While Ludwig and Boonstra sat in jail cooling their heels, the entire nation – and even Radio Netherlands – debated the RCMP's "dirty tricks." In the oil patch, people wondered why a company would risk its reputation with such tactics. Trial lawyers couldn't understand why the RCMP would foster terror in a community to solve a case about property damage. Many experts thought both the RCMP and AEC could have been charged with spreading false information. Others felt the bombing ruse would undermine the force's credibility. All in all, commentators found nothing good "in the RCMP debris." Trying to catch criminals is one thing, said an

Edmonton Journal editorial, but by "lying to the entire population and taking actions that raised public anxiety, the RCMP went too far."

Even diehard supporters of the industry raised questions about how the state ought to deal with single-issue militants intent on fighting pollution. "Whatever else he is now, Ludwig was once a utopian organizer who dreamed of changing his world peaceably, one religious community at a time," wrote Frank Dabbs in *Oilweek*. "When the mills of justice cease to grind in the criminal case, the oil industry will be faced, still, with the issue he raised long before the first act of violence at Hythe. Is there a connection between emissions from petroleum-producing facilities and human or animal health? Taking Ludwig and his Trickle Creek commune members out of the picture does not answer the question, because they are not the only ones asking the question."

Ludwig's children and relatives, of course, found the whole thing appalling. Trevor Schilthuis accused corporate power of teaming up with the RCMP to crush "two idiotic grandfathers who love their grandchildren dearly and who deem it their responsibility to protect the land entrusted to them."

Gwyn Morgan vigorously defended AEC's actions, taking out full-page advertisements in national and local papers. He explained in his public letter that AEC cooperated with the RCMP "to avoid injury or death. I might add this decision was taken with great care in what continues to be a highly charged and stressful atmosphere." He said the company had lied to the public only once in the past 25 years, in October 1998. "I regret that some people, including segments of the media, may feel upset at being misled by comments of AEC people following the staged explosion. Silence on our part was not an option because it would not have produced the necessary results requested by the RCMP." In interviews with reporters, he later pleaded a sort of naïveté: "I'm an expert at running an oil company. This has taken me well beyond my depth."

Relatives of Robert Wraight were disheartened but not surprised to learn of his dubious involvement. His mother, Colleen Ladd, said she hadn't seen him in 20 years and couldn't even remember his birthday. An aunt confided that he'd run away from home at 15 and that his father had done time for theft. "He's had a terrible life," added the aunt. "No self-esteem, no sense of belonging. He probably could be very easily influenced by whoever or whatever came along."

Members of the Church of Our Shepherd King felt grossly betrayed. Lois Boonstra typed out an open letter that spoke for everyone at the farm: "Bob Wraight was our friend and a guest in our home. He violated the sanctity of our home by what he did. He abused the intimacy we offered him and violated the trust we had established, especially our godly desire to help him with his family/marriage situation." She wrote that Wraight had been "relentless in trying to get us to play into his game of blowing up wells." The RCMP, she said, "knew of his relationship with us and instead of serving and protecting our family paid Bob to do us a gross disservice." She denounced Wraight's paid betrayals and said "the Lord will see to it that these violations are set straight."

In Hythe people couldn't believe the RCMP would blow up a gas well. "I have complete trust in the justice system and in the RCMP," declared the mayor, Frank Webb. "I think it's preposterous." A heavy equipment operator thought the bombing was just "a smokescreen." A retired farmer said it couldn't be true because "they'd lose their jobs." Others said a controlled explosion was a lot safer than some amateur running around the country blowing up sour gas wells. "It takes a thief to catch a thief."

The controversy so embarrassed the RCMP that Assistant Commissioner Don McDermid wrote a memo to his staff to "assure you that, contrary to the spin media are placing on this case, all aspects of this investigation were undertaken to current accepted practices of case law." The October blast was "absolutely essential in furthering the credibility of the agent" and was conducted "in a completely controlled environment." McDermid also said that the RCMP merely responded to media inquiries and didn't attempt to mislead anyone with its press releases. In fact, several papers received unsolicited faxes about the blast.

At the Peace River Correctional Institute, inmates treated Ludwig and Boonstra like abused heroes. Inmates jostled to sit beside "the mad bombers" at dinner and joked about their celebrated predicament. "Do I sense an explosive discussion here?" quipped one offender. Another inmate began breakfast each day by declaring, "These cornflakes just don't snap, crackle, and pop. They blow up in your face."

Several inmates also attended devotions as Ludwig read from the Old Testament. The number of aboriginal men with horror stories in the prison astounded both Boonstra and Ludwig. The inmates all told them that once the system gets hold of you, "it's hard to get out of here."

While Ludwig prayed for a successful bail hearing, Henry Pirker, the Austrian farmer concerned about pollution's wilting effects on plants, got his hands on a "preliminary assessment of emissions and air quality" in the Grande Prairie region. The report, commissioned by AEC West during Mike Weeks's tenure, had never made the news. According to Jacques Whitford and Environment Limited, the county regularly exceeded hydrogen sulphide guidelines at seven of thirteen air quality monitoring sites and routinely broke sulphur dioxide guidelines as well. In addition gas plants and flares in British Columbia sent tonnes of pollution into the county's airshed every day, nearly twice as much as was created by local gas plants. "There has been no monitoring of potentially hazardous by-products of solution gas flaring," said the study. It recommended an action plan to clean up the air.

After Pirker wrote about the study in the Grande Prairie *Daily Herald-Tribune*, he received an anonymous threatening letter (with numerous spelling errors). "If you are not happy here because of the pollution, we would suggest to you that you had better not use any motor vehicles anymore. You must go back to the horse and buggy days, and not drive any motor vashivles anymore. You are polluting the air you and we breath. You are defeating the purpose for which you are fighting – clean air. Either quit complaining, or get rid of your motor vehicles and get some horese to use." Just about everyone who has questioned industry's record in the Peace has received such letters.

While Ludwig was in jail, the Pembina Institute, an Alberta-based alternative-energy think tank, released *Beyond Eco-Terrorism:*

The Deeper Issues Affecting Alberta's Oilpatch. The report blamed ineffective government regulation, a rapidly expanding industry, and hard scientific evidence about the dangers of flaring for growing hostility to the oil patch. "Government indifference and a seemingly unstoppable industry are causing more and more Albertans to react with fear, frustration and anger. This is the fundamental cause of the problem in the Peace River country."

The report summarized several startling animal health studies. One reviewed the health of seven beef herds, about 1,200 cattle, in Sundre, home to one of the province's largest sour gas fields, over an eight-year period. Dr. Cheryl Waldner, a veterinarian, found that cattle breathing a lot of sulphur experienced higher rates of twinning and stillbirths. Cattle living downwind from flares had reproductive problems. "There is a stillbirth risk associated with sour gas flares." When Waldner concluded a presentation of her research to oilmen attending a Calgary conference on flaring in 1998, not one person in the audience of 300 got up to ask a question.

The Pembina paper pointed out other problems. Industrial investment in the field had climbed from $5 billion to $25 billion in seven years. While industry grew, the EUB's funding shrank by 23 percent and field staff dwindled by 19 percent. The results were entirely predictable, said the report: "Experiencing a dramatic growth in bad practice and pollution in the field and a loss of regulatory presence first-hand, the public's already limited faith in the government to act to protect their interests has evaporated." If industry and government didn't reverse "the erosion of public confidence," coalitions of farmers and landowners would probably use all their regulatory and legal options "to deliberately stop or delay further oil and gas development."

Rick George, president of Suncor, didn't disagree with that assessment. In a speech in May 1999 titled "Do We Get the Reputation We Deserve?" he described the sabotage as "scary stuff" but noted "it's too easy to attribute these actions to criminal activity and spend our time defending the good behaviour of our industry." He encouraged industry to pay more attention to environmental issues. "And if we don't directly address those concerns, they have the potential to turn into rage and fear."

After the Court of Appeal declined to get involved in the bail matter, Moreau finally secured a hearing before Alberta's second-highest judge, Associate Chief Justice Allan Wachowich. Moreau forcibly argued that Ludwig and Boonstra had been denied jail on the basis of false information provided by the Crown. For starters, Ludwig didn't have a criminal record; his smelly-crude attack on the EUB had resulted in a conditional discharge. And Boonstra had no record at all. Public documents also showed that the reverend paid his taxes, and on time, no less. Moreover, the allegations about a rising tide of violence in the Peace were patently untrue. With the exception of the RCMP bombing and the mysterious explosion on the Norcen road, there had been no violence in the Peace that fall. Indeed, Ludwig had even asked AEC if the company wanted to reopen negotiations in December. The RCMP, however, had instructed McGillivray not to reply.

Wachowich concurred with Moreau and released "the mad bombers" on February 19, but with the most restrictive bail conditions Moreau had ever seen. Wachowich forbade the two men to have any contact (Boonstra moved to Edson and stayed with Paul Belanger for several months) and prohibited Ludwig from leaving Trickle Creek unless visiting a lawyer. Ludwig also had to phone the RCMP in Beaverlodge three times a week. Neither man could touch a firearm or explosives.

Upon his release Ludwig asked for a truth and reconciliation committee, the kind the South Africans had set up to examine apartheid. "It's time we try to bury the hatchet between the parties, the industry and us, and try to discuss these things rather than run up more public money on police action." But nobody in government or industry seemed much interested in truth or reconciliation.

AEC's spokesman, Dick Wilson, said any land buyout deal was now out of the question. Moreover Ludwig didn't even have a property to sell because his bail surety had consumed its full value.

On April 19, 1999 – the sixth anniversary, coincidentally, of the FBI massacre of 86 Branch Davidians in Waco, Texas – Paul Moreau got a call around nine in the morning on his cellphone. It was Ludwig, whom he'd met with the day before to go over legal particulars for the upcoming pretrial.

"My van just blew up," said Ludwig.

Moreau was in a rush to get to court and didn't know why Ludwig was calling about car troubles. "Is it repairable?"

"I don't think so."

Moreau worried about Ludwig's bail conditions. He couldn't be wandering around Edmonton unless he was seeing his lawyer. "Phone the boys. Have them meet you. Okay?"

"So you are not going to get involved?"

"No, I'm not a car mechanic," said Moreau, hanging up.

When the lawyer checked his phone messages later that day, 15 reporters wanted to know what he thought about the van explosion. He rushed over to the Comfort Inn, where Ludwig and Mamie had stayed the previous night, to find the area cordoned off with police tape. Cops and television crews were standing around. Moreau borrowed a telephoto lens and zoomed in on Ludwig's Dodge van.

There wasn't much left of it. The door had been blown off and its roof had a huge hole. The vehicle looked as though a volcano had erupted above the gearbox. Shrapnel had shot so many holes through a nearby Cadillac that it looked peppered with machine-gun fire.

Moreau now comprehended Ludwig's call. "Holy Christ," he thought. "I nearly lost my client." He phoned Ludwig and apologized profusely. "Oh, my God, I just figured out what happened."

The blast had occurred as Ludwig stopped in the parking lot, about 12 metres from the van, to observe a plane. He had a suitcase in hand. Mamie was about 25 metres away, walking their dog. A hubcap and other debris flew past Ludwig's face. Something cut his forehead.

Edmonton police investigated the bombing and separately interviewed Ludwig and Mamie twice. They even asked for all Ludwig's clothes, to check for explosive residue. One spectator said he saw a flatbed truck speed away from the scene after the explosion. Police noted that a lot of people from the Grande Prairie area had stayed at the Comfort Inn that night to attend an oil and gas meeting.

Public speculation about the bomber's identity was as broad as the blast debris. Most people blamed a disgruntled seismic crew or an oil-patch crazy seeking revenge. Secord figured the culprit "didn't appreciate" Ludwig's stand against Big Oil. Others suspected a renegade RCMP officer. Even political cartoonists joked about the Mounties not having an alibi. A few wags believed that Ludwig may have set off the bomb himself to refocus media attention.

Ludwig believed the bombing was "industry related," as did most farmers and ranchers in Alberta. Many anonymous bomb and death threats had come to Ludwig's home; now the real thing had been delivered to his van. Whoever had designed the bomb knew what he was doing. Police couldn't tell if the explosive had been detonated by remote control because the blast vaporized the trigger mechanism. The bombing was the work of a professional.

Shortly after the blast, the managers of the Comfort Inn sent Ludwig a terse fax saying he couldn't stay there again. Ludwig said the feeling was mutual.

After the bombing the family applied to get the 30-30 back for protection and predator control. After much court work (the RCMP was vigorously opposed) the rifle was handed over to Renée Ludwig. When two Mounties gave her back the gun, she told them, "By the way, I'm the mother of the last child that died here because you men didn't protect him."

On May 3, 1999, Secord and Moreau walked into Grande Prairie's courthouse for Ludwig and Boonstra's preliminary hearing. Both lawyers wore black bulletproof vests. "I've got no desire to lay down my life for this or any other case," explained Moreau. "And I'm going to be standing next to Wiebo for three weeks." To enter the windowless courtroom, spectators and reporters had to pass through a metal detector. Two Mounties stood guard inside.

By now the Crown had pretty well thrown the Criminal Code at Ludwig and Boonstra. Each man faced a total of 18 charges that included mischief and mischief endangering life. On top of the nine charges related to conspiring or counselling with Robert Wraight to blow things up, the RCMP had added another five charges against each defendant for sabotaging the Norcen well. After new forensic evidence came to light, the RCMP also resurrected all the charges originally laid after the Suncor battery bombing and added two more against Ludwig and Boonstra: another mischief charge and possession of an explosive substance. Wraight's notorious claims about cop-killing never made it to the list; there was no evidence to support them. Nor did the police ever investigate the allegations throughout Operation Kabriole.

Ludwig thought the lawyers made a fine legal team: "Richard has public appeal and Paul has sharp teeth." The lawyers hoped to whittle down the charges and to quash four new mischief charges that had been laid against each of Trevor, Ben, Bo, Josh, and Fritz for the Norcen cement job.

The government signalled its opinion of Ludwig and the case by assigning the file to Steve Koval and George Combe, two middle-aged prosecutors. In 1986 they had handled Jim Keegstra's trial. Keegstra was a fundamentalist schoolteacher charged with teaching hateful and anti-Semitic material to high school students. Koval and Combe teased Secord and Moreau in court about their fashionable vests and wondered when they would get theirs.

One of the first witnesses was RCMP Sergeant Keith Hills, head of Operation Kabriole. He wore a brown suit and gold-rimmed glasses and spoke so softly he was often inaudible. He responded to questions with clipped sentences. Both Moreau and Secord sensed he didn't want to be there. He portrayed Ludwig as someone who had to be in control, perhaps a lunatic. He told the judge that Ludwig started out with petty vandalism and progressed to bombing: "Anyone who commits bombings is violent and may be mentally unstable."

Moreau asked if Hills had done a psychological profile to reach that opinion.

"No," said Hills. He added that he thought that "people who are rational do not commit bombings."

Next came the baby-faced informer, Wraight. He wore a blue

shirt with white stripes and dark green pants. Most of the families from Trickle Creek showed up that day to stare at the judge. Wraight couldn't remember much on the stand unless the judge allowed him to refer to his notes. On matters of important detail, his memory totally failed him.

"You don't remember who said what, do you?" Secord asked, speaking of the Norcen cement job.

"No," said Wraight.

The reason for Wraight's spotty recall soon became evident. He had been in a car accident in 1986. The impact of the crash threw his head back so forcefully that it sheared off the car's headrest. The accident left the young man in a coma for weeks. Afterwards he required extensive eye surgery and cognitive therapy.

"The surgeon took my eyes out and put them on my cheeks and worked on them," Wraight testified.

Moreau grilled him on the legacy of his brain injuries. "Did you suffer losses in thought processes?"

"Yes."

"Short-term memory?"

"Yes."

"Long-term memory?"

"Yes."

Wraight said he'd had to relearn how to tie his shoes. He'd mentioned the accident to Corporal Cox, he said, but had omitted crucial details about memory loss. Secord later jokingly reflected that the whole drama would make one hell of a movie. "We have an accused who is mentally unstable and an informant who's brain-damaged."

During the pretrial Ludwig prayed for no jail time and offered colourful commentary during recesses. "Now you can see the collusion," he said after Hills's testimony. "It's the little son of David against the big son of Goliath." One day he made a point of shaking Hills's hand outside the courtroom.

"So you're the man who's been hunting us down."

Hills smiled uneasily and said yes.

"I held his hand deliberately for a while longer than was comfortable so he couldn't get away," Ludwig said later.

Throughout the pretrial Secord and Moreau stayed at Trickle Creek in a guest room behind the communal kitchen. At dinner, when the setting sun lit up the farm's tall poplars like candles, one of the Ludwig boys usually read from the Bible and dutifully thanked the lawyers for their good work. Trevor, for instance, read from Psalm 94. "Lord, how long shall the wicked triumph? How long shall they utter and speak hard things? . . . But the Lord is my defence; and my God is the rock of my refuge."

One night Fritz, Ludwig's gangly red-headed son, offered a homely grace. "Dear Lord. Thanks for the wonderful day. For helping the lawyers do a good job and for helping Bob Wraight to repent for doing us in. And for Felicia for being four years old."

After a dinner of sunflower loaf, salad, and potatoes, the family presented Fritz's smiling daughter with a birthday cake. "She's happy, just like the name means," said Fritz. "I'm very happy she's here in the peace and quiet of this community, and I'm very happy I'm out of the system too." The lawyers and the family then sang "May God Bless You" to the tune of "Happy Birthday." Mamie gave her grandchild a big hug and Ludwig laughingly cautioned his wife to go easy. "After two bottles of wine, she just might crush the kid."

Moreau described the Crown's case against the family as a "big balloon. If we can pop it, it all goes boom." Each evening he and Secord reviewed binders of documents and newly released disclosures, looking for the pin with which to prick the balloon. Wiebo, Ben, Fritz, Trevor, and Bo all helped sort, compile, and collate the voluminous police records and transcripts produced by Operation Kabriole. The entire crew often worked until two in the morning. "We feel weak in all the things we are fighting. I think the match is very unequal," Ludwig said wearily one night. "But it's all right. Instead of griping about it, we might as well give ourselves to it."

One evening, while preparing for the cross-examination of Hills, Moreau read the sergeant's notebook. When he read about "heating the situation up by breaking off negotiations," he got upset. "This is incredible. I'm amazed he wrote this down. The RCMP are promoting crime and this is what they are supposed to prevent."

Moreau addressed that theme in court the next day, much to Hills's discomfort.

"Now, I'm just curious, Sergeant, about your concept of the obligation of a peace officer. Correct me if I'm wrong. I had always thought that the obligation of a police officer was to protect public safety and protect public and private property."

"That's correct," replied Hills.

"All right. Can you tell me how seeking to advance and promote a bombing of an oil or gas installation serves that duty?"

"Because I felt it was going to happen anyway. I wanted to be assured that I was in control. I felt there was going to be further violence."

"To your knowledge Reverend Ludwig was at this stage actively engaged in trying to negotiate a settlement with AEC?"

"I knew he wanted to reopen negotiations."

"And you were instructing AEC not to negotiate seriously with him but to simply string him along so that he wouldn't get too excited, right?"

"Until we were in control, yes."

"And then you instructed AEC to break off negotiations and heat the situation up?"

"That's right."

An older couple from Hythe attended the three-week pretrial every day. Their two sons worked at one of AEC's gas plants, and they believed the Ludwigs had done most of the sabotage. But they couldn't understand how the RCMP could lose sight of a ground vehicle under surveillance before the Hinton bombing, or why the RCMP would bother using malfunctioning listening devices. "I deeply feel the Ludwigs are responsible, but with the evidence the court's got, I don't know how it's going to turn. And this Wraight witness absolutely blows my mind. That's their key witness. Holy crow."

Wherever Ludwig and Mamie travelled, people now recognized the telegenic couple. Many gave them a thumbs-up sign or stopped to shake their hands. In Grande Prairie, Dawson Creek, and Edmonton, the story was the same. Even the Hells Angels welcomed the Ludwigs at an Edmonton pizzeria. Mamie started off the conversation with, "Well, we both kinda dress strange." The RCMP later suspected that motorcycle gangs might be involved in oil-patch sabotage.

At malls people pointed at the couple and declared, "There go the Wiebos." Whenever businessmen from Grande Prairie phoned down to Texas, the response was usually, "Oh, you're from Wieboland." Ranchers and farmers called every day to seek advice and to report on industrial transgressions throughout Alberta. People sent Bibles, fan mail, books, cheques for the legal fight. A blind musician in British Columbia, whose brother worked for AEC, mailed his own creation, a country music song called "Enough of the Insanity: The Ballad of Reverend Ludwig."

But the insanity hadn't ended just yet. Ludwig had still to go to trial.

Chapter 14
Lamentations

At 3:30 in the morning on Sunday, June 20, 1999, Brian Petterson, 19-year-old grandson of a wealthy construction-company owner, drove his green three-quarter-ton Chevy supercab into Hythe to drop off two tired pals. They'd all been at a noisy bush party, where local adults sold the young folks beer and drugs. On the eve of the summer solstice, night refused to fall, and Petterson's remaining passengers, Shaun Westwater, Chris Morgan, and Cody Murray, didn't want to go home. Nor did his girlfriend of two weeks, Karman Willis, a 16-year-old redhead who liked riding horses and listening to Faith Hill, the country star.

Petterson drove around Hythe's empty streets and met up with Dustin Dueck and his two fishing buddies, Todd Vatne and Kevin McNeill. They, too, thought the night was young. Dueck's light blue Chevy half-ton and Petterson's supercab formed a little convoy. As the seven boys and one girl headed northwest on Highway 43, the trucks passed Hythe's familiar landmarks: the Quonset hockey rink

("Home of the Champions") where Karman Willis played on the all-girls Colts hockey team; the little log cabin where Olive Stickney, Alberta's first elected councilwoman, used to serve saskatoon-berry pie to Alaska-bound tourists; the concrete-block Bigway store where everyone bought their bread; and the Tags station where Chris Morgan pumped gas.

Even at four in the morning, a warm summer light illuminated the flatness of the land. The drivers stopped or chatted on their cellphones about going trout fishing at a dugout. Someone mentioned that they had to pass Ludwig's place to get there. Exactly what was said among the teens nobody really knows. Hythe gossips generally agree that Karman didn't want to go to Trickle Creek.

The teenagers, of course, had all heard about Ludwig at the dinner table. Several of the boys' fathers toiled in the oil patch and worried about getting blown up at work. Todd Vatne's dad was a manager for AEC.

Like most people in Hythe, the teens' parents considered the bearded cleric "a fucking terrorist," "a goddamn hypocrite," "a megalomaniac." The home of such a fearful person, of course, had to be seen to be genuinely feared. Locals swear that's all the teens really proposed to do that morning. As one Hythe resident later said, "You don't go to the haunted house to scare the house, you go to get scared."

Curiosity had already got the better of at least two of the boys. A week earlier Petterson and Morgan had scared themselves silly out at Ludwig's place. They'd crept up late at night and pulled down the Jolly Roger that flew over Ludwig's infamous road sign, the one that warned trespassers: "BEWARE of the mounting anger of the local residents." The theft had given the boys a great adrenaline rush.

The kids knew the county road to Trickle Creek had been an ugly battleground in Ludwig's war. But heavy drinking has a way of erasing history and fear. Driving onto a farm with headlights flashing and engines roaring was something nearly every drunk teen in the Peace has done. But joyriding onto Ludwig's place – that would be the talk of Hythe.

On the Trickle Creek road the convoy passed two pipeline

rights-of-way and an abandoned farm whose previous occupants had died of cancer. The teens drove past the large "BEWARE" sign and right up to the wooden front gate. Dueck found it open. He turned into the yard, passed a white tent pitched near the garage, and arrived in front of the main log building with its ranch porch. Fear suddenly got the better of him and he quickly spun around in the yard and left. Petterson drove on, to the end of the road by the Boonstra cabin, before performing a 180 and eventually meeting Dueck back at the highway, some three kilometres from Ludwig's house.

The white tent sheltered four of Ludwig's daughters: Mamie Jr., 20, Salome, 18, Charity, 16, and Ishshah, 9. The girls had painted their rooms that day and were sleeping outside to avoid the fumes. When they heard the roar of Dueck's engine, they were too scared to get out and look. They knew the depth of local animosity and had heard about the death threats.

The first run emboldened the joyriders. They decided to go back for a second tour. This time Dueck drove 100 metres east of the main building and spun around in front of the windmill. Petterson followed but stayed in front of the log house, his truck's souped-up engine throbbing like thunder in the silent night. Petterson suddenly got the feeling he was being watched, or so he later said.

When Renée Ludwig, in the main house, heard the trucks the first time, she thought someone was "just screwing around." But when she heard them again, she got up and looked out the window. Seeing a pickup roar into the yard, she thought, "My God, they're coming to do us in." She didn't know whether to hide her children under the bed or run into the woods.

As Petterson turned his supercab just by the tent to leave, he heard a crack, then two or three more. "Gunshot!" he yelled, hitting the gas pedal and scooting up the road. When he turned around, he saw blood in the back of the cab. Karman was crying in pain. Shaun Westwater had been hit in the arm, and Karman appeared to be bleeding profusely from the chest.

When Ludwig's daughters in the tent heard the shots, they thought they were being fired at. "Lay down!" Mamie Jr. shouted to her younger sisters.

Dueck drove up alongside Petterson and yelled excitedly that his truck had also been hit. One of the boys called 911 while Petterson sped to the hospital in Beaverlodge, praying that Karman wouldn't die. Along the way the boys tossed a case of unopened beers onto the road.

As the vehicles disappeared in a frenzied cloud of dust, Ludwig stepped out of the main house in his underwear. The trucks and gunshots had awakened him from a deep sleep. He'd arrived back at the farm late that night after a long drive from Saskatchewan, where he'd been on an anti-industry fact-finding mission. Groggily assessing the scene, he hooked his thumbs in his underwear, as his children had seen him do many times. After family members came into the house looking for safer lodgings, they briefly discussed what they had seen and heard. Ludwig phoned 911. The operator said hello.

"Reverend Ludwig calling."

"What can I do for you, Reverend?"

"Just had a couple of vehicles, loud mufflers, run through the yard and the lawn here. You'll probably find a couple of bullet holes in their boxes."

"Okay. You shot at someone, sir?"

"Someone shot at them. Yes."

"Do we know who shot at them?"

"No, you don't. I don't think it's the first question you should ask," Ludwig added.

"Are they injured?"

"More interested in getting the criminals, not the victims, huh?"

"I'm wondering who was shot because I want to know who was injured, sir."

"Who was shot, you said?"

"Yeah, was someone at your place shot or was it someone in the vehicle shot, sir?"

"No one was shot. The vehicles were shot is what I told you."

Ludwig described the vehicles and provided one licence plate number.

"I just want to make sure the people in the cars didn't have guns," added the operator.

"Well, I think you should go find out, I think."

Ludwig added that the intruders threw beer cans in his front yard. He had no idea who they were, he said, but their trucks were definitely marked with bullet holes. "You got all the information we've got."

"Okay, how many shots were fired?" the operator persisted.

"I suggest you not bother us like you usually do," replied Ludwig.

"Okay, I'm just wondering how many shots were fired –"

"You just check, thanks very much," said Ludwig. Then he hung up.

Karman Willis's parents, Barbara and Gerald, got a call from an RCMP constable around five in the morning. He told them Karman had been in an accident and that they had better get to the hospital quick. Both parents suspected that the baby of their five children had been in a car accident caused by a drunk driver. That's how most young people got hurt in the Peace. Ged Willis, a former oil-patch worker and now an elk and buffalo auctioneer, planned to give "Kermit" hell for being out so late. But the lanky 52-year-old quickly swallowed his words at the hospital. When he and Barb found Karman fighting death, tearing at her breathing apparatus, they collapsed in tears. The girl died in an ambulance as she was being transferred to Grande Prairie. Later that morning Barb recalled the odd symmetry of life. Karman had just completed a scrapbook about her 16 years in the Peace.

Meanwhile, the police had stopped and detained Richard and Lois Boonstra at a roadblock at around five. Wakened by the truck noise, the couple had decided to drive to Dawson Creek for an early-morning coffee at the Alaska café or McDonald's. They didn't stop at the main house on their way out because Richard's bail conditions prohibited him from being there between 3:00 p.m. and 10:00 a.m. As they came out to Highway 59, they found a police cruiser. Boonstra knew the constable, having painted the young man's house. The Mountie said a girl had been shot and killed at Trickle Creek and that there was a homicide investigation. The Boonstras said they didn't know anything about it. "That's very surprising," said the Mountie.

The Boonstras spent the morning at the police station, where they eventually met harried and anxious Corporal Dale Cox, one of the key men in Operation Kabriole. Now the Willis case had landed in his lap. "I only want one thing," said Cox. "How do we get into Trickle Creek safely?"

The Boonstras offered to go in and talk to Ludwig, adding that there was nothing to worry about. Indeed, Ludwig had already invited the police onto the farm. But Cox decided to wait for a search warrant. Under a new cost-saving system every warrant in the province had to be processed in Edmonton. Cox and more than 30 constables waited 14 hours.

A 12-member RCMP SWAT team, dressed in camouflage gear and armed with automatic weapons, had surrounded the farm by midday and set up blinds in the bush. Their instructions had been simple: be prepared to use all your combat skills. Many half expected Wiebo Ludwig to come running out of his house with guns blazing, holding a child in his arms as a shield. Others expected to encounter booby traps and mines, even though children ran about the farm every day.

Late in the afternoon Ludwig and the boys walked out to the police blockade. They agreed to talk if the RCMP allowed two men to go back and look after the women and children, who had assembled at Boonstra's cabin. The RCMP promptly loaded all the men into a locked prisoner van while SWAT team members surrounded the women and children. After realizing that Trickle Creek was no Waco, they shouldered their weapons. Cox wanted to move the whole family into a Catholic church in town but later relented. It was safer to keep all the Ludwigs at Trickle Creek.

After answering some questions in Beaverlodge, the men returned to the farm later that evening. Ludwig sensed that the RCMP wanted to revive Operation Kabriole and investigate the shooting at the same time.

Ludwig's lawyer Paul Moreau got pretty much the same feeling. He spent most of Sunday negotiating with the police and Ludwig to avoid any more grief. He knew the cops had 12 to 15 suspects and no way to eliminate them. He also knew they didn't know what to do in the absence of a confession. At the very worst, from a legal perspective, it was a case of self-defence.

Donna and Bob Bilodeau heard about the killing of a 16-year-old girl at Trickle Creek on Sunday morning while driving in Edmonton. Donna cried and wanted to throw up. Bob stopped the car. Once Donna caught her breath, she wondered what she could have done to prevent the death. She felt strangely guilty and completely battered. "Maybe if I had told everyone how the RCMP didn't want to protect me. Maybe if I had said something, they might have realized the situation was serious. Maybe..."

Dymphny Dronyk, the emergency response planner, heard the full spectrum of Hythe's grief: "What is that asshole doing? We knew it would come to this and how dare they? What the hell were those kids doing there?"

When informed of the shooting, Sergeant Keith Hills ran to his bathroom and vomited his breakfast. He later said he had opposed the return of the 30-30, which he suspected was the murder weapon.

Mike Weeks, former manager of the Hythe Brainard plant, felt as nauseated as Hills. "No matter how you look at it, it's a young girl gone."

Peter von Tiesenhausen, the artist, heard about the shooting while driving on the 401 in Toronto. He knew the people he had grown up with would "never forgive Ludwig for this."

Linda Bruinsma, one of the churchgoers who had revolted against Ludwig 14 years earlier in Goderich, watched the drama unfold on television that week and experienced déjà vu. "He's stale. He still talks the same words with his rebukes and hasn't grown. He's taking no responsibility."

Allan Johnstone learned about Karman's death on the radio. "What a blow to the environmental movement," he thought. He then warmed up his fax machine. "I have documented 15 years of nighttime harassment by motorized teenagers... I take responsibility for my children's behavior!" Johnstone, whose wife had taught Karman in Grade 5, also felt profoundly guilty. He had given the Ludwigs an old .22 Mossberg that spring after watching Ludwig patrol the farm's perimeter with a machete. "I was visualizing someone breaking into their house. I never anticipated that defensive shots would be fired outside the family residence!" he explained in another fax, describing Hythe and Beaverlodge as Sodom and Gomorrah.

Johnstone told Paul Belanger, who phoned Mamie for confirmation. She was sombre and terse. Belanger, dismayed, thought, "It's going to be a circus now with the media."

On Monday night the people of Beaverlodge met to discuss the "murder" of Karman Willis. Reporters and cameramen, who had swarmed into town like blackflies, weren't invited and sulked outside. Inside, 200 citizens bristled with electric rage. Sergeant Dave MacKay and a crisis intervention psychologist stood at the front of the room to answer questions. Most of the citizens stood at the back, leaving the first few rows of chairs empty.

MacKay spoke about the investigation. More than 50 police officers were now collecting evidence at the farm, he said. Trickle Creek was like a small town, so the investigation would take time. The 35 people who lived there were presumed innocent until proven guilty. For the next half-hour the crowd cursed Ludwig, the media, and the RCMP, sometimes at once. MacKay stood there, patient and implacable, as one speaker after another charged the RCMP with being yellower than the stripes on their own pants.

"What investigation?" said one man. "We've put up with this bullshit for four years. We should lynch him." Many applauded and cheered.

"That's what every decent community does when confronted by death and terrorism," added another.

"Get him the fuck out of the country. He's not a Canadian," shouted a burly oil worker.

"They threw him out of Ontario and the United States – why can't we?" demanded another oil worker.

"The community cooperates with the police and that doesn't work. Can we Klan him?"

Then the women voiced their opinions. "We have to think of the Willises and their tragedy," offered one.

"There are two sides here," said an older woman with an Irish accent. "The kids were wrong to do what they did. And Ludwig is wrong to do what he did. How did he get his guns back?"

MacKay explained that a court order in April had forced the RCMP to return the 30-30 seized in the January raid.

After listening to more venting, Brian Peterson, a forestry consultant whose daughter had been Karman's best friend, noted that Ludwig had two advantages over the local community. "He speaks without emotion, and look – we're speaking emotionally. And he speaks as a united voice. That's what we need to do if we are to succeed and bring this thing to an end. I want to see this brought to an end."

"We're trying to do to Ludwig what NATO is trying to do to Milosevic in Yugoslavia," said a local businessman.

In the end, the community decided to select two or three spokespeople to "counteract" Ludwig's rhetoric. Two days later the West County Concerned Citizens group issued its first press release, at the Hythe hockey rink. It said the media was confused about who the victims were. "A child has been slain. The daughter of one of the most respected, hard-working families in the West County."

Many quietly took exception to the description. Everyone knew that Karman's dad had been a notorious barroom brawler as a young man. Ged had dispensed his own brand of justice, usually with five knuckles. Many half expected the blue-collar worker to drive over to Trickle Creek and pummel Ludwig senseless or shoot him dead.

Months later, when Ludwig phoned the family, Ged Willis's hands started to shake as soon as Ludwig's name appeared on the call display. He didn't think the bastard would have the balls to phone. Ludwig was interested in reconciliation, but Willis hung up.

The hunt for weapons at Trickle Creek became a nine-day ordeal. A day or two after the shooting, during the occupation of the farm, Richard Boonstra approached Corporal Cox with a list of needed supplies, including potable water. The members of the community – all 35 of them – were now quartered at Boonstra's 400-square-foot cabin. Cox seized the opportunity to take Boonstra for a drive down the Norcen road in a four-by-four. He said he'd wanted to speak to Boonstra alone for a long time.

"Wiebo doesn't like me. But I've got to tell you, I have a lot of respect for you. I've read the disclosures. It's obvious you're interested in the environment. Wiebo isn't. Wiebo is just interested in himself. He's a violent man; you're not." He told Boonstra what the RCMP was going to do to Trickle Creek. "If I have to, I will bulldoze buildings down. I'll drain the dugouts. I'll do whatever it takes, and I'm calling the shots. This place will be cleaned out. I know there are guns here but we can't find any. I've talked to Koval and Combe [the Crown prosecutors] and their telephone line is open. They are willing to cut a deal – you don't want to spend 20 years in jail, do you?"

"No, I don't," said Boonstra.

"It's my opinion that you haven't been given the whole story by this man. We've got to get this little guy."

Boonstra gave Cox a list of food, water, tools, and medicine the family needed while under house arrest. Cox glanced at the list.

"There's going to be no food, no money to buy food, no water, until we get what we want and until Wiebo gives us what we want."

"You mean to tell me you're willing to put children at risk and abuse children in this kind of situation?"

"Wiebo is doing this. You tell him that. Wiebo is stopping this. You talk to Wiebo and you get this thing on the road."

"I'm not comfortable being a middleman."

Boonstra related the incident to Moreau, who got on his cellphone and butted heads with the corporal.

"If we don't find what we are looking for, we'll knock down buildings!" yelled Cox.

"That's the last thing you'll ever do as a Mountie," vowed Moreau. In the course of the negotiations Moreau asked the Ludwigs where the 30-30 was and they told him. He then gave Cox instructions on where to find it – in the corner of the sheep shed. Even with directions, the RCMP still couldn't locate it. One of Ludwig's boys later walked the police to the shed and pointed out the gun that Ludwig had twice posed with for media photographs.

After the shooting, Ludwig made a habit each day of marching down to a police cruiser blocking the road, where he talked to a gaggle of reporters. They had come to drill for anecdote and emotion, and Ludwig proved to be an endless fountain of both. He knew the people of Hythe and Beaverlodge wanted a sacrifice, but he wasn't about to put his head on their platter. He spoke indignantly in defence of his family.

At first he said the teenagers and the police and the Willis family all had blood on their hands. He accused the community of glorifying the death of an irresponsible joyrider, suggesting the teenagers might have had guns and perhaps had shot each other by accident. (Although the boys and the police denied this, many farmers in the region still consider it a possibility.) Ludwig couldn't understand why the police hadn't charged the boys with drunk driving or trespassing. "Instead of laying charges where they need to be laid, they look at us." He accused the RCMP of creating an atmosphere of fear and blame by whipping up frenzied sentiments with their shed bombings and their town hall meetings.

"We could go the Waco route and hide and hunker down, but I never thought that was a wise route. Whoever played a role in stoking up the reckless teens were clearly liable for Karman's murder. So the townspeople got themselves a huge spanking and a very painful one and a sad one, but I know that spankings can work some good in good time. That's my hope."

Locals found Ludwig's lack of remorse and empathy intensely galling. Although he admitted now and then that he understood that Karman's parents had experienced "a great loss," he quickly returned to his theme: "They have to reflect on the part they played in it. It's a travesty of human behaviour to allow a 16-year-old out at 4 a.m. doing things like this to bother other people's lives."

Later Ludwig went so far as to hypothesize that one of his daughters might have fired the shot. "Supposing one of those girls had a gun in the tent, and thought the truck was going to run over them, and shot. Now imagine her confessing that. What goes in motion? A legalized system that is eager to get the Ludwigs."

On national radio programs Ludwig said he thought that Canadians were pampering their kids to death. He rebuked the police for not wanting to resolve the controversy and the government for failing to hold a proper inquiry into oil and gas pollution. On and on it went. John Ludwig, Ludwig's eldest brother, phoned from Edmonton and advised Wiebo to stop talking. "You may be 100 percent right, but this isn't the time to say it," he argued. But Ludwig didn't listen to him or to his lawyers that week.

As the people of Hythe and Beaverlodge heard more about their "painful spanking," they got even angrier. Len Racher, one of Ludwig's neighbours, a heavy equipment operator, offered to help the RCMP dig up the farm for free. "Ludwig is a cross between Hemingway and Rasputin. He's a fanatic. It's a clannish family and that's why I hold him totally responsible for the shooting. I don't think anyone wipes their ass out there without Wiebo's permission."

Fourteen businesses in Beaverlodge and just about every establishment in Hythe save the post office put up signs that read: "No Service for Ludwigs." More than 700 people signed a petition declaring, "Fear has become our reality. We are afraid of what the Ludwig family might do or incite others to do. We demand our provincial and federal politicians take decisive action to protect us." A handmade cardboard sign saying, "We Hate Ludwigs," appeared in Hythe just above one that said, "We Love Seniors." Someone from Beaverlodge created a website that said Ludwig's latest resident at Trickle Creek was "Chucky," a murderous Hollywood puppet with the devil's social insurance number: 666.

Beyond the Peace, Canadians debated the merits of shooting drunken teenage trespassers at four in the morning. Many agreed that Ludwig had a point about parental responsibility. Scores of angry faxes bombarded the mayor's office in Beaverlodge, supporting Ludwig. "No matter how innocent they claim their actions were, they had no business being on private property," wrote one citizen. Another asked, "What would the reaction of the community have been had the truck run over and killed one of the occupants of the farm?" Something called the Canadian Workers' Party threatened to send 100 armed guards to protect the Ludwigs if rednecks in Beaverlodge didn't leave Ludwig alone. Even the Willis family received anonymous hate mail.

During the search of Trickle Creek, the RCMP released descriptions of various items seized at the farm. By the end of June most people in Hythe and Beaverlodge believed that tear gas, an arsenal of guns, bomb-making supplies, an assault rifle similar to an AK-47, and a variety of terrorist handbooks had been found at Trickle Creek.

In truth, apart from the 30-30, the "arsenal" mostly consisted of three .22-calibre rifles, including a sawed-off gun used for killing pigs and cattle. Most Alberta farmers own such weaponry. The "tear gas" turned out to be pepper spray, an item every berry picker owns in the bear-rich Peace, and several carbon dioxide canisters used for making soda pop. (Robert Wraight had abandoned the canisters in a boat behind a shed.) The "assault rifle" was a Norenco 7.62-mm, a popular deer-hunting rifle sold to the family by Wraight. The "terrorist manuals" included a government document, available at any gas station, that told farmers how to remove stumps and beaver dams, and how to make a dugout with dynamite. Other "terrorist" reading material included *The Poor Man's James Bond* (donated by environmentalists) and *Harvest of Rage*, a book about the Oklahoma City bombing loaned to the family by a university professor. Josh Ludwig says the family hid it under some straw, knowing what the RCMP would think of it.

On July 9, the RCMP arrested Ludwig and Boonstra and charged them with breach of bail for having firearms or ammunition at Trickle Creek. Everyone agreed that the arrests were designed to appease the people of Hythe and Beaverlodge. The Crown argued that Ludwig should be kept behind bars because he was a despotic mind controller and must have known where every gun was on the farm.

A judge released Boonstra but prohibited him from being within 10 kilometres of the farm. Ludwig, meanwhile, spent the next two weeks in the Peace River Correctional Institute in isolation. "For several nights I was suddenly euphoric and happier than I'd ever been in my life," he later recalled. He realized that most of the pain in life was really the fear of pain. On July 22, a judge found the breach-of-bail charges specious and ordered Ludwig's release, confining him to Trickle Creek except to go to court or meet with his lawyers.

After his release Ludwig got a mysterious call from Scott Sutherland, who claimed to represent several businessmen in British Columbia.

Sutherland proposed a meeting in Edmonton and a plan to help move the Ludwigs out of the Peace and harm's way. Ludwig showed up at the Mayflower Inn smelling a rat. Sutherland was dressed in black clothes and alligator boots. "You were the environmental sunshine boy until Willis got killed," Sutherland told him. He then promised to pay Ludwig's relocation expenses. "We want to help. But we need to know who killed Karman Willis." Ludwig said he didn't know, and the police didn't know either, and then he left. He suspected Sutherland worked for either the Canadian Security Intelligence Service or the RCMP. "They baited a hook with smelts and there was a problem: no fish."

Several months after the shooting, Chris Harvey, an Alberta farmer, wrote to the CBC about a show it did on the death of Karman Willis. He noted that the Ludwigs, the Willises, and the RCMP were so consumed with self-righteousness they couldn't see the larger picture. Wouldn't it be wonderful, asked Harvey, if "a member of the Ludwig community admitted they had lost their temper and fired at the truck of trespassing rowdies?" If the teens' parents, who may have encouraged the joyride, admitted they were wrong? If the saboteurs "expressed regret for taking the law into their own hands?" If the oil companies admitted "they had caused pollution and had been evasive and insensitive to citizens' complaints to avoid responsibility?" Wouldn't it have been wonderful if the RCMP admitted "they had been less than zealous in dealing with the mounting problems?" Harvey noted that "there have been many deadlocks around the world that have been broken by just one person admitting error, apologizing, and trying to make amends."

No one yet knows how wonderful such truth-telling could be. Months after the death of Karman Willis, hatred still clouded the Peace like a smoking flare. One day it assaulted Fritz Ludwig, his wife, Dania, and his sister Salome when they stopped at the Valhalla variety store to buy chocolate bars and a newspaper. It was 6:30 in the evening and the family was on the way home to Trickle Creek after visiting Dania's parents, the Boonstras, who were staying at Carl Bryzgorni's farm in Sexsmith. Valhalla has only one variety store and it's as spotless as a Scandinavian kitchen. Dania left Fritz happily bouncing little Dirk on his lap in the community's beat-up old Sprint.

As Dania dealt with the cashier, two men walked in. One of them, a tall fellow with an advancing beer belly and a blue baseball cap, ran angrily to the cashier.

"What are you fuckin' selling to these people for?"

The 16-year-old cashier, frozen in fear, didn't say a word.

"You don't sell to these fuckin' people." He turned to Dania and spat, "You bunch of fuckin' cocksuckers."

He spilled her money across the counter, grabbed the paper, and put it back on the stand. "You don't serve these people!"

Dania plucked up the paper and returned it to the counter. She gathered her money and her courage. "This is not your store and you'll have to talk to the manager about that," she said.

"I fuckin' will talk to the manager," shot back the man. "You fuckin' cocksuckers."

As he turned to leave, the man let go another blast: "Next time I see you on the fuckin' road, I'll fuckin' kill you."

After the two men left, the one in the blue cap headed over to the Sprint and abruptly opened the passenger door. He caught Fritz and Salome unawares: "If you can't buy in Hythe, you shouldn't be able to fuckin' well buy here, you cocksuckers." He slammed the door and swore as he got into his white pickup. "I'll fuckin' kill you if I see you on the road, just like you fuckin' killed Karman." And then his menace, the collective wrath and despair of the Willis clan, sped off down Highway 59.

Dania asked the cashier if she knew the man. She said no. Dania added, "I'm sorry about that."

"No, I'm sorry. They shouldn't be treating you that way."

Dania paid and left. She didn't stop shaking for hours.

A couple of days later, the owner of the Valhalla variety store sent Trickle Creek a short note. It read: "I am sorry, but until all the issues in the past and the recent past are resolved, I can no longer serve you in the store. I ask that you do not try."

Over in Beaverlodge, meanwhile, a group of teenagers attacked Allan Johnstone's house. The wannabe brushfire anarchist had gone to the local high school to complain about threats made against his two daughters. He'd ended a conversation with staff by shouting, "Long live the Ludwigs." Classmates of Karman Willis heard the outburst in the hall.

Shortly afterwards "out of control, foul-mouthed, alcohol abusing, motorized juvenile delinquents" threw pop bottles through his front window, annihilating the family's television. Rocks and eggs followed several nights later. Oil-patch workers blocked Johnstone's travel downtown and often followed him and threatened to beat him up. Vandals tried to take down the house's "For Sale" sign. Even after Ben and Josh Ludwig boarded up most of the windows with plywood, the intimidation continued.

Following the attacks Johnstone donned a bright orange target sign over his camouflage jumpsuit in a desperate attempt at humour. He wrote up his own obituary and faxed it throughout town ("Kentucky fried chicken should be served at the grave side and the bones thrown on my casket!"). After vandals threw beer bottles through his 11-year-old daughter's window (she was in bed at the time), Johnstone sent out another urgent fax, saying he was under siege. "However, this is good publicity for the Ludwig trial in February." His terrified wife, Esther, didn't agree.

In the fall of 1999 four representatives of the West County Concerned Citizens secretly met with Ludwig and the head of each family at Trickle Creek. Ludwig's brother John acted as mediator. John Ludwig knew what it was like to lose a child; one of his daughters had been murdered by her husband 25 years earlier. The psychopath often wrote letters from prison threatening to eat John's heart. John, who knew that his brother had a way of putting his finger on public sore points, had no faith in the justice system.

The representatives of the WCCC were Doug Burdess, Hythe's grocer, Brian Peterson, the forestry consultant, Rob Everton, the Ludwigs' closest neighbour, and Reverend Chris Donnelly of the Beaverlodge United Church. Donnelly, who ministered to the Willises' spiritual needs, spelled out three starting points: no media, complete cooperation with the RCMP, and a renunciation of violence.

Ben wanted to know what the community feared from Trickle Creek. Everton said they were afraid someone would blow up a well. "Once you condone violence, you have fear."

"We have a lot more to fear from your community than you have to fear from us," replied Wiebo. "That is why we are moving out. You have a lot more weight, tradition, and history behind you in an area where we have some serious reservations about the oil and gas industry. Your lives are connected with it, where we want to divorce ourselves more and more from it." He added, "I can see how you are angry about what happened to Karman Willis and it has to end. But the RCMP have used the occasion to investigate us and not Karman Willis's death."

Ludwig and his boys repeated the need to reconcile with the RCMP and industry as part of any peace initiative. The WCCC reps didn't agree. "It's not whether you were right or wrong in your oil-field battle, but I fear for my family," said Peterson. He agreed that the RCMP needed to deal with the family neutrally.

After a final prayer, the participants agreed to continue talking. Ludwig reminded them: "Man makes his plans but God directs his path."

In late November, the talks collapsed. The WCCC raised concerns about Ludwig's bail conditions and erected a sign at the foot of the county road, on Everton's property. The sign said, "Remember Karman," and cited a passage from Genesis about Cain and Abel and Jesus' rant against hypocrisy in Luke: "For there is nothing covered that is not revealed." In a 14-page letter Ludwig rebuked the WCCC and quoted Psalms: "The wicked plots against the righteous and gnashes his teeth at him."

Despite more threats, and the verbal abuse Ben had been subjected to while eating at McDonald's in Dawson Creek, the family announced at the end of the year that they had changed their mind about moving. To the chagrin of most local citizens, Ludwig had decided to stay put. "We have a continued burning interest," he explained in a news release, "in developing Trickle Creek as a viable visionary alternative to the prevailing destructive lifestyles round about us.

"Shalom."

Chapter 15

Judges

The trial of the oil-patch saboteurs began on February 11, 2000, in Room 412, a windowless box on the fourth floor of Edmonton's courthouse, before Justice Sterling Sanderman. The soft-spoken former cowboy had a reputation for fairness, smart judgments, and not wearing socks in court. When Secord and Moreau learned that Sanderman would preside, they recommended that their clients elect a trial without a jury, which they did.

Much was at stake. Eight of the 18 charges against Ludwig and Boonstra concerned mischief endangering life; each carried a maximum sentence of 10 years. The other counts, including counselling or conspiring to do mischief and possession of dynamite, carried lesser penalties. To Paul Moreau the most serious charge of all, however, was a new extortion charge levelled at Ludwig alone. Justice Leo Wenden, who oversaw the pretrial, added this surprise when he committed the whole mess to trial, three weeks after the shooting of Karman Willis. The extortion charge carried a maximum sentence of 14 years and gave Moreau many sleepless nights by suddenly connecting three separate incidents with one motive. But in a move that calmed both lawyers, the Crown abruptly dropped the charges against Bo and Mamie for the Suncor bombing and the charges against the Ludwig boys and Trevor Schilthuis for the Norcen cement job. To Secord that meant the Crown really didn't have much faith in its case at all.

The Ludwig trial made the nightly news for eight weeks. It attracted dozens of oil-patch contractors, members of the Christian Reformed Church, Buddha-worshipping environmentalists, curious students, right-wing kooks, disgruntled ranchers, people from Hythe, and Ludwig's mother, once or twice. Mamie and Wiebo made a point of shaking hands with every newcomer.

One of the regulars was Bob Bilodeau. After his dismissal from Beaverlodge, the Mountie received treatment for his post-traumatic stress disorder and went on medical leave. He had filed a long and detailed grievance against the RCMP for the way it had treated him, his wife, and the local community, and he had become something of a pariah. In his inch-thick brief to the RCMP, he pointed out that he had called the facts correctly and that history had, sadly, exonerated him.

On the first day of the trial, Bilodeau bumped into Ludwig and his brother John outside the courtroom. The former adversaries chatted for several minutes like war veterans.

"How are you, old soldier?" asked Ludwig.

Bilodeau, gracious and professional, said he was just fine and shook hands. Ludwig told John how Bilodeau had attempted to disarm a snowbank near Trickle Creek.

"Disarm a snowbank?" asked John.

Bilodeau explained the theatrics, even laughed a bit.

"I'm glad that there is room for humour in these struggles," said Ludwig.

Bilodeau asked how the family was doing.

"The family is doing well. We are not divided. You know there is a lot of power in a loving family life."

"In the end, that's all you ever have left," said Bilodeau.

For its case the Crown had accumulated enough documentation, including transcripts and CDs, to fill an entire set of encyclopedias. Prosecutor George Combe, a tall man with a slight hunchback, had the unlucky job of tying it all together. He proposed a singular theory of avarice to explain the sabotage against Norcen and Suncor as well as all the conspiring and counselling with Robert Wraight. He claimed that Ludwig and Boonstra, upset by pollution, were leaning on industry to get more money for their property. "And how would that pressure be applied?" asked Combe dramatically. "Through vandalism." The prosecutor called it "a bomb and bargain strategy."

Moreau called the Crown's approach a good example of "bathtub litigation." The state had filled the tub of justice with so many charges that it hoped something would form a ring when the evidence all drained away. Moreau and Secord's job was to make sure there wasn't much of a ring left. They considered Robert Wraight "a lawyer's wet dream" and concentrated their energies on disproving the extortion charge.

They did so with vigour. On March 30 Justice Sanderman threw it out.

Over two months all the principals took the stand and told their stories. Sergeant Keith Hills testified about Operation Kabriole, uttering short sentences through gritted teeth. He said the RCMP hadn't wanted to provoke Ludwig into committing a bombing but wanted to create "an opportunity that would happen." During Hills's testimony Ludwig held up a homemade sign: "Conspiring and counseling with AEC."

Sergeant Dave MacKay fought back tears as he described the mistrust and fear in Hythe and Beaverlodge during the height of the sabotage campaign. "I've never met more terrified people." Lois Boonstra thought they were crocodile tears.

Corporal Dale Clarke described his respectful encounter with Ludwig in Grande Cache after the Suncor battery bombing. Yes, he had some sympathy for the man's plight, said the gentlemanly officer. He also understood the fear of oil workers who found explosives strapped to pipelines. "Look at the money all of this is costing. Maybe if lab tests had been done on emissions...," suggested Clarke.

Overwhelmed by the heartfelt testimony, Mamie Ludwig burst into tears. Ludwig retreated with his wife to a corner and hugged her.

Ed McGillivray recounted his story of the long negotiations and their unhappy ending. During his testimony Ludwig approached McGillivray at a recess. He congratulated the general on his publicly voiced desire to reduce flaring in the oil patch. "My hope is that after all of this is over, we can get that done," said Ludwig. "I realize going to court is not fun and wish you the best."

McGillivray chuckled and said, "Okay."

Leonard Lau, a Vancouver forensic chemist, testified that Ludwig had residue on his hands consistent with commercially used explosives after the Hinton bombing. Moreau argued that such nitrates might have come from handling a firecracker or even moss in the bush.

Dale Cox, now a sergeant, whom Ludwig called "the sheriff of Nottingham," talked about all the hissing and static on the Nagra tapes collected by Wraight. To enhance their courtroom appeal, Cox had contracted the services of an audio specialist, Peter D'Amico, before the trial.

A rotund little fellow with splashy shirts, D'Amico explained to the judge how he digitally enhanced the tapes using all kinds of new technology. He insisted that removing the static and highlighting Ludwig's voice wouldn't affect the context. "Somebody being angry doesn't change into Shirley Temple," he said. The technician also described how he turned the tapes into three sets of CDs: a general wash (no static), "triple enhancements," and what Secord dubbed "the greatest hits collection."

D'Amico compared his $70,000 effort to that of peeling an onion. But Secord argued that D'Amico was dealing with just half a vegetable in the first place. Even with triple enhancements a lot of words couldn't be heard. When Secord suggested "a portion of the onion is rotten because the ear can't hear the conversation," D'Amico got upset: "You are misusing the onion, sir."

Despite D'Amico's efforts, the tapes sounded rough in the courtroom. Justice Sanderman hunched over his desk, like a man hard of hearing, whenever the Crown played its "greatest hits." After days of debate on whether to reject the tapes as evidence, Sanderman permitted the CDs to be cited. He reasoned that their contents worked just as well for the defence as for the prosecution. He vowed, however, to listen only to the general wash, and if he couldn't hear something clearly without a transcript, he wouldn't count it as evidence.

The inability of the nation's police force to make a simple tape recording astounded Christie Blatchford, a columnist with the *National Post*. She had fun describing the tapes: "Sometimes it sounds like they taped in a wind tunnel; sometimes in a bronchial ward of a hospital; sometimes smack in the middle of the world's busiest restaurant. They are filled with static, and all manner of background noises, including chirping birds, shrilling children, whistling, barking dogs, clanking dishes, running water and once, amusingly, the sound of a toilet flushing, which was duly followed by a noise familiar to every woman in the world – the contented song of a happy man who has just relieved himself in an entirely satisfactory manner."

Robert Wraight wore the same clothes he'd bought for the pretrial the previous fall. He stood nervously with his hands folded over his belly button. His memory hadn't improved much but he had been coached to answer questions crisply. As he identified voices on the tapes and talked about the Easter Bunny and explained that he'd done what he did so no one would get killed, he looked like a forlorn DJ. When the defence played the Abel Ryan video, Wraight cried openly, along with most of the Ludwig family in court. "That shouldn't have happened to anybody."

After hearing some of the informer's testimony, Sanderman declared his evidence "tainted" because his prime motive was money. The remark left the prosecution nearly speechless.

Some days more happened outside the courtroom than in it. Ludwig usually began and ended each day with commentary for the press, a habit that sorely irritated the judge. At the end of March, Bilodeau couldn't contain himself any longer and held his own press conference. He said the trial had started in the middle of the story and he wanted to talk about its beginning. "If this thing would have been dealt with when it was still a relatively small issue, maybe we wouldn't be here today. Maybe Karman Willis would be still with us." The RCMP made no comment.

The lengthy trial took its toll on everyone. Secord came down with the flu and Moreau developed a serious eye infection. Like Roman soldiers at a crucifixion, the press corps started to make bets on how many charges Ludwig would be nailed on. Sensing his legal vulnerability, Ludwig sweated so heavily in the final days of the trial that he carried around a little bottle of perfume. Boonstra, whose name was rarely mentioned in court, became almost an invisible player.

During the trial the Ludwigs stayed at a house south of Edmonton owned by a 75-year-old Ukrainian farmer named Bill Pankiw. Pankiw owned two quarter-sections of land on which Imperial Oil had abandoned a number of oil wells, flare pits, and battery sites without a proper cleanup. Pankiw had spent $45,000 and nearly a decade to get the sites properly reclaimed, with less than satisfactory results. He couldn't talk about it any more without turning red in the face. ("Talk about a crooked bunch of bastards.") On account of his generosity and sympathy with the Ludwigs' struggle, the RCMP tapped Pankiw's phone for a year.

Just prior to the verdict, Allan Johnstone, the tireless comprehensivist, sent Ludwig and Boonstra a cheerful fax. It began with a quote from George Bernard Shaw: "The Reasonable Man adapts himself to the world. The man who listens to reason is lost. Therefore all progress depends on the unreasonable man or woman."

Johnstone assured the men that if the verdict went badly, "you may be comforted by the fact that I am available to give your wives emotional counseling during your prison sentences – and my counseling is not limited to any way! . . . Over and out, Allan."

To hear Justice Sanderman's verdict on April 20, more than three dozen citizens from Hythe chartered a bus down to Edmonton, a distance of 500 kilometres. It took nearly an hour to get more than 200 people through the metal detectors that day. The spectators included a landman whose father, a farmer, idolized Ludwig and an oil-patch contractor who believed flaring was "a grotesque waste of public resources."

The people from Hythe and Beaverlodge, including several grim-faced teenagers, occupied one section of the court like a Greek chorus. Brian Peterson and Rob Everton wore blue-and-white "Remember Karman" buttons. Scores of reporters occupied another wing of the room, including a correspondent from the *New York Times*. Bilodeau was there; so was Sergeant MacKay.

Mamie and nearly half the family sat in the front row. "I feel there is another judge listening here today," said Mamie.

For two hours Sanderman spoke as deliberately as a schoolteacher as he walked through the charges against the two men. The crowd listened with the expectant tension of a group of theatregoers looking for the moral in a difficult play by Ibsen. The judge had no doubt that some of the environmental issues raised by Ludwig and Boonstra were valid, but he didn't dwell on them. He didn't believe Wraight was a liar, just an honest person with a faulty memory who admitted that he had difficulty recalling events. "A liar wouldn't do that."

Sanderman acknowledged that the quality of the tapes was abysmal and that he had reviewed only the "general wash" version. He didn't recommend such listening to anyone. He noted that Ludwig and Boonstra never trusted Wraight and did "toy with him." But their "troubling and suspicious" conversations supported no conspiracy to commit mischief of any sort. He dismissed all the conspiracy charges and found Boonstra innocent of any wrongful counselling.

Ludwig, however, was another matter. Sanderman described the reverend as a cunning, careful man who sparred effectively with words and had an inordinate interest in dynamite. Ludwig, he added, either spoke in riddles or talked plainly. He characterized Ludwig and Wraight's conversations about buying dynamite as "plain talk." After explaining how Ludwig picked up the fake sticks at the Bi-Lo station, the judge convicted him on two counts: counselling to possess an explosive substance and attempted possession of fake dynamite. At that point the tense citizens of Hythe, fearful that Ludwig might somehow walk without a conviction, issued an audible sigh of relief.

Then Sanderman dealt with the cemented Norcen well site decorated with flaming straw bales. He described it as a "macabre scene" and concluded that Ludwig "was integrally involved." Based on the videotape found at Trickle Creek as well as Wraight's testimony, the judge convicted Ludwig and Boonstra of mischief by interfering with the lawful use and enjoyment of property.

That left the five counts on the bombing of the Suncor battery, what Sanderman called the "most serious allegations in the entire indictment." He talked at length about the death of Abel Ryan, the long trip to the Suncor site, and RCMP lab tests that found nitrates on Ludwig's hands. He concluded that Ludwig was in the vicinity and "set off the bomb."

Upon hearing this statement a court regular and Ludwig supporter stood up and accused the judge of putting an innocent man in jail.

"Have her removed!" snapped Sanderman.

Following the outburst he convicted Ludwig on two of the Suncor charges: mischief by destroying property and possessing an explosive substance. He dismissed related charges against Boonstra, saying the evidence mysteriously placed the man 80 kilometres away.

Next Sanderman dealt with Moreau's abuse-of-process arguments. "The theory that AEC and the RCMP were conspiring to get Mr. Ludwig and Mr. Boonstra was without foundation." AEC was just an aggrieved party seeking results.

Sanderman, however, was troubled by the timing of the RCMP's shed bombing. He said the police's lack of foresight could "be severely criticized. Their investigative goals outstripped their common sense. The RCMP selfishly considered their desires to advance their investigation rather than to consider the needs of the community and their obligation to preserve its general well-being."

At the end of Sanderman's delivery, the people of Hythe and Beaverlodge stood up and politely clapped. Moreau shook Ludwig's hand before guards handcuffed him and took him away.

"I'm sorry it didn't work out better," the lawyer said.

"It could have been much worse," said Ludwig reassuringly.

Boonstra quickly left the building without talking to reporters.

He tearfully admitted later that day that he was surprised by Ludwig's conviction. "Very much so. But we are not despairing. That's not part of the game."

Moreau stood on the court steps and confessed a deep disappointment. He felt Sanderman had given the defence a fair shake but thought five convictions were a heavy blow, given the quality of the evidence. He lit a cigarette and watched the reporters drift away from their scrums with the people from Hythe. "You know," he said, "I'm convinced I haven't heard the whole story."

On April 26 Justice Sanderman sentenced Ludwig to 28 months in jail and Boonstra to just 21 days. He called the reverend a "zealot" and warned him that the world wasn't black and white. In a 20-minute speech Ludwig admitted to making mistakes and quietly noted that the legal process had managed to avoid what mattered: pollution in rural Alberta. It was "the cauldron in which all churned."

The trial of Wayne Roberts, the man accused of shooting Patrick Kent, took place in an airy Calgary courtroom six months after Ludwig went to prison. With the exception of a few Calgary reporters, no one covered it.

Crown Prosecutor Larry Stein painted Roberts as a cold-blooded killer who didn't want a well in his backyard and who "picked the time and place to rid himself of Patrick Kent and KB Resources." Stein suggested that Roberts had shot an unarmed and defenceless man with an execution-style coolness.

Roberts, unlike Ludwig, testified in his own defence. When Stein implied that he was motivated by money in his soil-contamination fight, the rancher got very angry. "I think you've got me a little bit wrong here, Mr. Stein. What happened at my place was a confrontation, pure and simple, between two men." He accused the Crown of charging him with first-degree murder instead of manslaughter because the victim was "a vice-president of an oil company in Alberta, where oil dollars feed the provincial government coffers."

The rancher's two astute lawyers, both from Nova Scotia, patiently argued that Roberts had shot Kent in self-defence. To support their case they called in two prominent American ballistics experts and Vietnam veterans who testified that it was entirely possible that Kent "was standing or semi-erect when shot." In addition, no bullets were ever found beneath the body, suggesting that Kent had indeed been shot while charging Roberts.

During his final argument for the defence, Blaise MacDonald unfortunately called Roberts a "straight shooter." After regaining command of his metaphors, he argued that Kent had a "dark side" and that the two men "played a crazy game" in which both raised the stakes that day.

After 15 hours of deliberation a jury convicted Roberts of second-degree murder. Justice Peter Martin later described Roberts as a "dangerous man" and sentenced him to 15 years in prison without once mentioning the backdrop to the case: environmental contamination and the relentless drive of the oil industry. The omission stunned MacDonald, who says he learned a lot about Alberta during the trial. "It's like the three blind mice. I'm not saying the judge didn't have reason to reach the conclusions he did, but there is a pattern of bullying by authorities in Alberta that's worth being sensitive to. There are a lot of farmers in the same circumstance as Roberts."

The well that cost Patrick Kent his life, sent Wayne Roberts to prison, and confirmed Wiebo Ludwig's view of the murderous inevitability of the war against Big Oil was recently reactivated. It produces 15 barrels of crude oil a month, worth about $450.

Epilogue

The RCMP pronounced itself "very pleased" with Ludwig's conviction. Assistant Commissioner Don McDermid believes there might never have been a conviction if Robert Wraight hadn't become an informer. Nor does McDermid have any regrets about working with AEC. "It's important to remember that they were the victims in this case, and we always work with the victims in terms of solving crimes."

Sergeant Keith Hills retired to the town of Peace River in January 2001. In March a drunk driver struck him and his wife while they were strolling on the highway by their home. Hills was killed; his wife, Linda, sustained serious injuries but lived.

The RCMP accused Sergeant Bob Bilodeau of conducting himself during the trial "in a disgraceful manner which brings discredit to the RCMP." Bilodeau hired Ludwig's lawyer, Paul Moreau, to represent him and finally settled out of court. He now drives a truck part-time. His wife, Donna, returned to college to earn a degree in social work. "Extremists," says Bilodeau, "are ordinary people with their backs against the wall. But in a civil society you can't declare private wars."

Sergeant Dave MacKay remains detachment commander of Beaverlodge. He recently completed a major investigation of the Horse Lakes Indian band, after which several adults were charged with molesting children.

For his role in Operation Kabriole, Corporal Dale Cox was promoted to sergeant. He does not talk to the press.

Gwyn Morgan, the CEO of AEC, said Ludwig's conviction enabled his company to "turn the page and carry on with our lives." Yet none of the convictions were related to sabotage at AEC's installations. He called Ludwig's complaints about flaring and gas plant emissions "unfounded." His company donated $750,000 to the Alberta Ecotrust Foundation to help with community programs for the environment.

At AEC, turning the page has meant not talking about Ludwig or pollution. Morgan, his senior executives, former employees, and AEC contractors all declined to be interviewed for this book. "This story is over," said the media spokesman, Dick Wilson. Ludwig and the saboteurs cost AEC an estimated $10 million in security and damage to property. "You wouldn't believe the enormousness of the problems this thing caused the company," said one retired employee. "The fiscal side was astronomical."

According to Ottawa's National Pollution Release Inventory, AEC's Hythe Brainard plant released 12 tonnes of poisonous hydrogen sulphide into the atmosphere in 1999, along with half a tonne of carbon disulphide. The company identified the source of the pollution as "fugitive releases." In the same year AEC's Sexsmith plant released more than 18 tonnes of hydrogen sulphide. In 1998 Alberta's Environmental Protection Branch fined the Sexsmith plant $16,000 for exceeding its hourly emission rate for sulphur dioxide.

AEC's record on flaring and venting hasn't noticeably changed. In 2000 the company bought Amber Energy Inc. and vigorously defended its record of venting raw gas into the air in the Fort McMurray region. The volume of gas vented could have heated

25,000 homes for a month. As usual the EUB scolded AEC and said the waste was unacceptable, but no fines were levied for lost revenue to the government or for fouling the air.

Ed McGillivray is no longer AEC's director of environment, health and safety, although he still works for the company.

Mike Weeks, the former gas plant manager, now spends alternate months in Libya and the Peace. A central part of his job is flare reduction. He has remarried and has renovated a bungalow near Sexsmith.

After two years of record profits, AEC merged with PanCanadian Petroleum to become EnCana – North America's largest independent oil and gas company. Morgan remains the CEO of the $30-billion corporation. He is also a big fan of President George W. Bush's new energy plan, which calls for greater Canadian oil and gas imports. To meet the energy demands of the United States, EnCana and other firms will have to drill another 200,000 wells on public and private land in Western Canada over the next decade. Forty percent of that gas will be sour – the largest concentration in the world.

Forensic tests established that Karman Willis was killed by a .30-calibre weapon but could not pinpoint which one.

Each year the town of Hythe holds a memorial hockey tournament in Karman's name. Many people in Hythe believe that the Church of Our Shepherd King is a cult, and they answer questions about the Ludwigs with extreme anger. "They're sheltering a murderer, and anything is justifiable to get them," spewed one gas plant worker. Other residents wonder if the shooting of Karman Willis didn't underscore the community's own problems, including the lack of a teen recreational centre and the inability of parents to talk seriously to their teenaged children. "What are we dealing with?" asks one mother. "Ludwig, or a society that is crumbling and thinks that anything is okay for a dollar? There are no principles and morals left. There are no guidelines for our children. The oil companies have no accountability; the police accept no accountability; Ludwig holds no accountability. Why does all of society accept no accountability for their actions?"

To date the seven teenagers involved in the joyriding refuse to talk about that fateful night. Doug Burdess of the West County Concerned Citizens says the boys just aren't ready to talk. Since the shooting, one of the teenagers has taken to slashing his arm with razor blades and has been charged with vandalizing oil-field equipment. The others have retreated into a code of silence. Many in the community feel guilty and troubled. "We made Wiebo Ludwig into what he turned out to be. We were enablers," says Richard Harpe, who farms north of Trickle Creek. He hopes the Ludwigs will eventually move and be gone. "I think there's some worry that it isn't over yet." He is also troubled by industry's assault on the region. "We know that sour gas is responsible for a lot of health problems. The Peace has the highest per capita rate of cancer in Alberta." Yet the EUB and the Alberta government, he says, stand around like unconcerned spectators.

Ged and Barb Willis still live a grief like no other. They have turned Karman's bedroom into a shrine, complete with candles and a large photo of their daughter. "Something has got to happen," says Ged, "or else it's going to drive everybody nuts." Barb says, "They're mad at industry for stillbirths, and we're not supposed to be mad because they killed our daughter."

In spring 2001 police charged 32-year-old Derek Willis, Karman's older brother, with assault after he attacked Trevor Schilthuis in Beaverlodge. Willis accused him of killing Karman and didn't stop kicking and beating him until he discovered that Schilthuis wasn't one of Ludwig's sons.

The *American Journal of Industrial Medicine* recently pointed out that hydrogen sulphide guidelines for workers and downwinders are based on very different realities. Rural residents come in all states of health and have the expectation that their air will be free of toxic gases. "While levels of hydrogen sulphide as high as 10 ppm appear to be acceptable for workplace exposure, community levels as low as .250-.300 ppm can create an unacceptable nuisance condition." No agency in Alberta has acknowledged that conclusion.

The Northern River Basin Human Health Monitoring Program, a government study group, documents and evaluates the health of people living in the Peace. It shows that they suffer from rates of respiratory infections, pneumonia, stillbirth, endometriosis, asthma, and neurological problems nearly three times higher than those of people living in Calgary and Edmonton. Ken Saro-Wiwa's people in the flare-saturated Niger Delta suffer from exactly the same ailments. Experts suspect that a polluted airshed is partly to blame. More studies have been promised.

In Grande Prairie many citizens believe that "the powers that be" chose to minimize both the miscarriages and the sabotage campaign from the beginning. "The last thing the industry wants to do is fess up to being responsible," says one. "Everybody was playing ostrich, hoping nothing would happen." In addition the RCMP didn't want to spend money on mischief caused by true believers with a righteous cause. All in all, Ludwig got the classic runaround. "He was treated shabbily by authorities, and people thought they could do that because he's different and flaky. It was a great clash between two of Alberta's great principles. It pitted a man looking for peace in the wilderness, a man whose beliefs rejected Mammon, against oil-money greed that runs the province and has the justice minister's phone number on its Rolodex. They clashed, and in a province governed by oil wealth, Ludwig had to lose."

The Alberta government, which has conducted perfunctory reviews of all oil and gas legislation and recommended different forms of mediation, has declined to tighten pollution standards. Some of the most glaring polluters are the 61 sour gas plants exempted from 1988 pollution guidelines. They remain the largest source of sulphurous emissions and groundwater contamination in the province. The industry argues that taxpayers should pay for any upgrades.

During the Ludwig trial, Alberta and three other provincial governments agreed to spend $16.2 million to study the health effects of flare emissions on human health, cattle, and birds. "In particular, greater scientific knowledge is required in order to understand the potential impacts of flare emissions." No results from the study are expected before 2006.

After the trial the EUB denied Ludwig's latest request for an inquiry. Though the decision made no mention of the death of Abel

Ryan or the toxicity of flaring gases near a community of 36 people, "the Board acknowledges that high levels of industry activity, a growing population, especially in rural areas, increasing sour gas development and changing values had led to a need for greater attention to landowner concerns at an early stage." The EUB acknowledged that in 1998 daily flaring within a 10-kilometre radius of Trickle Creek released enough gas to heat more than 5,000 homes.

The EUB has doubled its field inspections and set up an alternative dispute mechanism for landowners and oil companies. It has also published basic pamphlets on landowner rights and well reclamations, something never available to Ludwig. And in 2000 the EUB set up a committee to review sour gas regulations. The committee visited 12 cities and towns, including Grande Prairie. All the participants told them what Ludwig had been saying for years: that both industry and the regulator were "vague and unresponsive" on sour gas issues. Most denounced the EUB as ineffective and biased. Downwinders cited the same health problems their forefathers had cited 40 years earlier: respiratory illnesses, bloody noses, nausea, asthma, premature births, cancer, sick or dead livestock. Just about every community described the continued establishment of sour gas wells and plants in populated communities as deadly and irrational: "Greed and profit have been put ahead of public safety," testified one. Most also noted that current setback distances and emergency response planning provided little comfort or protection.

In its final report in December 2000 the committee agreed "that further improvements must be made." Some of the committee's 87 recommendations included better health studies, improved field audits, smarter enforcement of existing laws, and greater neutrality "when dealing with the public." The report also pointed out some glaring failures: "The EUB's single mobile air quality monitor is not considered adequate to address the number of issues and concerns that exist." The EUB says it will implement all 87 recommendations and has already given "the highest priority to sour gas complaints."

No one in rural Alberta expects the recommendations to be acted on. In 2000 the regulator approved a sour gas well in a crowded

Calgary suburb that even oil executives opposed, recertified a sour gas pipeline that had leaked and knocked down a senior citizen, and denied a public hearing on a sour gas well next to a provincial campground. Out of thousands of applications, it rejected only one proposed sour well. In that case more than 100 landowners and farmers in Rocky Mountain House strenuously opposed a proposal by Shell. Most locals suspect the EUB would have approved the well if the National Film Board hadn't been making a documentary about how the regulator treats landowners.

Flaring remains an unrelenting concern for rural Albertans living downwind of wells, batteries, and gas plants. Although industry has voluntarily reduced the amount of gas it burns by 50 percent since the Ludwig saga began, the province still flares or vents enough gas to heat half the city of Calgary every year. Worldwide, Big Oil flares enough toxic gas into the air every year to heat more than 18 million homes.

New research at the University of Alberta recently found that the amount of raw toxic gases escaping into the air at a flare stack increases eightfold when the wind blows. In some parts of Alberta the wind never stops blowing. Scientists have also found that every flare site emits its own unique blend of developmental or neurological toxins. To date the government of Alberta has introduced no legislation to force companies to conserve gas, to stop flaring, or to pay royalties on flared or vented gas.

Many farmers and ranchers in western Canada sympathize with the Ludwigs. Most don't support violence, but all agree that the mayhem brought national attention to a problem that industry and government have ignored for 40 years. "He achieved in six months what we couldn't do peacefully in 10 years," says Phyllis Bocock, a dairy farmer.

Alberta farmers and ranchers have recently scored several legal victories. Doug Jones, a rancher and former schoolteacher, won $325,000 from Mobil Oil after a judge ruled that groundwater contamination had sickened his herd from 1982 to 1992. Jones believes that industry's refrain of "Deny, deny, deny" doesn't work any more. Another landowner, who developed facial paralysis and neurological damage after being exposed to flare emissions, settled out of court and signed a confidentiality agreement. Wayne and Ila Johnston, whose herd was devastated by a pipeline leak, finally reached an agreement with Shell. Richard Secord has now filed some two dozen tort claims against industry. "I'm getting to a point where I can't take on any more." The claims include gross water contamination, continuous flaring, cancerous benzene emissions, and sour gas leaks resulting in neurological damage and livestock losses.

Ludwig's campaign against flaring and sour gas has been taken up by a regional celebrity. In 2001 Kelly Sutherland, an eight-time world champion chuckwagon driver, started a campaign to limit flaring near people and their livestock east of Grande Prairie, after several companies lit up the countryside around his home like a birthday cake. He says that pollution from a flare stack can eat away a thoroughbred's lungs and turn him into a "roarer" – an animal starved of oxygen after running half a mile. He accused the companies of being indifferent to the concerns of rural people. "If you're living in Calgary, I don't suppose the flaring bothers you too much." He eventually got the flaring near his own home stopped.

Alberta's oil and gas industry admits that relations with landowners have reached an all-time low. Some companies won't attend public meetings about proposed sour gas wells without bodyguards. Many landmen will now work only in pairs.

Tensions between mineral rights holders and landowners are also rising throughout British Columbia, where the Crown owns 90 percent of all mineral rights, and the western United States, where the federal government holds about 40 percent. In Colorado, for example, oil firms don't even have to compensate surface owners for damages caused by drilling. Ludwig identified the source of the rage a decade ago: the imbalance between the rights of landowners, the environment, and the rights of oil and gas operators. Many American environmentalists fear that George W. Bush's energy plans will bring Alberta-scale problems south of the border.

In a time of continental energy shortages, the EUB expects more than 20,000 oil and gas wells to be drilled in the province in 2001; about a third of them will be sour gas wells. Alberta's northern forest has now been fragmented by 1.3 million kilometres of roads, seismic lines, and pipelines. Less than 10 percent of Alberta's forest land remains unfragmented. Although the Amazon rainforest gets all the publicity, the forest of the Peace has suffered an identical fate.

The identity of the saboteurs remains a mystery. Richard Boonstra suspects that cells of individuals acting independently may have been responsible. Wiebo Ludwig would like to give up their identities and the whole unbelievable story but says certain legal fundamentals prevent him from doing so. He also notes that much of the sabotage ended when Bob Wraight left the area. Members of the RCMP believe that the Ludwigs definitely had help and that several people from British Columbia and southern Alberta participated in the sabotage campaign. People around Hythe swear that members of the Ludwig or Boonstra families committed most of the vandalism. Allan Johnstone believes that Ludwig's dynamite supplier, a true sympathizer, lived somewhere near Sexsmith and died of cancer in 2000.

The campaign of the saboteurs has become part of Alberta folklore. When landowners want to make a point with an aggressive oil company, they threaten "to do a Ludwig." Henry Pirker believes that parents in the Peace will one day tell their children, "You be good or Wiebo will get you."

Sabotage against oil and gas installations remains a substantial hidden cost of doing business in the province. Millions of dollars' worth of vandalism goes unreported every year. Lax pollution rules, ambivalent regulators, and the province's ethos of rugged individualism have made the jurisdiction a growth centre for eco-terrorism.

Carl Bryzgorni, the organic farmer who supported Ludwig, died of lymphonic cancer on March 23, 2001. He blamed his illness on exposure to toxic gases flared and vented near his farm. One of the wells in question was owned and operated by AEC. Mamie Ludwig wrote to Gwyn Morgan at AEC after Bryzgorni's death: "We have experienced many tragedies, as you are well aware of. Would it not be a matter of urgency for you to begin the process of reconciliation – to heal the deep wounds and scars of those you have hurt?" Morgan didn't reply.

Wayne Roberts, serving 15 years at the Edmonton Correctional Centre for the murder of Patrick Kent, has appealed both his conviction and his sentence. He and his wife, Jean, have launched a multimillion-dollar lawsuit against KB Resources and Petro-Canada over the contamination of their land. Jean, who manages a local co-op store near Olds, says, "I would never, ever own land with any connection to the oil and gas industry, whether it was a well, a pipeline, or a nearby gas plant. The government and the judicial system have no interest in assisting landowners in maintaining their property rights." The source and extent of contamination on their land have not yet been determined.

Paul Belanger concentrates on his environmental consultation business. He says he's been swamped with orders to design straw bale homes powered by solar or wind energy. He regards Ludwig as an enormously learned man with "some warts and flaws and egos. The only real blemish in this effort was the death or murder of Karman Willis." He calculates that industrial pollution from gas plants, batteries, and flares in rural Alberta kills about 1,000 people a year. He predicts that landowners will eventually launch a class-action suit against the industry, and that Big Oil will one day face the same sort of legal troubles that now plague the tobacco industry. Belanger doesn't think the war in the Peace is over. "Wiebo has learned a lot and he's going to make more waves. I'm not sure how or where, but I'm sure there will be surprises."

Bob Wraight and his family now live in the interior of British Columbia. They home-school their children and cultivate lives of relative isolation – no one wants to associate with "a snitch," says Wraight. To make ends meet, he does odd jobs; his wife is unemployed. He refused to change his name under the witness protection program: "If you do that, you're left with nothing." He feels misunderstood and unappreciated. "I'm not proud of what I done, but I'm not ashamed of it either. I've never been one to turn a blind eye. If there's a purse snatcher, I'll chase him as far as I can run." He collected AEC's $100,000 reward.

After the trial and the attacks on his home, Allan Johnstone left his family in Beaverlodge and became the region's first "political refugee." For several months he lived in his car in Quesnel, B.C., while writing his memoirs for the *Radical*, a left-wing newspaper. He later moved to Edson, where he sleeps in a $50 sleeping bag that Robert Wraight sold him. He says that Ludwig is a con man – "but I love him." He recently met with his wife, Esther, and his two daughters and reports that "our marriage is strained but still exists."

Richard Boonstra served out his 21-day sentence and returned to Trickle Creek to resume his role as an elder. He says that Ludwig's absence has proved just how genuine and rooted the community's faith has become. "There is basically one spirit, one mind, and one God. Christ in you, and you in Him. All of these beautiful mysterious things that we experience here – the Lord has favoured us. And we are as amazed as anyone."

In January 2001 the RCMP again raided the farm. This time four dozen Mounties retrieved listening and tracking devices planted after the shooting of Karman Willis. In March, 17 members of Ludwig's family, including 11-year-old Ishshah, received perfunctory letters from Alberta Justice: "Take notice that you were the object of the interception of private communications." Several Ludwig friends and supporters received similar letters. A month later the family filed a 200-page report on "RCMP bias and abuses" to the RCMP Public Complaints Commission and the Solicitor General of Canada.

Industrial activity around Trickle Creek has continued unabated. Loggers clear-cut half of another quarter-section along the Trickle Creek road, and oil and gas companies have drilled three more wells within five kilometres of the farm. In the spring of 2001, seismic testing was done half a kilometre from Trickle Creek's residences.

AEC has applied once again to convert the sweet gas pipeline north of the farm into a sour gas one; the family plans to oppose the conversion, as it did in 1998. When Anderson Exploration proposed to drill three new wells just northeast of the farm, Ben Ludwig emphatically objected. He also invited Anderson, along with other companies, to purchase the farm.

Anderson soon reduced its proposal to one sweet gas well. It also offered to relocate "sensitive residents" during any test flaring and to construct a "closed system" to eliminate low-level emissions. But the company said it was not prepared "to purchase your property as a solution to your concerns."

The Ludwig boys work as drywallers in eastern British Columbia. The women, virtuous and thrifty as ever, raise the children, salve wounds, and plant gardens, just as Proverbs advises – for a virtuous woman "looketh well to the ways of her household and eateth not the bread of idleness." The family is still awaiting a public inquiry into gas-field pollution, miscarriages, sabotage, and the shooting of Karman Willis. It has also asked the government of Alberta to help it move out of the Peace.

Wiebo Ludwig served his 28-month sentence at a minimum security prison in Grande Cache. Prison officials expected a rebellious inmate; instead, they got a model prisoner who took woodworking courses and studied the Scriptures. From jail he wrote to Suncor and apologized for the Hinton bombing. "Even though my own hands never touched the explosives that were allegedly used in that bombing, I have for quite some time used explosive rhetoric carried by media clear across this country." Ludwig then suggested that Bo, the father of Abel Ryan, may have "acted upon his anger and sheer frustration" by blowing up the battery. "If the bombing was indeed not a 'set up' – which considerable evidence in court seemed to suggest – then I believe one of my sons probably did do it, though to this day he vehemently denies it, which too is understandable."

In a prison interview Ludwig said that he doesn't feel guilty just because he's been convicted. "The guilty ones" – the oil companies – "escaped conviction." He does plead guilty to being different, outspoken, angry, desperate, and fearless. "I have represented quite a different mind. I admit that, and that opens me to being targeted." He notes that Jeremiah, the prophet of grief, walked into places wearing a sticky ox hide instead of a suit and tie. "There are better ways to communicate and more politically correct ways, but they are anemic, bloodless, and don't carry any punch."

Lisa Ling of the Correctional Service of Canada wrote a 33-page intake assessment on Ludwig. "Mr. Ludwig impresses this writer as minimizing, rationalizing and denying personal responsibility while painting himself as a victim. For example, he alleges that he has been threatened with death and had his van blown up (April 19, 1999) and suggests it was at the hands of a vindictive oil and gas industry. He appears to be full of self-pity and blame. His comments, inflection, and word selection leaves the writer with the view that either he does not really understand his behaviors, or more realistically, he doesn't care. His articulations are totally devoid of remorse or appropriate victim empathy." Ling, who is divorced, found his views on women "unenlightened and scurrilous." She concluded that Ludwig's skills at manipulation were finely honed. "Wiebo Ludwig in my view, is a thrill seeker, craving fantastic and uninviting behavior. Calculated risks seem to be thoroughly planned and enjoyed." Her report played a key role in the denial of Ludwig's application for early parole.

Ludwig wrote a 17-page letter contesting the assessment. He pointed out a number of errors – for example, the family's making 750 to 1,000 bottles of wine a year, often gift-wrapped for friends, was hardly "an illegal business engagement" – but mostly he was upset that Ling repeated falsehoods circulated by some members of the RCMP. One has the children of Trickle Creek carrying fanny packs full of ammunition – an allegation he said has no basis in fact. Another held that Harmony, Ludwig's eldest daughter, had conceived a child while her husband, Trevor Schilthuis, was out of the province – also untrue. "What amazing and perverse invasive interest as to what goes in the bedroom privacy of the people's lives at Trickle Creek," wrote Ludwig. "It boggles the mind and gives one the creeps." Ludwig also pointed out that his family was a "family," not a "following," his property a farm, not a "compound," and that he did not believe in "getting even." "The entire idea of that is repugnant to our fundamental religious position which teaches that vengeance belongs to God; that He will repay." Finally, he pointed out that his name is not "the subject," but "Wiebo (Arienes) Ludwig, son of the late Harm Jan Ludwig."

Ludwig was released from prison on November 15, 2001 and returned to his home in the sour gas fields of northern Alberta.

Sources

Over three years I interviewed more than 100 people in and around Hythe, Beaverlodge, and Grande Prairie, Alberta. Some were farmers, some were gas-field workers, and some were just spectators. I also talked to relatives and associates of the Ludwigs throughout North America, including people in Goderich, Ontario, and Sioux City, Iowa; some were dismayed by Wiebo Ludwig's behaviour while many friends and in-laws admired the man. No one was indifferent. I talked to gas executives and oil-patch employees residing in Calgary and to health experts such as Dr. Kaye Kilburn in Los Angeles, California. Many people spoke on condition of anonymity, out of fear of Ludwig or the oil and gas industry. With the exception of Robert Wraight and AEC executives, I interviewed all key players in this story at length.

The residents of Trickle Creek have been keeping detailed records since 1990. They shared with me their lively diaries, logs of local industrial activity, hundreds of letters, transcripts of public hearings, and videotapes of everyday life as well as their conflicts with indus-try. After repeated cross-checking with other sources, I found their diaries, despite some key omissions, to be a very reliable record of what happened in the bush. The diaries, other documents, and other information about the family can be found at <www.wiebo.net>.

The pretrial and trial of Wiebo Ludwig and Richard Boonstra released a flood of documents. In particular, RCMP transcripts of Robert Wraight's undercover conversations and records of Operation Kabriole helped me reconstruct key events in this tale. RCMP tran-scripts of statements taken from Wraight, Ludwig, and Boonstra also proved enormously helpful.

The following works provided useful information.

Alberta. Energy and Utilities Board. *Response to Inquiry Request From the Ludwig, Schilthuis, Boonstra, Wraight, Bryzgorni and Johnstone Families and Dr. W. O. Scott.* Calgary: the Board, May 9, 2000.

———. Environmental Protection. *The Final Frontier: Protecting Landscape and Biological Diversity Within Alberta's Boreal Forest Natural Region.* Edmonton: March 1998.

———. Occupational Health and Safety. *Lost-Time Claims and Fatalities Involving Chemicals as the Source of Injury: 1983-1987.* Edmonton: December 1988.

———. Provincial Advisory Committee on Public Safety and Sour Gas. *Public Safety and Sour Gas.* Calgary: Energy and Utilities Board, December 2000. See also <http://publicsafetyandsour gas.org>.

Alberta Energy Company. *1997 Annual Report.* Calgary: AEC.

Bott, Robert. *Our Petroleum Challenge.* Calgary: Petroleum Commu-nication Foundation, 1999.

———. "Sour Gas: Questions and Answers" [pamphlet]. Calgary: Petroleum Communication Foundation, 2000.

Brody, Hugh. *Maps and Dreams: Indians and the British Columbia Frontier.* Toronto: Douglas & McIntyre, 1981.

Canada. Correctional Services. Intake Assessment: Wiebo Ludwig [form]. Prepared by Lisa Ling. July 7, 2000.

Canadian Association of Petroleum Producers. *Managing Human Exposure to Benzene in the Upstream Oil and Gas Industry.* Calgary: CAPP, November 1997. Publication 1997-0014.

———. *Upstream Petroleum Industry Glycol Dehydrator Benzene Emissions Status Report.* Calgary: CAPP, 1999. Publication 1999-0008.

Clean Air Strategic Alliance. *Animal Health Workshop: Proceedings.* Edmonton: the Alliance. Held in Sundre, Alberta, November 29-30, 1999.

———. Survey on Gas Flaring – Results [typescript]. August 1997.

Foreman, Dave (ed.). *Ecodefense: A Field Guide to Monkeywrenching.* 3rd edition. Chico, California: Abbzug Press, 1993.

Galveston Houston Association for Smog Pollution. *Hydrogen Sulfide Petition to EPA* [online]. January 25, 1999. <http//www.neosoft.com/~ghasp>.

Griffiths, Mary, and Tom Marr-Laing. *When the Oilpatch Comes to Your Backyard: A Citizen's Guide to Protecting Your Rights.* Drayton Valley, Alberta: Pembina Institute, February 2001.

Hanan, Zahava. *Heading for Home.* Sussex, England: Book Guild, 1995.

Hemminki, K., et al. "Community study of spontaneous abortion; relation to occupation and air pollution by sulfur dioxide, hydrogen sulfide and carbon disulfide." *International Archives of Occupational and Environmental Health.* Vol. 51 (1982).

Heschel, Abraham. *The Prophets: An Introduction.* New York: Harper & Row, 1969.

The Holy Bible. Authorized King James Version. London: Oxford Crown Edition, 1978.

Jones, David C. *Feasting on Misfortune: Journeys of the Human Spirit in Alberta's Past.* Edmonton: University of Alberta Press, 1998.

Kilburn, Kaye. "Exposure to reduced sulfur gases impairs neurobehavioral function." *Southern Medical Journal.* Vol. 90, no. 10: 997-1006 (October 1997).

Kilburn, Kaye, et al. "Hydrogen sulfide and reduced sulfur gases adversely affect neurophysiological functions." *Toxicology and Individual Health.* Vol. 11, no. 2 (March/April 1995).

Levine, Mark. "The Souring of the Good Reverend's Nature." *Outside Magazine.* December 1998.

Life Application Bible. King James Version. Wheaton, Illinois: Tyndale House Publishers, 1989.

Marr-Laing, Tom, and Chris Severson-Baker. *Beyond Eco-Terrorism: The Deeper Issues Affecting Alberta's Oilpatch.* Drayton Valley, Alberta: Pembina Institute, February 1999.

Milby, Thomas H., et al. "Hydrogen sulfide poisoning: clarification of some controversial issues." *American Journal of Industrial Medicine.* Vol. 35 (February 1999).

Morris, Jim. "Lost Opportunity: EPA Had Its Chance to Regulate Hydrogen Sulfide." *Houston Chronicle.* November 8, 1997. See also "The Brimstone Battles" at <www.HoustonChronicles.com>.

Mostrom, M.S., and C.A.J. Campbell. *1994 Livestock Field Investigations of Two Ranches Associated with a Pipeline Break.* Edmonton: Alberta Research Council, 1998.

Nikiforuk, Andrew. "Blood and Oil: The Killing of Patrick Kent." *Canadian Business.* December 25, 2000.

———. "Holy Terror." *Saturday Night.* February 1999.

———. "The Riddle of Pincher Creek." *Harrowsmith.* October 1986.

North, Gary (ed.). *Tactics of Christian Resistance.* Tyler, Texas: Geneva Divinity School Press, 1983. Christianity and Civilization Series.

Palango, Paul. *The Last Guardians: The Crisis in the RCMP and in Canada.* Toronto: McClelland & Stewart, 1998.

Pirker, Henry. "Damage to Native and Agricultural Vegetation in the Sour Gas Areas of North-Western Alberta." Paper presented at the Fifth National Science Meeting of the Ecological Monitoring Coordinating Office, Environment Canada, Vancouver, January 19-27, 1999.

———. "Domino Effect of Pollution from Sour Gas Fields: Failing Legume Nodulation and the Honey Industry." Paper presented at the Third National Science Meeting of the Ecological Monitoring Coordinating Office, Environment Canada, Saskatoon, January 21-25, 1997.

Saro-Wiwa, Ken. *A Month and a Day: A Detention Diary.* New York: Penguin, 1995.

Stacey, E.C. *Beaverlodge to the Rockies.* Beaverlodge, Alberta: Beaverlodge and District Historical Association, 1974.

Staples, David. "Of Faith and Fury." 2 parts. *Edmonton Journal.* December 11 and 12, 1999.

———. "Only Finding a Killer Will Free Prisoners of Pain." *Edmonton Journal.* April 9, 2000.

Steele, Kevin. "An Explosion Waiting to Happen." *Alberta Report.* February 9, 1998.

Stelfox, Brad, and Bob Wynes. *A Physical, Biological and Land-Use Synopsis of the Boreal Forest's Natural Regions of Northwest Alberta.* Peace River, Alberta: Daishowa-Marubeni International Ltd., September 1999.

Stenson, Fred. *Waste to Wealth: A History of Gas Processing in Canada.* Calgary: Canadian Gas Processors Association, 1985.

Steward, Gillian. "Who Really Benefitted From the Sale of AEC?" *The Post.* Parkland Institute, Edmonton. Fall 1999.

Strosher, M. *Investigations of Flare Gas Emissions.* Edmonton: Alberta Research Council, 1996.

Sulloway, Frank. *Born to Rebel: Birth Order, Family Dynamics and Creative Lives.* New York: Vintage Books, 1997.

Waldner, Cheryl. Beef Herd Health and Productivity and Exposure to the Petroleum Industry in West-Central Alberta. 1989. Thesis submitted to University of Saskatchewan.

Walton, Dawn. "Stigma Haunts Man Who Told on Ludwig." *Globe and Mail.* September 2, 2000.

Acknowledgments

This book probably began in Pincher Creek in 1986, when I first interviewed ranchers poisoned by sour gas. Their tales have haunted me ever since.

As every author knows, a work of nonfiction is generally the labour of one demented individual roundly supported by family and friends. And this difficult book would never have taken shape without the good work of many relatives, assistants, helpers, and researchers.

Let's start with my beautiful wife, Doreen. She kept me sane and connected to the real world and to my three patient boys when I felt lost in this narrative. My eldest son, Aidan, suggested the title of the book after attending Ludwig's trial. "It just seems obvious," he said. No matter how late I returned home at night, Keegan waited up for me. And Torin always greeted his tardy and tired father with a broad, forgiving smile.

Ed Struzik and Julie Parker opened the doors of their Edmonton home as only friends can do while I recorded doings in a provincial courtroom. Their generosity and humour refreshed my spirit, which money woes – the writer's bane – had sorely eclipsed.

Sid Marty deserves credit for being Sid Marty and for often asking after the health of the "Wiebomeister." Heather Pringle patiently listened to my exploits and doubts while working on her own book, about mummies. We took turns appalling each other with tales of sour gas and uncorrupted flesh.

Philip Hanneman, a tireless crusader for landowner rights, offered an endless stream of invaluable insights and documents on how the oil industry operates in rural Alberta. Mike Sawyer, executive director of the Oil and Gas Council, provided contacts and objective accounts of the pillage of the boreal forest.

This book could never have been written without the unqualified cooperation of the Ludwigs and the Boonstras at Trickle Creek. I thank them for their warm hospitality, many fascinating conversations, and fine glasses of homemade wine. As Wiebo Ludwig often noted, "If you don't dance with the rest of them, you seem out of step." I have tried hard to respect that fine truth, but on several points of fact and interpretation we simply disagree.

Many people in Hythe and Beaverlodge spent long hours retelling incidents and explaining their views. They included Brian Peterson, the Evertons, the Willis family, the Smiths, and Doris McFarlane. Dymphny Dronyk provided much critical feedback. Björn Sommervold (the only person in the book identified by a pseudonym) shared intriguing tales from the trenches. Allan Johnstone sent me a boatload of faxes until I asked that he stop. Paul Belanger reviewed important events and environmental issues over the phone. Under the worst circumstances, Jean Roberts graciously spent many hours recounting events that led up to the shooting of Patrick Kent. Before being muzzled by the RCMP, Bob Bilodeau outlined the war against Big Oil as well as the finer details of police procedures. Sergeant Dave MacKay was also generous with his time. Richard Secord and Paul Moreau patiently explained many legalities.

Many ranchers and farmers, including the Bococks and the Johnstons, described their sour gas experiences with a saddening soberness.

A number of oil patchers told me their tales. Thanks go to Jack Evans, Kerry Sully, Terry Brooker, Ron Fipke, and in particular Mike Weeks. The people at AEC chose to have nothing to do with this project and I thank them for it — they made me dig harder.

John and Paul Readwin, my officemates, helped solve inevitable computer hassles. Scott Steele, my editor at *Canadian Business* magazine, inadvertently helped finance this book with a string of bank-saving assignments and published my first account of the killing of Patrick Kent. Assignments from the *Globe and Mail* and *Saturday Night* magazine also helped in the research for this book.

Last but not least my publishers, the folks at Macfarlane Walter & Ross, deserve credit for taking on this very unconventional tale. Gary Ross, my editor, magically transformed an unwieldy manuscript into something more like a sleek thriller. Barbara Czarnecki attacked errors and vague passages with a dogged and refreshing thoroughness. And Adrienne Guthrie cheerfully helped Macs talk to PCs and made sure nothing went awry.

As the author, of course, I am responsible for any mistakes this book may contain and whatever life it may assume. It contains many unsolved mysteries and haunting questions and lingering sins. The real world often works that way. Sometimes it takes a book to remind us of other possibilities. I hope this is such a book.

Readers with comments, corrections, questions, or additional stories can contact me at andrew@andrewnikiforuk.net. For updates on this tale, check the following website: <saboteursandbigoil.com>.

Index

Abel Ryan video. *See* Ludwig,
    Abel Ryan
Aberhart, William, 18
Absolute Seismic, 44
acid, sabotage with, 59
AEC (Alberta Energy Company)
    appeal for government action by,
        147–148
    cost of saboteurs to, 64, 87, 251
    description of, 44–46
    Dymphny Dronyk and, 51–52
    Gwyn Morgan and, 113–119,
        164–167, 211, 251, 252
    Hythe Brainard plant shooting and,
        106–107
    Ludwig buyout and, 130–132,
        136–141, 221
    private security deployed by, 62,
        64, 69–70, 80–83, 106, 108, 109,
        117, 128

public meetings held by, 137–138,
    164–167, 189–190
Ranchmen's and, 40
reaction to Ludwig's conviction of,
    251–252
report commissioned by, 213
Agent K4209, 168–169
    See also Wraight, Robert, as
    undercover agent
Aguila Exploration, 44, 47
air monitoring, 98
Alberta Agriculture, 96
Alberta Cattle Commission report
    (1994), 84–85
Alberta Ecotrust Foundation, 251
Alberta Energy Company. *See* AEC
Alberta Environment, 100, 175, 177
Alberta mineral rights, 14–15
Alberta Research Council, 83, 99
Albright, Donald, 11–12

injunctions, 60
Interline Security, 143
Iroquois. See HMCS *Iroquois*

Jael, 94
Janzen, Jake, 9, 138
Jentze, Sandy, 190
Johnston, Al, 169–170, 184
Johnston, Wayne and Ila, 98–101,
   181, 257
Johnstone, Allan ("Alien"), 76–80,
   81–82, 83, 85–86, 89, 90, 91, 106,
   119, 120, 147, 163, 202, 229–230,
   237–238, 245, 258, 260
Johnstone, Esther, 77, 79, 229, 238,
   260
Jones, Doug, 256
Jones, Roundhouse, 144
"Joseph," 39

K Division, 70, 75, 88, 142, 146–147
Kabriole. *See* Operation Kabriole
KB Resources, 172–178, 248, 259
Kelly, Shel, 62, 67–68, 69–70, 72–73,
   80, 83, 86, 88–90
Kent, Patrick, 172–173, 174, 175–181,
   248–249, 259
Kerhoulas, Karry, 178
King, Jim, 47
Kipling, Rudyard, 140
Klein, Ralph, 31, 45, 147, 187
"Knights of the Round Table," 144
Kostuch, Martha, 101
Koval, Steve, 162, 232
Kubrick, Stanley, *Spartacus,* 205

Ladd, Cheryl, 211
Land Stewardship Council (LSC),
   123–124, 126, 128, 131–132,
   136, 138
Lau, Leonard, 243
Lawrence, Wayne, 38
lawyers, Ludwig's and Richard
   Boonstra's. *See* Moreau, Paul;
   Secord, Richard

leaks. *See* sour gas, accidental release
   of; sour gas, deliberate release of
Leismeister, Rick, 191
Levine, Mark, 204
Lieverse, John, 120, 122
Ling, Lisa, 261–262
livestock. *See* sour gas, livestock and
Loberg, Gerald and Emily, 191
Locke, John, 93
Lougheed, Peter, 45
Louisiana Pacific Wafer Board Plant,
   31
LSC. *See* Land Stewardship Council
Lubicon Indians, 95–96
Ludwig, Abel Ryan, 148–149, 157, 158,
   162, 166, 204, 206, 244, 247, 261
Ludwig, Anna, 5, 6
Ludwig, Ben
   abused verbally, 239
   Anderson Exploration and, 260–261
   arrest of, 69
   arrives at Trickle Creek, 4
   building work and, 10, 26, 261
   house of, 14, 37
   letters written by, 43, 94
   marriage of, 13
   Ranchmen's and, 14, 16, 17, 37
   RCMP searches and, 154, 209
   recognized by Bilodeau, 66
   Robert Wraight and, 158, 196
   suspected in cementing incident,
      110, 218, 241
   testimony of, 31, 34
   trial and conviction of, 93–94
Ludwig, Bo (Wiebo Jr.)
   arrest of, 153
   arrives at Trickle Creek, 4
   marriage of, 13
   suspected in cementing incident,
      110, 218, 241
   suspected in Hinton bombing, 162,
      164, 241, 261
   testimony of, 31, 35
Ludwig, Caleb, 4, 199, 208–209
Ludwig, Charity, 4, 225

Moreau, Paul, 209–210, 215–216, 217–221, 228–229, 232, 240–241, 243, 245, 247–248, 250–251
Morgan, Chris, 223–224
Morgan, Gwyn, 113–118, 119, 125, 127, 130, 131, 132, 140, 144, 145, 146, 147, 164–168, 169, 211, 259
See also AEC (Alberta Energy Company)
Morin, E.J., 24
Mosher, Cal, 49–50, 59, 113
Munro, Al, 63, 88, 92–93, 156, 162
Murray, Cody, 223

Nagra tape recorder, 170, 183–184, 186, 188, 196, 200, 201
See also technical problems of RCMP equipment
nails in tires, 53, 55, 58, 80
National Film Board, 256
National Pollution Release Inventory, 251
National Post, the, 244
NATO, 231
navy. *See* Canadian navy
Nazis, 35, 74
New York Times, the, 246
Niger Delta, 46–47, 254
Norcen Energy Resources Ltd., 53, 55, 120–122, 123, 128, 132, 133–134, 136, 137
  bombing on road of, 202
  cemented wellhead of, 111, 247
Northern River Basin Human Health Monitoring Program, 253–254

Occupational Health and Safety, 25, 35
Oilweek, 211
Oklahoma City bombing, 235
Old Testament, the, 7, 213
Omniyak, Bernard, 95–96
Operation Kabriole, 147, 148, 150, 154, 162, 168–169, 186, 199, 201, 203, 205, 210, 218, 220, 228, 242, 251

See also Wraight, Robert, as undercover agent
Orphan Wells Program, 175
Our Shepherd King church. *See* Church of Our Shepherd King
Our Stolen Future (Theo Colborn), 85
ozone, 96

Pankiw, Bill, 245
patriarchy. *See* headship
Patterson, Donald, 88, 93–94
Paulson, Ron, 23
Peace River Arch, 15
Peace River Correctional Institute, 212–213, 235
Peace, the, 1–2
Pembina Institute, 213–214
Pembina pipeline, 139
Peterson, Brian, 231, 238–239, 246
Petro-Canada, 174, 259
Petterson, Brian, 223–226
Pfau, Ron, 134–136
Pharisees, the, 9
phone tapping, 148, 245
See also surveillance
Pickell, Blake, 87, 150–151
pipeline bombs, 139
See also bombing
pipeline sabotage, 87–88, 89, 133–134, 139, 142–143
"pipepecker," 87–88, 133–134
Pirker, Henry, 96, 213, 258
police. *See* RCMP
pollution. *See* global warming; ozone; sour gas, environment and
Poor Man's James Bond, The, 235
post-traumatic stress disorder (PTSD), 55
Precision Drilling, 150
Prefontaine, Phil, 14–19
press conferences, 164–167, 244–245
See also media statements
Prince, Phil, 33, 35, 36–37

The text of this book is set in Minion. Inspired by the beauty and elegance of classical, old-style typefaces of the late Renaissance, Minion was designed in 1990 by Robert Slimbach.

Text design by Terri Fong
Typesetting by Marie Jircik
Maps by Visutronx

Photography credits
CP Picture Archive: p. 5, bottom (Edmonton Sun/Dan Riedlhuber); p. 7, top (Adrian Wyld), bottom (Walter Tychnowicz). Paw Meggeson, Danish National Police: p. 4, lower left. Radical Press, Arthur Topham: p. 4, lower right. RCMP: p. 3, bottom. Southam/Edmonton Journal: p. 1 (Rick MacWilliam); p. 5, top (Greg Southam); p. 6, top (Greg Southam), bottom (Rob Ganzeveld). Trickle Creek: p. 1, inset; p. 2, both; p. 3, top; p. 8, bottom. Willis family: p. 8, top.